Two Surre
Village Schools

The story of
Send and Ripley Village Schools

Ripley School in 1912

Send School in 1924

Newark Priory.

Send & Ripley History Society
Surrey

ISBN 0 9509961 81

Designed by John Ashcroft
Printed in England By
The Knaphill Print Company Ltd
Lower Guildford Road
Knaphill
Woking
Surrey
GU21 2EG

Cover picture:
Original water-colour painting of Ripley High Street by Charles E Shaw 1896,
formerly owned by Cedar House Galleries, Ripley.
Photographed by K H Bourne MSc in 1997

Contents

Introduction   5

Acknowledgements   7

Illustrations   9

Guidance on Pupil Lists in Chapters 1-9   12

Guidance on Pupil Lists in Chapters 10-20   13

A Word about Money   13

The First 50 Years

Chapter 1. The Early Years at Ripley   17

Chapter 2. New Masters   21

Chapter 3. Lessons and Leavers   24

The New Century

Chapter 4. War and Peace   33

Chapter 5. William and Kate Blaxland   38

Chapter 6. After the War   41

Chapter 7. Sporting Activities   46

Chapter 8. Frederick Dixon   49

Chapter 9. Farewell   55

Pupil Lists for the school at Ripley, 1847-1968   59

List of Masters and Mistresses of the school at Ripley   72

And So to Send

Chapter 10. The New School at Send   75

Chapter 11. Lancelot and Jessie Rawes   82

Chapter 12. Jimmy Rogers   93

Chapter 13. Events and Changes   97

Chapter 14. Send School in Wartime   102

Chapter 15. Miss Stella Perrin   106

Chapter 16. The Post War Years   109

Chapter 17. A Small Boy Remembers   117

Chapter 18. The Red Cross Years and After   124

Chapter 19. Changes Ahead   129

Chapter 20. The Final Years   132

Epitaph§   135

Pupil Lists for the school at Send, 1854-1972   136

List of Masters and Mistresses of Send School   146

Sources   147

Introduction

This is the story of the two schools that provided the first elementary education for the poorest children in the Parish of Send and Ripley, in Surrey.

It was a new concept that such children should receive any education at all, for, at the beginning of the 19th Century, educating the children of the labouring classes was considered unnecessary, and the government of the day was reluctant to be involved in providing any state education for two reasons.

They said that the country could not afford it, and they were convinced that education would make the lower orders rebellious, and give them ideas above their station!

The lowest paid people were the agricultural workers and it was their children who grew up with little or no education. The parents were very dependent on the beneficence of the people they worked for, and put their children to work from the earliest possible age to help the family income.

Self-help was considered an essential policy for poor people.

It was left to the church to offer any teaching, but then only to help people to learn to read so that they could understand the Scriptures better.

However, there were men of goodwill at that time, who thought all children should be given some elementary education for the future good of the country, and they put continual pressure on the government, who finally yielded and in 1833 released the first money towards part-funding a state education.

The road to full-time education was not an easy one and the progress made in the village schools of Send and Ripley is told in the story. Chapters I-9 are about the school at Ripley, and Chapters 10-20 continue with the school at Send.

It is a story set against a background of national, international, and local events. The children and their teachers play their part, and many are named in the pages, in photographs, and in the Pupil Lists that accompany the story.

There are over 5000 names in the Pupil Lists, of children who attended the schools at Ripley and Send, covering the years 1847-1972.

Acknowledgements

Many people have helped with the making of this book. They have offered documents, photographs, and personal memories of their schooldays, including those of their parents and grandparents, to bring the story to life and to put on record their own part in it. There are too many to thank by name in print, and there is also the risk of leaving some persons out. The authors wish to thank all those who helped in any way, for their contributions have greatly enriched the story.

However, there are three people who worked along with us and we feel they should have a personal acknowledgement here.

The first is Jane Bartlett, who looks after the photographic archives for the Send and Ripley History Society. Jane diligently searched out every photograph to do with both schools, and interviewed many elderly residents in Ripley village, jogging their memories and encouraging them to put 'names to faces' in many of the photographs. She did this over a period of time with the result that school groups from past years have become more interesting and identifiable.

The second person is Pat Clack. Pat's connection with Send School covers many years from the 1930s, first as a pupil, then as a parent and finally as the school secretary until 1972 when Send School closed. Pat has a remarkable memory for faces and details and she too has put many 'names to faces'. She has also provided photographs and memorabilia, and sought out others in Send village who were able to add to the story.

The third person is my husband Les, who spent countless hours typing in the pupil names to make the Pupil Lists. He also read the script as it was prepared, and encouraged and supported us with constructive suggestions. His expertise on computer matters was tested to the limit when occasional disasters befell the authors and he was able to put us back on track!

To these three people we give our special thanks for their time and continuous interest.

Illustrations

water colour painting by Charles E Shaw, 1896 — Front & back cover

Ripley School in 1912, Send School in 1924 — Frontispiece

Children sitting in a gallery (19th Century) — 17

Drawing of Send and Ripley National School from School Plans, 1847 — 18

Application to National Society for Aid to build a new school at Ripley, 1846 — 19

Portrait of Thomas Marriot Berridge, Master 1852-1862 — 21

Mrs Marshall's Infants School with Poppy Day group in front of building, 1919 — 22

Page one from Ripley National School log-book, 1885 — 25

Handy book of Object Lessons and List of lessons for 1888-9 — 26

Class with Joseph Lewis, Master 1882-1893, and teacher Miss Dedman, 1890 — 27

Balance Sheet for Ripley Infants School Building Fund, 1899 — 29

Class with teacher Miss Dedman, 1900 — 33

Ripley National School Report, 1902 — 34

Never Absent Never Late Postcard c1905 — 35

Arthur Nash, AA Motor Scout, 1909 — 37

Class with teacher Miss Goff, 1909 — 37

Girls with decorated float at festivities for the Coronation of George V, 1911 — 38

William Blaxland, Headmaster 1910-1935 — 39

Class with teacher Mrs Goldsmith, 1919 — 42

Class with teacher Miss Clay, 1923 — 43

Class with teacher Mr Tarr, 1923 — 43

Class with Mr Blaxland, Headmaster, and student teacher Miss Sale, 1923 — 44

Class with teacher Mrs Goldsmith, 1923 — 44

Class of children with teacher Miss Cosson, 1927 — 45

Football team with teacher Mr Hughes, 1931 — 46

Netball team with teacher Miss Bullard, 1934 — 47

Class with teacher Mr Hughes, 1934 — 48

Class with Mr Blaxland, Headmaster 1934 — 48

Frederick Dixon, Headmaster 1936-1961 — 49

Canteen staff serving meals at Ripley School, 1950s — 50

Children dancing on Ripley Green at Coronation celebrations, 1953 — 51

Mr Dixon, Headmaster, with pupil Celia Baker, 1953 — 52

Newspaper cuttings of prize-winners, and blessing of school Coronation Bible — 52

Three pupils, 1950s — 53

Pupils, 1960s   53

Mr Dixon's book The Straight Furrow, 1986   54

Jeffery Reynolds, Headmaster 1961-1968   55

Ripley School, 1980   56

Church Row, 1990   56

Ripley School bell on display at the Surrey Local History Symposium, 1983   56

Ripley School bell in brick shelter in the grounds of Ripley C of E Primary   57
    School in the Georgelands estate, 1997

Painting of Send National School and Schoolhouse, 1924   73

Application to National Society for Aid to build a new school at Send, 1853   76-77

Plan of School Site from Trust Deed, 1854   78

Receipts for salaries paid to Frederick North and Mrs Sarah North, 1859   78

Ground plan of Send School showing new Infants Room, 1870   79

South elevation of Send School showing new addition, 1870   80

Fourth Standard certificate awarded to Florence May, 1887   81

Technical room in Send School playground, c1900   84

Class with Lance Rawes, Headmaster, 1908   85

Weekly attendance postcard, 1915   85

Group of children with Lance Rawes, Headmaster, and teacher Mrs Rawes, 1915   85

Never Absent Never Late Postcard, c1915   85

Christmas Day Gifts Certificate, 1915   86

Illuminated address presented to Lance Rawes, 1921   88

School group of children with Lance Rawes, Headmaster, 1922   89

Interior of classroom with children, 1923   89

Page from Send School logbook, 1923   90

Illuminated manuscript presented to Mr and Mrs Rawes, 1924   91

Lance and Jessie Rawes outside their home on Send Hill, 1940   92

Portrait of Lance Rawes at County Hall Kingston, 1940   92

Mr and Mrs Sex outside their home on Send Hill, c1930   93

Swimming certificate awarded to George Masters, 1929   94

Send School netball team, 1924   95

School group with Miss Palmer, 1928/29   95

Send School football team, 1933/34   96

Silver Jubilee medal, 1935   98

Hand drawn plan of playground, c1930s   99

School report of Pat Gibbons, 1935   100

Two school photographs of Jean Smallbone and Pat Gibbons, 1930s   100

Frontispiece of commemorative book for Miss Lancaster's funeral, 1938   101

Three evacuees   102

Dig For Victory food poster and pamphlet, 1940   103

Elsie Lancaster Memorial Prize   105

Registration of Stella and Cicely Perrin from Ripley Admissions Register, 1920   106

Send Schoolhouse, 1972   106

Royal Garden party invitation, 1946   108

Frontispiece of Riverdale book, 1936   109

Managers Report to Subscribers for 1941-1946   110

School staff group, 1946   110

Send School football team, 1949   111

Rose Queen float, 1953   111

Coronation seat, 1953   112

Class with teacher Mr Donaldson, 1954   112

Class with teacher Mrs Brown, 1954   113

Class with teacher Mrs Donaldson, 1954   113

Class with teacher Mrs Godwin, 1954   114

Class with teacher Mrs Birjac, 1954   114

Class with teacher Miss Palmer, 1954   115

School staff, 1954   116

The centenary climbing frame, 1954   116

Side entrance to Send School, 1972   117

Send School showing flights of steps to the sunken playgrounds, 1972   119

David Porter, 1961   120

Send School interior plan, 1950s   121

School children playing outside Send Red Cross hut, 1956   124

School canteen group in Sandy Lane with School Secretary Mrs Gale, 1956   125

Chairs being carried from Red Cross hut to the pavilion, 1956   125

Children outside pavilion in the recreation ground, 1956   125

Cartoon by Mr Donaldson, 1956   128

Wedding group of Nick and Kyra Somerfield, 1961   128

Small boys in egg and spoon race, 1962   129

May Queen Jenny Harris, 1956   130

Children maypole dancing at May Day celebrations, 1956   131

May Queen Linda Peacock with children from fancy dress parade, 1965   131

Miss Perrin's last entry in Send School log-book, 1971   133

Christopher M Brown, 1972   134

The Old School, 1990   135

Pupil Lists for Chapters 1-9

The names of pupils at the first school built in Ripley in 1847 have been gathered
from several sources.

1847 - 1853

The names are from the Census Returns for Ripley 1841 and 1851,
and the Census Returns for Send 1841 and 1851.

1854 - 1899

The names are from the Census Returns for Ripley 1861, 1871, 1881 and 1891.
In the main it is only children whose parents were agricultural labourers who have been included
from these returns. Additionally for 1885-1899 some names are taken from the Ripley National
School log-books for those years, but the father's occupation is not stated.

1900 - 1918

The names have been taken from the Register of Baptisms for the parish of Ripley.
In the main these are children of agricultural workers, and additionally, names have been taken
from the Ripley School log-books for those years, but the father's occupation is not stated.
Names have also been included in the above lists where relatives have offered the information.

1919 - 1968

An Admissions Register for these years gives details of dates of pupils' admission to the school,
and also dates of leaving. From this register it has been possible to determine how long each
child stayed at the school. Only children who stayed at the school for longer than one year have
been included in the list.

The Pupil Lists appear at the end of Chapter 9

The ages of the children have not been given in the Pupil Lists.
The date beside the name indicates that a child of that name was at the school on that date
except for the years prior to 1919 where the names have been gathered
from a variety of sources and there may well be errors and omissions.

*(NB. Children with the same surnames are not necessarily siblings.
They could be cousins, or not related at all.)*

Family historians should always check the original souces

There are indexes to the Census years, and to the Parish Registers, that may be consulted
at the Send and Ripley History Society Museum in the High Street in Ripley.

Pupil Lists for Chapters 10-20

The names of pupils at the school in Send have been gathered from several sources.

1854 - 1899

The names are from the Census Returns for Send 1861, 1871, 1881, and 1891.
It is mainly children whose parents were agricultural labourers that have been included from
these returns.

1900-1922

The names have been taken from the Register of Baptisms for the parish of Send.
Again these are mainly children of agricultural workers.

1922 - 1972

There was no Admissions Register for these years (as there was for Ripley)
and the names included in the Pupil Lists have been taken from the following sources:

Local people with long memories about their families;
Names that appeared on the backs of old school photographs;
Also, names taken from the Send School log-books for these years.

The log-books for Send School start in 1922.
There may well be errors and omissions.

The ages of the children have not been given. The date beside the name indicates
that information was given from one of these sources that a child of that name
was at the school on that date.
Any additional information will be appreciated.

The Pupil Lists appear at the end of Chapter 20

A Word About Money

Prices referred to in the text are quoted in "old money"
before decimalisation changed our money system in 1972.
Comparison with the present day seems to distort the value of the costs in bygone days,
so have not been made. The following explanation may help
£1 = 20 shillings; 1 shilling = 12pennies (d); a florin = 2 shillings;
half-a-crown = 2 shillings and sixpence; 4 farthings or 2 half-pennies = 1 penny
240 pennies = £1

The First 50 Years

Ripley Church & National School
Vicar Revd C.R.Tate

Chapter 1

The Early Years at Ripley

In 1847 a school was opened in Ripley High Street, next to the Church, which was to bring about great changes to the lives of children from poor families. The school, built with financial aid from the church, local subscriptions and a government grant, was to provide the first part-state-funded elementary education ever offered to the children of the poor in the villages of Send and Ripley.

Children in the gallery in the classroom.

The school in Ripley was first known as the Send and Ripley National School because the two villages formed one parish at that time, and it was built to accommodate 80 boys and 80 girls of the labouring class living in the parish. Although the building was really one large hall, a moveable wooden screen separated it into two schoolrooms. Each schoolroom had a separate entrance, side by side, with the words BOYS and GIRLS cut into the stonework over the doorways, and above these doorways there was an alcove which housed the school bell. The bell would be rung to call the children to school.

Each schoolroom had a gallery. This was a tiered wooden fitment, with benches and desks, where the children sat and could see and be seen by the Master or Mistress. The picture below shows what a gallery looked like but does not show Send or Ripley children.

The name of the first Master of the new school is not known but there was a Mistress as well- Miss Catherine Bartlett, aged 20, whose father James Bartlett owned a private school in Ripley.

The word NATIONAL in the name of a school meant that it was affiliated to the National Society for Promoting the Education of the Poor in the Principles of the Established Church. This was the education society of the Church of England and was always referred to as the National Society. It was one of the two societies that were given the task of administrating the first grants of money given by the state towards the building of schools for the poor. The other was the British and Foreign Schools Society, the society of the Nonconformists, and their schools were known as British Schools. Both these societies had already made progress in setting up schools for the children of the poor since 1813.

Much local fund raising had preceded the opening of the school in Ripley, for one of the conditions of qualifying for a grant was that half the cost of the building must be raised locally. The Vicar of Send and Ripley, the Reverend Henry Albany Bowles, had succeeded in raising £180 from his more affluent parishioners by 1846 when he applied to the National Society for aid.

The Application for Aid form that he submitted (see page 19) gives details of the quality of the proposed school building, and the materials used. It also shows that a significant number of poor children in the parish were already receiving some part-time education at the church and at Dame schools, at their parents' expense. These were children of the class of people, mainly agricultural labourers, that could be expected to send their children to the new school, and all were expected to be absorbed into this when it opened.

The land on which the school was to be built had to be secured on a long lease or be given. The Reverend Bowles gave the glebe land next to the church in Ripley to the Trustees, the Vicar and the Churchwardens, with the consent of the patron Lord Onslow and the Bishop Sumner. The Trustees then set up a School Committee to deal with the administration of the school and its continued funding, which also had to be assured locally.

NORTH.
Ripley National School · 1847

A Ladies' Visiting Committee was also set up, the members being the wives of the Churchwardens and other ladies of importance in the parish. Their task was to visit the school regularly to see that it was being run properly. The children, whilst being in awe of these Lady Visitors, often benefited from their interest and generosity, as will be seen later.

The parents had to make their contribution too and were expected to pay one penny (1d) a week for each child. This was known as Children's Pence and would go towards paying the salary of the Master and Mistress. The children were also expected to do some work during the school day which could be sold to raise funds. This would be sewing or basket making, or some rural craft with which they were familiar.

The required grants were awarded and the total sum for the building of the school was £420.

The architect was Henry Woodyer, well known in Surrey.

Now that the school was open, it was under the guidance of the National Society, and the first and most important subject that had to be taught was Religion since the National Society was insistent that this should be at the heart of education. The Liturgy and the Catechism were to be taught daily and each child would be examined by the Diocesan Inspectors to make sure that it had been properly instructed. Attendance at church each Sunday was expected and the building was to serve as a Day School and a Sunday School, being often referred to as "the Schools".

The children were to be taught to read and write so as to be better able to study the Bible and to understand their religion. Instructions for conducting the school were provided by the National Society which also arranged cheap school supplies.

The Master and Mistress were helped in the daily task of teaching the children, by monitors and monitresses. These were older boys and girls who were taught the lessons for the day by the Master before school started. This was known as the Monitorial system and was that on which the education of the masses was founded. It was thought to be a cheap and efficient way to teach large numbers of children. The monitors were paid a small sum for their efforts, so it was a job much sought after.

Children were taught to form their letters and numbers using a sand tray, an inexpensive piece of equipment that could be used over and over again just by smoothing out the sand. Each child had to practise to perfection

Application for Aid towards {building, ~~enlarging,~~ fitting up,} of {~~one or~~ two, &c.} *School-rooms* for {Boys, Girls, ~~or Infants~~}

~~together with a~~ **Residence** ~~for a Teacher or Teachers,~~ at *Ripley (Parish of Send & Ripley* {~~in the~~ Surrey} *Post-town of* { *Ripley*

The Schools {are to be} *United to the* NATIONAL SOCIETY {state which} *Send Ripley* A.D. 18

It is intended to purchase a house to be converted into a School-room, instead of building a new one, the circumstance must be clearly stated, and a Surveyor's certificate be forwarded, which may shew the actual present condition of the building, and what its state will be when the undertaking is accomplished.—The date of erection must be also mentioned, and the purpose to which the building was originally applied.

---

1. The Population of the *Parish* for which the Schools are intended, as {was *1556* and now is about *1570. Chiefly Agricultural* taken in the year 1841
State whether it is manufacturing, mining, agricultural, or commercial.

2. The existing Provision for Education gratuitously or at a very small charge in Schools connected with the Church is as follows:

	Sunday or Daily.	ACTUAL ATTENDANCE.			ACCOMMODATION.		
		Number of Boys.	Number of Girls.	Number of Infants.	Number of Boys.	Number of Girls.	Number of Infants.
No. 1.	Sunday	60	70		Held in the Church in a private room		
No. 2.	3 Dame Schools	10	53	5			
No. 3.							

Be pleased to state whether any, and which, of the above existing Church-of-England Schools are to be merged in the School for which aid is now solicited. *all excepting one*
will be merged into this and eventually all the
The existing Provision for Education gratuitously or at a very small charge in Schools not connected with the Church is understood to be *about 10*

3. The new Schools, allowing an area of six square feet for each child, will accommodate *80* Boys, *80* Girls, and ——— Infants. in *2* rooms, to be Sunday and *Day* Schools.

4. The instruction in the Schools is to be afforded at the rate of *1* a week, or *1/* a quarter, from each child.

5. The estimated annual charge for Master and Mistress, Books, &c. &c. is about £ *85* and the means by which that annual charge is to be met are *Annual Subscriptions (£35 already promised, £15 or £20 more expected — Annual Sermons — Weekly Payments and the produce of the work.* so that there is a reasonable prospect of the Schools being permanently carried on.

6. There is accommodation provided for *60* Children in the *Gallery & Chancel* *100* of the {parish district} Church. {Send Ripley Gallery}

7. The Boys' School-room is to be internally *24* long, *20* wide, and *23* high, to the ceiling; making an area of *382* or *6* to each child.
The Infants ditto ditto ditto ditto do. and do ceiling; ditto or to each Infant.
Where there is an open roof, state the height to the wall plate. *A foot nice of slate roof*
If it is intended to add a Teacher's residence, state the number and size of the rooms.

8. The materials are to be as follows: *foundation Flint & Concrete*; *floor Paving tiles* *walls Flint* and , feet thick; *roof Best Memel* and the property is to be held on the following legal tenure, viz. *Glebe Ground conveyed & trusteed by permission of Patron & Bishop*
and is to be conveyed to the following Trustees, viz. *Rector & Churchwardens*
so that it will be legally secured for the purpose of educating the Poor in the principles of the Established Church.

9. The entire estimated Cost of the undertaking is £ *425* which sum includes the expense of conveyance, the value of any ground, labour, or materials given, viz. conveyance, £ *5 or 10*; ground, £ ——; building, labour, and materials, £ *384*; fittings-up, £ *35*

10. The exertions that have been made to provide means to meet the estimated cost, actually raised or promised, are {viz. {by Subscriptions in money . . . £ *130 already given* by Collections after Sermon . . . £ by Donations of ground, materials, cartage, labour, &c. valued at . . £

So that the total means already provided or promised to meet the cost are . . . £ *130*
The only further local source of funds is *Contributions not yet promised but confidently expected* which is expected to produce about . . . £ *50*

Total means raised, promised, and expected . . . . £ *180*

To be signed by the Incumbent, as well as the Applicant or Secretary of the School Committee. {(Signed) *H. Albany Bowles Rector of Send & Ripley* *Applicant*
This *29th* day of *April* *1845*

To be transmitted through the Bishop of the Diocese, for his Lordship's approval and counter-signature. {Approved by me,

N.B.—It is particularly requested that a copy may be preserved of the Application, and also a copy of any further correspondence that may take place relating to it.

☞ A Draft of the Conveyance is required to be sent to the National Society before the Deed is engrossed.

before moving on to a slate and slate pencil. And each of the children had to bring a piece of rag from home to clean the slate!

Words were learned from reading sheets, which were fixed to the wall, and each child had to master all the words on one sheet before moving on to the next. The reading sheets started with two-letter words, then three-letter words and so on. This was learning by rote. The monitors would take groups of children and stand around the reading sheets helping them to master the words. After that, they were able to have reading books called Primers.

Number work was done in the same way. The same sum was repeated until the child got it right and then the next sum was given and the procedure repeated.

Physical exercise was called Drill and took the form of military style marching. No area was set aside for this activity other than the playground outside.

The school day was in two sessions, morning and afternoon, and the school was closed for two hours at mid-day when the children went home for their dinner. Those who lived too far away brought food from home and ate it outside the school.

Discipline in the classroom was strict but not harsh. The National Society did not approve of physical punishment. It regarded praise and encouragement as being more conducive to learning, and even approved the giving of small prizes as something for the children to strive for. The Lady Visitors often provided the prizes.

No Admission Register is available to name the first children to attend the school. However, a list of those who were likely to have attended when the school opened in 1847 has been compiled from the Census Returns for Send and Ripley for 1841 and 1851. They are mainly children of agricultural labourers and they would have been between the ages of five and ten years in 1847.

The first pupils at Send and Ripley National School in 1847

BAKER	Abraham	CHILDS	Edward	HOPKINS	Henry	SALMON	John
BAKER	Emma	CHITTY	Ellen	HOPKINS	Peter	SANDERSON	Margaret
BIRD	Eliza	COLLYER	Cozbi	HOPKINS	Sarah	SIMMONDS	Charlotte
BIRD	Ellen	COOPER	Ann	JACKMAN	Elizabeth	SIMMONDS	Emma
BIRMINGHAM	Ann	COOPER	James	JELLY	Eliza	SIMMONS	Francis
BRACKLEY	Jemima	COOPER	Jane	KILLICK	albert	SIMMONS	Sarah
BRACKLEY	John	COX	Emma	LAMBERT	Fanny	SMITH	Ellen
BURDETT	Ellen	COX	George	MANDEVILLE	Elizabeth	SMITH	Henry
BURDETT	Emma	COX	Robert	MANDEVILLE	Martha	SMITH	James
BURDETT	George	DANCE	James	MONK	Harriett	SMITH	John
BURDETT	Jane	DANCE	Sarah	MONK	Lydia	STEER	Abraham
BUTLER	Alfred	DAWS	Frances	NIGHTINGALE	Ann	STEER	Eliza
BUTLER	Emma	DAWS	Harriett	NIGHTINGALE	Charles	STEER	John
BUTLER	John	DENYER	Edmond	NIGHTINGALE	Clara	STEER	Mary
CARTER	Rachell	DENYER	Henry	NIGHTINGALE	James	STENNING	Mary
CARTER	Rebecca	ELMES	Joseph	OFFORD	Edward	STENNING	William
CARTER	Samuel	ELSTON	Emily	OFFORD	William	TICE	Mary
CARTER	Sarah	FALKNER	Henry	PENDARY	Shadrach	TICKNER	Emma
CHALCROFT	Edmund	FALKNER	Mary	PERCY	James	TUBBS	Eliza
CHALCROFT	Edward	FURLONGER	Ann	PETER	Ellen	TUBBS	Henry
CHARMAN	Stephen	FURLONGER	Eliza	PETER	Rose	WADE	Elizabeth
		GANDE	George	PETER	William	WADE	Jane
		GANDE	Mary	POTTERTON	Jesse	WAKEFORD	John
		GARMENT	Abram	POTTERTON	William	WALKER	James
		GARMENT	Daniel	PULLEN	Lucy	WATSON	Emma
		GILES	Elizabeth	PUNTER	Charles	WATSON	Mary
		GRAY	Maria	RAGET	Emma	WATSON	William
		HARMS	Margaret	REIGATE	Emma	WEBB	James
		HEDGCOCK	Jane	SALE	Hannah	WHEELER	Charles
		HEDGCOCK	John	SALE	Reuben	WHITE	James

Chapter 2

New Masters

Thomas
Marriott
Berridge

In the 1851 Census for Ripley, John Weight names himself as the National Schoolmaster. He may well have been the first Master of the school in 1847 but there is no documentary evidence to confirm this. In 1852 he left the school, and Thomas Marriott Berridge became the new Master. He was to stay for 10 years, and together with Miss Bartlett they taught the children with the help of the monitors.

Monitors, when they reached the age of 13, could apply to be apprenticed as pupil teachers. Pupil teachers were apprenticed for five years to a school and the Master was paid extra for training them. They attended a Pupil Teachers Centre one day a week and helped the Master with the teaching of the older children on the other days. The pupil teachers were paid £10 a year rising to £20. They could then go on at the age of 18 years, if they passed the Queen's Scholarship Examination, to one of the Training Colleges set up by the National Society and become Certificated Teachers. This assured them of a regular salary and a pension.

Records of the Dame Haynes Charity (of Send) show that in 1871 they paid for two girls to be apprenticed as pupil teachers, one at Ripley and one at Send, and no doubt they had paid for other girls and boys to be apprenticed before that date, as this charity goes back to 1702 and was set up for 'the apprenticing of poor children'.

Census Returns for Send and Ripley in 1851 show that the population was increasing and a decision was taken to raise funds for another school to be built, this time in Send. This school was opened in 1854 as the Send National School and will be the subject of later chapters.

Names of pupils who would probably have attended Send and Ripley National School between 1848 and 1853, before the Send children had their own school, have been gathered from the Census Returns for Send and Ripley 1851 and are included in the Pupil Lists at the end of Chapter 9.

After 1854 the school in Ripley became the Ripley National School for the children of Ripley. The accommodation was overcrowded, even without the children from Send, and a new classroom was added in 1859 with more fund-raising, this time by the Rev. Charles Richmond Tate who was then the Vicar of Send and Ripley. Mr Berridge was still Master at the school, but now there was a new Mistress, Mrs Mary Ann Forder, in place of Miss Catherine Bartlett.

In 1861 a separate Infants School was opened in Rose Lane, Ripley, for the Ripley children. It was built with a gift of money from Mrs Charles Marshall of Ripley Court,

The Poppy Day group, 1920

on a paddock which was part of her property. It was always known as Mrs Marshall's Infants School. Although it formed part of Ripley National School it did not receive any funding from the National Society, and the School Managers paid a rent to Mrs Marshall for the use of the school building. The children started their education there and were transferred to the National School when they were "of an intelligent age". The first Infants Mistress was Mrs H Reynolds.

The photograph shows Mrs Marshall's school building some years after it had ceased to be used as an Infants school. In 1918 it had become the clubhouse for the Ripley Post of the Comrades of the Great War. Standing in front of the building are the members of one of the first Poppy Day groups in 1920. Some of the men shown in the photograph could no doubt remember starting their schooldays there.

Mr Berridge left Ripley National School in 1862 to become the Principal of Ryde House School in Ripley High Street. This was a private day and boarding school for boys, the pupils coming from a wide area.

Gabriel McConnochie was appointed as the new Master of Ripley National School, with Mrs Mary Ann Forder as Mistress.

* * * * *

The year 1862 saw the introduction of a system of inspection which became known as Payment by Results, in which all children aged 6-11 years were to be examined annually by Her Majesty's Inspectors (HMIs) and the schools would be given grants per head only if the Inspectors were satisfied that each child examined had reached the required standard for his or her age, in the three Rs (reading, writing, and arithmetic). Children were not promoted to the next Standard, or Class, until this was achieved, and the grants were graduated by the child's record of attendance.

The object of the Inspection was to see that the country got value for the money it was spending on elementary education, and to encourage better attendance at school. Sadly, the system had a disastrous effect on the teaching in the schools, as it led to the exclusion of all but examinable subjects.

A few years later, in 1870, an Education Census was made throughout all the parishes in the land. The aim was to make sure that sufficient school accommodation was available to make compulsory attendance a viable proposition. School Boards were set up to fill the gaps in areas not covered by the voluntary bodies, either by building new schools or taking over inefficient ones.

The Church was not happy about the possible outcome of this, but the Report on Ripley National School in 1871 was favourable. There was enough accommodation for the 156 children, plus the 83 infants in Mrs Marshall's School and there was no need for a School Board to take control. No doubt James W Strickland who was now the Master, and his sister Harriet who was the Mistress, heaved a sigh of relief!

It must not be presumed that all children went willingly to school! They had to face the strict discipline of a regimented day, and some had a long walk to get there. A high standard of cleanliness was expected of the children, too. Hands and fingernails were inspected daily, and hair had to be kept tidy. Girls wore pinafores over their dresses. These were made of white cotton trimmed with broderie anglaise and had to be clean at all times; they can be seen in several of the photographs.

Parents, too, were often uncooperative in the vexed problem of regular attendance at school by their children. They would keep the children at home for many reasons. If the mother became ill, the eldest girl would have to stay at home to look after the younger family members. The boys would often be kept away to give a hand on the farm or with the animals, or simply to run errands. And some children never went to school at all. In the Census Returns for Ripley in 1851 and again

in 1861, there were several boys aged nine whose occupation was farm boy, or agricultural worker, instead of 'scholar'. The low incomes of agricultural labourers (the average wage being less than 10/- a week at that time) meant that families desperately needed any money their children could earn.

Poor attendance figures were a constant cause for concern for the schools, as low attendance meant less money from the grants. But laws were now about to be passed to improve the situation, and attendance at school for all children became compulsory in 1876.

The School Attendance Officer

In 1877 the first paid School Attendance Officer was appointed by the Board of Guardians in Guildford, for the parishes of Ripley, Send, Ockham and Wisley. His salary was around £80 a year.

He was Charles P Frye and his job was to seek out children in his district who were of school age and ensure their regular attendance, reminding parents of the financial penalties of not sending their children to school. He had to visit his schools and check the registers and would go looking for those who were absent; special vigilance was necessary to see that children who should be in school were not out at work. Parents and employers still tried to ignore this enforcement by law, but the diligence of the School Attendance Officer gradually changed the situation.

A certificate had to be issued by the School Attendance Committee in Guildford, set up by the Board of Guardians in 1877, before a child could leave school. Several criteria had to be met: the child had to have reached a certain Standard in the school, to have attended school a certain number of times and to have some employment to go to.

Mr Frye served his four parishes well for 14 years, and his untimely departure will be mentioned later.

Chapter 3

Lessons and Leavers

The logbooks for Ripley National School start in 1885. They are a rich source of information, as the Master had to record on their pages events of relevance to the school. He also mentioned children by name for a variety of reasons, for example on 2nd October 1885 he wrote "Admitted Edith Dines. Heard that Joshua Butler was away ill. Annie Tickner returned to school." - see next page.

All visitors were noted and the weekly visits of Mr Frye, the School Attendance Officer, were also recorded. One of the Managers would call regularly to examine the registers and he would write his own note to that effect in the logbook and sign it. One of the Lady Visitors also would come regularly, and she usually examined the needlework done by the children – again see next page

The Annual Report on the school by the HMIs, given to the Master after the Inspection, would have to be copied into the logbook and signed by the School Correspondent.

There was also the annual Diocesan visit and inspection, another important event in the school year and another report to be copied into the school logbook.

The annual inspection by Her Majesty's Inspectors was a day to be feared by pupils and teachers alike, for their funding depended on the children reaching the set standards.

Ripley National School usually had a fair report but there was often an unfavourable comment about the Drill. In 1886 the HMI reported ' Marching is poor being defective in time' and in 1887 the comment was 'Marching is a failure' and in 1888 the HMI reported 'Much in the elementary work is pretty good except Marching which is still weak'. Obviously there was no grant given for Marching in those years! However, there was always a half-day's holiday for the children after the Inspection was over.

As time went on, grants were being made for other subjects, and singing, needlework, history and geography were now included. The government was more committed to funding elementary education, through the grants and by paying some of the salaries for the teachers.

Each month the Master gave a lesson on Objects and Animals. He chose from a pre-pared list and would no doubt draw his lesson from books printed for this purpose, one such book being *The Handy Book of Object Lessons* by J B Walker. In the Ripley logbook the Master, Joseph Lewis, wrote on 15th October 1885 "gave lessons on the Tiger and the Shoe", and again on 13th November 1885 he wrote "gave lessons on Glass and the Whale". The aim of the lessons was to broaden the children's knowledge of things outside their rural lives. These Object lessons had to be approved by the HMI when he visited. See page 26.

The school leaving age had always been at 10 years old or earlier, but from 1876 children could leave school to go to work only if they had passed the Second Standard and had attended school 250 times in the two previous years. This ensured that some education had been achieved. But from 1881 half time work was allowed to any child over 10 years who had passed the Fourth Standard and had attended school regularly for five years, thus limiting the number of children who could leave.

Once again parents and employers resented this, the parents because they needed the extra income, and the employers because they lost their source of cheap labour. But the Government was determined to see that every

1885.

1

Sept. 11th — Resumed schoolwork after holidays. Admitted three boys. Mary Colborne became monitress in place of Sarah Morey. No visitors. Children learned new song, "The Sparrow on the Tree". Lessons done very well especially needlework. Average 75.4

Sept. 18th — Numbers higher. Examined Class III in reading and arithmetic – thought both pretty good. School visited by Mrs Frye. Annie Tickner Harriet Bonner and Margaret Butler still away.

Sept. 25 — Registers checked and found correct
           H. Hooper. Correspondent.

Sept. 25th — School visited by Mrs Frye and the Revd H. Hooper. Examined needlework and thought it improved. The Tees family left, removing from the village. Admitted two children named Snelling Average 83.6

Oct. 2nd — Admitted Edith Dines. Heard that Joshua Butler was away ill. Annie Tickner returned to school. Gave lessons on the sheep and on coffee. Average 83.5

This is page one from the log-book of Ripley National School, 1885.

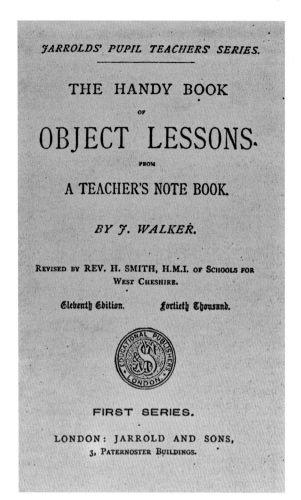

A Handy Book of Object Lessons (left)
and (above) a list of lessons for 1888-9

child benefited from the elementary education offered.

The work of the Attendance Officer, Mr Frye, must have become increasingly difficult as time went on, for in May 1890 the School Attendance Committee had a complaint put before them that Mr Frye had not visited Ripley school for six months, and that on his last visit, he had been asked to leave by the Master, Mr Lewis, because he had used *bad language* in front of the children. Mr Frye was called to account for his behaviour and after admitting that he was unwell, and apologising, he was allowed to continue in the job. But, sadly, a year later it was reported that he had become insane and had "been removed to the Surrey County Asylum at Brookwood".

In 1890 Miss Caroline (Kate) Dedman had commenced duties as an Assistant Teacher. She was a former pupil who had started at Ripley National School in 1871 at the age of five. Later she had been made a monitress, and then she had been apprenticed to the school as a pupil teacher.

Another logbook entry in 1893 noted that Miss Caroline Dedman had been appointed as a Certificated Teacher. She was to remain at the school for some years and can be seen with the children in some of the photographs.

More educational changes were on the way, and in 1893 the school leaving age was raised to 11 years without exception.

While parents wanted their children to leave school as soon as possible to go to work,

A class at Ripley National School in 1890 with the Master, Joseph Lewis, and Assistant Teacher, Miss Kate Dedman

it was also their desire to get them admitted to school as early as possible. On 6th March 1894, James A Roach, the Master, recorded in the logbook "Admitted two aged three years" and a former Master, Mr Lewis, had recorded in 1887 that he had admitted a boy aged five "who had not attended a school before". Instances of children starting school at the age of three continued to be recorded.

Entries in the logbook also tell us that slates and reading sheets were still being ordered for use at the school in 1894, as well as a new Object Lesson Book.

In 1894 there was a special mention for a girl named Rose Tice. She was presented with a silver thimble for diligence and proficiency in Needlework, the gift of Miss Onslow who was a school Manager. Miss Onslow was one of the daughters of Major Pitcairn Onslow, and the family lived at Dunsborough House on Ripley Green.

Miss Dedman came in for praise in March 1895 when there was an influenza epidemic, and the Master had written in the logbook on 11th March "All teachers away ill except for myself". The following day he wrote in the logbook "Miss Dedman has bravely crawled down to help a little" but three days later he wrote, "Miss Dedman obliged to give up again".

Many of the children who had also been ill recovered in time to go on the Band of Hope

outing to Hampton Court in May 1895, and there was another outing in July 1896, this time to the Crystal Palace.

The Crystal Palace was so called because it appeared to be made entirely of glass. It was built in 1851 to house the Great Exhibition and was originally in Hyde Park. Later it was moved to Sydenham in South London. It was surrounded by 100 acres of grounds and became one of the chief pleasure resorts of London.

Schoolmasters and Mistresses came and went at Ripley National School, some staying just a few years, exceptions being Joseph Lewis and his wife Ann who stayed for eleven years.

They all had one continual problem, that of dealing with absenteeism. Despite new laws and fines, children still stayed away from school from time to time. Apart from childhood illnesses and bad weather, there were seasonal absences-for example, on the first day of May children traditionally went 'a-Maying' dressing up and going round to the big houses with baskets of flowers and a small maypole and chanting,

"May Day's the first of May, Give us a penny and we'll run away."

Village events such as a ploughing match or a fair, or cover beating for the shoots on the big estates nearby, would also keep the children away from school.

The effort to encourage children to attend school regularly is reflected in 1896, when children who had been attending properly for a full year were presented with a new dress or a suit of clothes, the gift of the Hon. Mrs Stuart Worsley. She was one of the Managers of the school and lived in Ripley House. The lucky children to be the first to gain these prizes were Mary Hyde, William Hyde, Emily Liffard, Fred Perrin and Annie Wigman. This prize-giving became an annual event and was something well worth striving for by every poor child.

Sheer poverty hit one family, in the same year, as the entry in the logbook records "Two children taken into the Workhouse". By contrast the school must have been very proud of one pupil, Sydney Green, who also in 1896, won a scholarship to Guildford Grammar School, "fully funded for three years".

The Hon. Mrs Worsley, who was the mother of Lady Lovelace, was a good friend to Ripley National School. She came to its rescue in 1896 when the school was in real danger of closing and being taken over by a School Board. The school's accommodation was not sufficient, the Voluntary Subscriptions were not forthcoming and the Final Notice of Closure was about to be issued when Mrs Worsley offered a substantial gift of money that solved the problem and allowed the school to continue.

*****

But there were lighter moments ahead, for in 1897 the nation was looking forward to celebrating the Diamond Jubilee of Queen Victoria. She had been 10 years on the throne as a young queen when the school had opened, and now the country was going to celebrate 60 glorious years of her reign. There was a national holiday on 22nd June for the country to celebrate the event and Ernest John Cosier Young, the Master, recorded in the logbook that "children from the school joined in the Jubilee Procession and had their photographs taken". An extra week was also added to the summer holiday that August because of the Diamond Jubilee.

A new classroom was planned at the Ripley National School. It was to be an Infants classroom and would result in the closure of the Infants school in Rose Lane known as Mrs Marshall's School, as there would now be enough room for the infants in the main school. The Jubilee Room, as it was called, was opened in 1898 by the Bishop of Winchester, having been paid for by a big fund-raising effort involving the whole village; the balance sheet published in 1899 and reproduced on the next page, shows how this was achieved; the names of the subscribers make interesting reading as do the sums raised.

The head of the Infants school in Rose Lane, Florence Gilbert, was invited to continue as the Infants Mistress in the new room.

1899 saw the start of the Boer War, in which Great Britain was fighting the Dutch settlers in South Africa. The first men to go were the Reservists, and this must have caused considerable hardships because on 7th November 1899 a logbook entry records "Collection made amongst children towards the Fund for the relief of the families of the Reservists".

And in 1899, as the 19th Century came to a close, the school leaving age was raised to 12.

Below is a list of children known to be monitors at Ripley National School some of whom went on to be Pupil Teachers. The dates cover the years 1861-1896.

AVERY Ada 1888
BROWNING Agnes 1891
BUTLER Ada 1889
COLBOURNE Mary 1885
COLLYER Ada 1891
COLLYER Edith 1885
COX Ellen 1885
DEDMAN (Kate) Caroline 1879 and Pupil Teacher
DIBBLE Evelyn 1885
EVANS Isabella 1891
FARMER Kate 1891 and Pupil Teacher
GOLDSMITH Ethel 1885
HIGGINS Edith 1885
HIGGINS Kate 1891 and Pupil Teacher
INGRAM Helen 1885
KEARVELL Ann 1883
LEWIS Sarah 1885 and Pupil Teacher
PANTLIN Jesse 1861 and Pupil Teacher
PULLEN Edith 1885
PULLEN Ethel 1893 and Pupil Teacher
SINK Annie 1885
SPOONER Helen 1885
STENNING Ellen 1884 and Pupil Teacher
STRUDWICK Eliza 1861 and Pupil Teacher
TICE Mary 1885
TICKNER Kate 1885
WILLIAMS Alice 1888
WOODS Ellen 1896

Ripley Infants' School Building Fund.

1899. PAID.	£	s.	d.
March 1st.			
Cost of Building as per Contract	699	0	0
Extras (allowed)	25	0	0
Architect's Commission	10	0	0
Messrs. Peak & Lunn's Plans	12	10	0
Advertising, Printing, etc.	2	12	6
£749	**2**	**6**	

1899. RECEIVED.	£	s.	d.
March 1st.			
Donations (as per list)	515	0	9
Grants—Winchester Diocesan Society	40	0	0
„ National Society	45	0	0
Concerts and Entertainments	61	15	8
Offertories	3	18	10
Children's " Brick " Cards...	4	4	11
Opening Ceremony (Collection)	8	0	4
Rummage Sale	20	0	0
Collected by Cards (as per list)	51	2	0
£749	**2**	**6**	

DONATIONS.

	£	s.	d.
Berridge, T. M., Esq. ...	10	6	6
Boreman, The Misses ...	1	1	0
Buckland, G. R., Esq. ...	5	0	0
Deacon, W. S., Esq. ...	80	0	0
Deacon, Mrs.	20	0	0
Eager, Miss		10	0
Farmer, Mrs.		10	0
Farr, Mr.	3	0	0
Finn, W. J., Esq. ...	5	5	0
Friend, A	10	0	0
Geale, Mr.	20	10	0
Gibbons, Mr.		5	0
Grant, W. M., Esq. ...	10	0	0
Green, Mr.	20	0	0
Jordan, Mr.	1	10	0
ing, G. Maitland, Esq. ...	10	10	0
King-Noel, Captain The			
Hon.	5	0	0
Lambert, C. E., Esq. ...	2	2	0
Lovelace, Earl of ...	26	0	0

	£	s.	d.
Lancaster, A. H., Esq. ...	5	5	0
Leigh - Bennett, H. C.,			
Esq., M.P. ...	10	0	0
Lucas, Mr.	10	0	0
May, W. H., Esq. ...	5	0	0
Money, Rev. G. ...	5	0	0
Moon, Rev. Sir E. G., Bart.	1	0	0
Morey, Mr.		5	0
Neville, Colonel ...	10	0	0
Onslow, Earl of ...	34	0	0
Onslow, the Misses ...	1	15	0
Paulton, Mrs.	5	0	0
Pearce, R. M.. Esq. ...	10	0	0
Pearse, F. E., Esq. ...	5	6	6
Phillips, Canon... ...	3	3	0
Pledger, Mr.	1	10	0
Rutson, Mrs.	10	0	0
Rendel, Lord	5	5	0
Sinclair, Mr.	1	0	0
Smallpeice, Miss ...	2	2	0

	£	s.	d.
Sutcliff, J. H., Esq. ...	15	15	0
Sutcliff, Mrs. ...	2	2	0
Sutcliff, the Misses ...	2	0	0
Stuart - Wortley, Hon.			
Mrs. J.	27	7	9
Tice, Mr. A. ...	2	0	0
Tuke, Rev. F. H. ...	3	0	0
White, Mr. D.		10	0
Wigman, Mr.		5	0
Wilson, A., Esq. ...	4	0	0
	414	0	9
Collected by the Rev.			
F. J. Oliphant and the			
Rev. C. A. Skelton...	101	0	0
£515	**0**	**9**	

Donations Collected by Rev. F. J. Oliphant and Rev. C. A. Skelton.

	£	s.	d.
A.C. and A.M.C. ...	1	1	0
Agar, Talbot, Esq. ...	1	0	0
Anon	1	0	0
Ashcombe, Lord ...	10	0	0
Awdry, C. Esq.... ...	2	2	0
Bank Interest	2	11	2
Bashford, J. W., Esq. ...	1	1	0
Bowles, Rev. A. H. ...	2	2	0
Bowring, Rev. E. F. ...		5	0
Bramwell, Rev. A. ...	1	1	0
Buttemer, Rev. A. ...		10	6
Carwardine, Mrs. ...	1	0	0
Churchill, C., Esq. ...	5	5	0
Cooper-Cooper, Mrs. ...	1	0	0
Cumberlege, Rev. S. F.	1	0	0
Currey, C. H., Esq. ...	2	2	0
Edwards, Rev. A. T. ...	1	0	0
Friend, A	5	0	0

	£	s.	d.
Friend, A	1	1	0
Friend, A	1	0	0
Friend, An old	2	2	0
Fox, Mrs.	5	0	0
Goldingham, Mrs. ...	1	0	0
Guildford, Bishop of ...		10	6
Harris, Rev. J. M. ...	7	0	0
Hopkins, Rev. F. ...	3	0	0
Knight, Capt.	1	0	0
Lancaster, A. H., Esq. ...	2	2	0
Lawes, Col.	1	0	0
Littlejohn, Rev. C. P. ...	1	1	0
Lusk, A., Esq.	1	0	0
Oliphant, Rev. F. J. ...	2	1	8
Percival, S., Esq. ...	5	0	0
Phillips, Canon F. G. ...	2	2	0
Phillips, F. G. P., Esq....		5	0
Riley, A., Esq.		5	0

	£	s.	d.
Rural Dean	10	0	0
Scott, Mrs. F. J. ...	1	0	0
Skelton, Rev. C. A. ...	3	0	0
Stevens, R. N., Esq. ...	1	1	0
Storey, W. C., Esq. ...	2	2	0
Thorn, J. M., Esq. ...	1	1	0
Wermig, G., Esq. ...	1	1	0
Wigram, L., Esq. ...	5	0	0
Willan, Col. F.	1	0	0
Winchester, Lord Bp. of	1	1	0
Wyatt, Rev. J. P. ...		10	6
	102	7	4
Less Printing & Postage	1	7	4
	£101	**0**	**0**

Collected by Cards.

	£	s.	d.
Berridge, Miss	11	3	6
Drew, Mr.		3	1
Eglinton & Tice, Misses		3	2
Gibbons, Mr.		3	10
Goodman, Mr. T. S. ...	5	10	0
Green, Miss	6	3	6

	£	s.	d.
Henton, Mr. D. ...		8	8
Hill, Mr. A.	3	13	0
Pearse, F. E., Esq. ...	5	0	0
Pledger, Mrs.	3	18	6
Skelton, Mr.	1	9	6
Sutcliff, Mrs. (Balance)...		6	3

	£	s.	d.
Sutcliff, the Misses ...	2	15	0
Tedder, Mr.	5	1	0
Tuke, Mrs.		7	6
Turner, Mr.	3	15	6
	£51	**2**	**0**

J. H. SUTCLIFF, *Hon. Treasurer*, Fairfield House, Ripley.

Balance Sheet for Ripley Infants School Building Fund, 1899 • *Copyright of Surrey History Service*

The New Century

Ripley.

Chapter 4

War and Peace

The dawn of the 20th Century passed without comment in the school logbook, and a new Headmaster, G W Ward, with his wife as Assistant Mistress, took over the school.

The Boer War was still being fought in South Africa and the school made a collection for War Funds in January 1900, there being much public concern for the fate of British soldiers and civilians caught up in the sieges of two towns in South Africa.

Ladysmith, a town in Natal, was relieved in February 1900 after having been besieged by the Boers for four months. And a child baptised in Ripley in March 1900 was named after the event; she was Alice Ethel Ladysmith Perrin.

But it was another town, Mafeking, in Cape Province, under the leadership of General Baden-Powell, which had withstood a siege of seven months, that caused the British nation to go wild with delight when it was relieved in May 1900. The newspapers reported that there was riotous rejoicing in London and around the country, and a national holiday was given on 21st May to celebrate the Relief of Mafeking. However, the war in South Africa was not over yet.

On 12th June 1900 the Reverend Tuke presented a framed picture of Queen Victoria to the school. No mention is made of the reason for the gift; it could have been to mark either the Relief of Mafeking or the new century.

The death of Queen Victoria is not noted in the logbook (she died on 22nd January, 1901) nor was a day-off recorded for national mourning or the funeral.

The passing of the great Queen made no impact on the school but on 2nd June 1902 the next Headmaster, Harry Tilbury, wrote in the logbook in red ink "Peace Proclaimed", and the school had 'Peace Celebrations' on 6th June that year, marking the end of the Boer War.

Although Queen Victoria had died at the beginning of 1901, the coronation of her son

Here is Miss Kate Dedman and her class in 1900

Ripley National School.

REPORTS, ACCOUNTS, &c.

FOR YEAR ENDING FEBRUARY, 1902.

Report of the Religious Instruction by the Diocesan Inspector, January 23rd, 1902.

Mixed School.—" The work has suffered considerably owing to sickness among the children, and several changes in the staff. There is every prospect of the School doing well in the future. The Upper Class showed much interest in its work, and is being well taught on the right lines. The Middle Division was somewhat weak. Standards I. & II. showed a creditable knowledge of Bible History."

Infant School.—" I was much pleased with these two classes. In both of them the children were bright, interested, and well-informed, answering readily and accurately. The results reflect credit on the teachers."

A. B. MILNER, Diocesan Inspector.

Report of His Majesty's Inspector, February, 1902.

Mixed School.—" The School is now reorganised after a change of teachers, and promises to do very well with its present staff."

Infant School.—" A good Infant School."

NOTE —The " Highest Grant " was earned in the Mixed School for the first time this year. The Infant School again earned the " Highest Grant."

BIDDLE AND SON, TYP., GUILDFORD.

Edward VII had been delayed due to his ill health and the war. The Headmaster recorded in the logbook that the school held "Coronation Celebrations on 20th June 1902", so the children must have been very happy to have two celebrations in the same month!

The Managers of Ripley National School published their Reports and Accounts in 1902, the reports of the Diocesan Inspection and that of His Majesty's Inspector being printed for all to read. There is also a list of names of those people who supported the school by a voluntary rate and donations.

The Balance Sheet shows, amongst other items, the cost of the teachers' salaries. In 1902 the joint salary for the Headmaster and his wife was £150 per annum. The Managers were advertising for an Infants Mistress at £65 per annum, and an Assistant Mistress, Miss Grace Laura Hill, had just been engaged at £35 per annum. There was possibly one other

Assistant Teacher. The Pupil Teacher rate was still at £10 per annum and the caretaker was being paid £20 a year. Monitors were paid one shilling and sixpence a week. The combined salaries for the whole school staff for the year came to £330 6s 8d.

The Education Act 1902 created Local Education Authorities (LEAs) which took over the duties of the School Boards. Board schools became Council schools. The LEAs were now responsible for the expense of conducting the schools in their areas, including the voluntary schools, but the cost of maintaining the buildings, remained in the hands of the schools' local supporters. New rules about Pupil Teachers came into force in 1902, which meant that they could not teach in schools until they were 16 years old. Up till that time they had been apprenticed to a school at the age of 13 and 'learned on the job' whilst attending a Pupil Teacher Centre one day a week.

Never Absent, Never Late Card showing Albury Park

Now they were to be given bursaries by the local authorities to enable them to attend secondary schools, as special pupils being trained as Pupil Teachers. No longer were "children" being allowed to teach other children.

In January 1903 Mr H J Best and and his wife Caroline, came to the school as Headmaster and Assistant Mistress. They were to stay for seven years. Mr Best continued to report improvements in attendance figures and more children were being awarded prizes and medals for good attendance. The Local Education Authority was also issuing picture postcards as **Never Absent Never Late** incentives, and books were now included as prizes for achievement *(see previous page)*.

In 1905 the School Managers were pleased to report that 40 children had obtained medals for having attended every single time through the previous year.

The school was now celebrating Empire Day on May 24th each year. This event was inaugurated in 1902 as a permanent memorial to Queen Victoria, the date chosen being Her Majesty's birthday. The children would be told about the countries of the British Empire and sing the National Anthem. Prizes for good attendance and achievement were given out by the Managers on this day to the children who had earned them, and the rest of the day was a holiday.

On 22nd January 1908, on the anniversary of the accession of King Edward VII to the throne, a flag and flagstaff were formally presented to the school
Thomas Marriott Berridge, one of the Managers, gave the flag, a Union Jack, and Lady Lovelace offered a tree from her estate to be made into a flagstaff. This was erected by the school entrance and can be seen in some of the later photographs. There was a public ceremony of "hoisting the flag" for the first time and the children had the Union Jack explained to them. Saluting the flag was now added to future Empire Day ceremonies.

A giant step was taken in the same year

towards improving sanitation in Ripley School when after complaints and concern over the school "offices" the buckets were replaced by automatic flushing closets.

During these years Evening Classes for Adults were well under way at the school and grants were being received for the adult students. There were good reports and praise for those who "after a hard day's work on the farm, were prepared to give up their free evenings to study to improve their skills and knowledge". However, the adults were not prepared to face a visit by His Majesty's Inspectors in the same way as the children were and, after attendance dropped sharply when this was first attempted, no further Inspections were made and the Evening Classes continued with good results until the outbreak of war in 1914.

*****

There was a serious diphtheria epidemic in 1908 and many children throughout the country died. Mr Best recorded in September 1908 that "two children at Ripley School" had died in the Guildford Isolation Hospital. They were Doris Peters and Hilda Barratt. Hilda had been a prizewinner two years running for good attendance at school. Later in the same year, another girl, Bessie Fuller, also died of diphtheria. Concerns were expressed by the School Managers that sick children were being sent home from the Isolation Hospital too soon and infecting other children in their families. Bessie appeared to have caught the disease from her sister, and died as a result. The Medical Officer for Health was called in to examine all the school children.

In the following year Mr Berridge died, aged 79 years. He had been one of the earlier Masters of Send and Ripley National School and had taught there for 10 years before leaving in 1862 to start his own private school in Ripley. He had continued to take an active interest in village affairs and especially the village school. He became one of the Managers of Ripley School and served the school well for many years, resigning only a year before his death.

*****

Arthur Nash, the father of a family of children who went to the school in Ripley in 1909 was an AA Motor Scout. He worked in the Ripley/Guildford section and would call out teasingly to his children as he cycled past them on his way to work,

"Hurry along !" then "You've got plenty of time!" A lot of boys and girls must have known him.

Mr and Mrs Best left Ripley School at the end of 1909 to take charge of another school. They were presented with gifts of a silver teapot and a tea service from the Managers, and a clock from the staff and children. The photograph below may have been taken to mark the occasion. Mrs Ivy Sopp, neé Carter (who was at the school in 1909) has named some of the children in the photograph. Ivy who is standing next to the teacher, Miss Goff, remembers being taught in the tiered gallery and chanting the Alphabet and Number Tables. She won a school prize in 1914, a book called *Meg's Children*.

Amongst those in the photograph are;
Lally Billingshurst, Lily Townsend, Louis Caffin, Annie Brown, Ivy Carter, Miss Goff (teacher)
Sidney Smith, Alfred Charman, Alfred Chandler, Emily Chandler,
Mabel Nash, Ivy Budd Lily Carter, Gertie Fuller, Mabel Biggs, Maggie Watson.

The Automobile Association started in 1905 and for the first few years the Motor Scouts patrolled their areas by bicycle.
At first there was no uniform and they wore AA armbands over a cycling jacket and a large AA badge, which fixed onto the jacket buttons.
But in 1909 they were issued with a uniform. Here is a photograph of Arthur Nash, Motor Scout no 25, in his new uniform with his bicycle.
The photograph is by courtesy of his grand-daughter, Mrs Ann Munday.

Chapter 5

William and Kate Blaxland

In **January 1910** William Blaxland and his wife Kate came to the school as Headmaster and Assistant Mistress. They were to stay for the next 26 years.

That same year the gallery was removed from the Infants School and new desks were bought. The Inspectors declared it an "improvement". They had asked for galleries to be removed years before but schools had been unwilling to lose them.

*****

In May 1910 King Edward VII died after a short reign of nine years, and a new king was proclaimed. He was George V known as the Sailor King because of his previous connections with the Royal Navy. He had been educated as a professional naval officer and had seen service throughout the world, but on the death of his elder brother the Duke of Clarence in 1892 he was forced to relinquish his career to assume the duties of heir-apparent.

Ripley Village celebrated the Coronation of George V and Queen Mary on 22nd June 1911 with a procession of floats representing the countries of the Empire. One photograph shows several girls beside a float, holding shields with the names of the provinces of South Africa. The girls were probably pupils at the school, but their names are not known.

Coronation mugs were presented to all the Ripley children and the festivities continued with tea and sports for all, at Ripley Court.

The country settled down to the reign of the new monarch, and rural life continued its daily round, unaware that life was to change for many of them in a few short years. And in 1913 the Countess of Lovelace presented the prizes to the school. She was the daughter of

Girls with the South Africa float

the Hon. Mrs Worsley who had been such a benefactor to the school in earlier days.

Mr Blaxland soon became involved with village affairs, as was expected of him. He was obviously a busy man outside school hours.

In writing of an excursion for the children of Ripley and Ockham in July 1913, organised by Mr Blaxland, Albert Fuller, a pupil at the school, wrote "We all know and greatly appreciate all that Mr Blaxland has done and is doing for Ripley and so many are the calls on his time that we think Mrs Blaxland can see him only at mealtimes!". Albert then goes on to report on the outing to Dover by train, "We left school at half-past five and arrived at Guildford by brakes at about seven o'clock. When we arrived at Dover, Mr Blaxland took us along the Admiralty Pier and we saw some gunners sighting and loading the big guns and training them on targets towed out to sea ... then Mr Blaxland came and took us round to the mailboat 'Victoria' and we were shown over it by Captain Blaxland".

(Mr Blaxland later wrote in the logbook in 1916 that he had to take leave of absence

William Blaxland, Headmaster of Ripley National School

from school to attend the funeral of his brother who had drowned while piloting a vessel in the North Sea, the steamer having struck a mine.)

War was looming and in 1914 the country was mobilizing its troops and calling for volunteers to join the fight. The logbook records that in May 1915 "the military hurriedly took over this school for military purposes ... The military 'occupation' of the school only lasted four days and then school returned to its normal routine". The war that was to involve nearly every nation in the world

became known as the Great War, the war to end all wars. Over 100 young men from Ripley joined the forces and saw service in Europe.

Walter Sidney Smythe, a young teacher who had been at the school for two years, joined up in 1914, the vicar of Ripley left in 1915 to become Chaplain to the Navy, and in 1917 Mr Blaxland went to the war leaving R H Green in temporary charge of Ripley National School.

All three men survived the war, but 28 of the young Ripley men did not return. A note in the Ripley Parish Magazine records that "Mr Allwork has made an oak frame for a Roll of Honour to be a permanent record of those who have gone to fight in the Great War. It is hoped to find a resting place for this in the Vestry after Peace is concluded". The names of those who lost their lives are recorded for posterity on the war memorial in front of Ripley church.

Those who returned joined the Ripley Post of the Comrades of the Great War, formed in 1917 for ex-service men. Their clubhouse was the old infants school building in Rose Lane, which had been purchased by Sir Wilfred Stokes in 1918 as a meeting place for them. *(See Chapter 2.)*

At the beginning of the war the health of children must have been a cause for concern because in 1914 Surrey Education Committee set up School Care Committees in every school in the county, "whose duty will be to the health of the children whilst at school, that is, medical inspections followed by medical treatment at low cost to the parents ... and to see that children have an opportunity to continue their education after leaving elementary school". Medical inspections were to be compulsory and free but not the treatment, and Ripley Care Committee discussed the best means of raising money to carry out the recommendations of the inspections with regard to adenoids, tonsils, eyes and teeth.

The Fees were to be as follows:

- *for adenoids, including stay at clinic hospital = £1.6s 0d*
- *for teeth, from 1s 6d*
- *for eyes, to include two visits = 10s 6d*
- *for spectacles, from 7s 6d*

The Ripley Parish Magazine reported that "The Committee have agreed to ask parents to subscribe at least a half-penny a week, when possible one penny, and to send the money each Monday morning to the Head Teacher. Those parents who do not subscribe regularly *will get no assistance from Surrey Education Committee or from Ripley Care Committee*. The parents that do, will not be called upon to pay anything further towards the fees".

Some parents would appreciate the means to save towards medical treatment for their children when needed. However, for other parents it was just another hardship to find money out of an already over-stretched wage.

It was nothing new for poor people to be persuaded towards thriftiness. 'Penny Banks' had been a feature of Victorian days when people were encouraged to save regularly for clothes, boots, coal, and blankets. The school would be the paying-in point each week, and regular savers would get a bonus added as further inducement to keep up the payments. As far back as 1869 there was a 'Clothing Club connected to Ripley school ... by 1d a week subscriptions to which donations are added by inhabitants...' and a Children's Clothing Club at the school was still ongoing in 1901.

By 1918 Ripley Care Committee was giving cod liver oil, Maltine, and Eastons Syrup on medical recommendation *"but only to children whose parents subscribe regularly"*. It was the thin edge of the wedge, but it *was* the beginning of medical care for children in school.

*****

The Great War was coming to a close but there were still problems and shortages at home. The Ministry of Food had to make sure that even the harvest from the hedgerows would not be wasted, and on 21st September 1918 the logbook entry reflects this: " at the request of the Ministry of Food, and with the consent of the Managers, groups of children are being sent out to gather blackberries".

It was recorded that they collected 108 lbs of blackberries over the next few days. This was probably made into jam, as that was a quick way of preserving the high vitamin content of the fruit. Bread and jam was the usual teatime fare for most families with children.

The children of Ripley School made other contributions, too to help the war effort. In December 1915 they had given a concert during the holiday to raise money on behalf of war funds, and in the autumn of 1917 they had collected two tons of horse-chestnuts for the Ministry of Munitions - for use as animal food!

Chapter 6

After the War

Armistice Day was announced on 11th November 1918. Ripley spread the good news that hostilities had ceased by ringing the church bell, and Ripley School "hoisted the flag at the school at 2pm" and the school bell was rung. During the War no clocks were allowed to strike and no bells rung. The school bell had no doubt remained silent too during those years.

It was commented in the next issue of the Ripley Parish Magazine that the ringing of the school bell at the same time as the church bell was not harmonious to the ears, and should not be repeated! However, the old school bell could survive such criticism. It was a permanent reminder of its own value to the village. It remained faithful to the end, as will be seen later.

Another important milestone for children happened in 1918 when the school leaving age was raised to 14 years.

Mr Blaxland and Mr Smythe returned to Ripley School in January 1919. The Vicar did not return to the village having been offered a living elsewhere. Mr Blaxland immediately succumbed to the influenza epidemic, which was sweeping the country in the aftermath of the war. He was absent for several weeks, but recovered and took charge of the school again.

Shortages were still affecting the lives of the villagers, for in April 1919 Mr Blaxland reported that there was no fuel in the school, and none to be had of any coal merchants, so the older boys were sent to the school garden to collect pea and bean sticks to make fires in the classrooms.

On 18th July 1919 there were Peace Day Celebrations, "the children were making costumes" (possibly to join in the village celebrations), and there was to be an extra week's holiday owing to the King granting an extra week for Peace.

*****

The fallen were not forgotten. On 11th November 1919 at 11am, by command of the King, there was to be a two minute silence observed throughout the country in memory of the brave fallen. The children took part in this and the reason for the observance was explained to them.

*****

The year ends on a happier note, for the last logbook entry for the year, on the 19th December records "The children are very excited about Christmas, probably due to being the first real Christmas remembered, as the war caused cessation of all festivities"

Overleaf is a photograph, taken outside the front of the school in 1919 which may have been taken as part of the Peace Celebrations to mark the end of the war. The children look to be dressed in their best clothes. The girls have white pinafores over their dresses and most are wearing boots, except for two girls in shoes and knee-high socks. Some of the boys have large white collars whilst two are wearing sailor suits. The teacher is possibly Mrs Eugenie Goldsmith, nee Proudlock, who had taught at the school before her marriage and had returned in 1919.

Only one child is identified here. She is Vera Nash who started school in 1919. She is in the front row, the fifth girl from the left. Her older sister, Mabel Nash is in the 1909 group. The photograph is by courtesy of their niece, Mrs Sheilah Higginson.

An **Admissions Register** book for Ripley National School starts on January 1919 and gives the dates of all children entering and leaving the school. It gives other details, too, including father's name and home address.

Infants' class with Mrs Goldsmith in 1919

From this register it is clear that many children left after a short time, so only those who were at the school for at least one year have been included in the Pupil Lists which can be found at the end of Chapter 9.

In 1921 there was again a major problem of keeping the school warm, for on 16th April Mr Blaxland reported in the logbook " very cold ... heavy snow ... no coal in the village due to the miners'strike". However, happier occasions were to be recorded.

There was a special school holiday in the following year. On 28th February 1922, a holiday was granted by King George V for Princess Mary's wedding day. She was the King's only daughter and had the title of Princess Royal. The Ripley School children celebrated with a paper-chase.

On the 26th April 1924 another holiday was granted, this time for the wedding of the Duke of York to Lady Elizabeth Bowes-Lyon. *In 1936 this bridal pair became King George VI and Queen Elizabeth.*

The same year, 1924, the whole school in four "char-a-bancs" visited the Imperial Exhibition at Wembley.

Bad weather was recorded in the logbook on 13th February 1925 when an extremely stormy day with floods resulted in ten children being taken home in a farm wagon as floods were rising and roads were impassable to pedestrians.

*****

In 1923/24 photographs of the children were taken inside the classrooms. This gives a glimpse of how the children were taught at that time. The children faced the front of the classroom where there would be an easel carrying a blackboard on which the teacher would write using sticks of chalk. When finished with, the writing was easily rubbed off with a cloth or duster.

Children sat two to a desk, (sometimes three if they were infants). And these desks were of an interesting design. They are on a heavy iron frame with bench seats that tip up to allow access from either side. The desk tops are of wood, probably oak, and each top

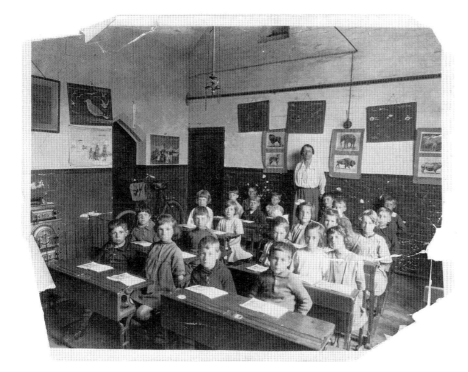

The Infants' classroom with the teacher Miss Rosalie Clay who had taught at the school since 1917.
Note her bycycle standing in the corner of the classroom!

The Middle School classroom with the teacher Frederick W. Tarr who taught at the school from 1923 – 1925. This is the Jubille Room built in 1898.

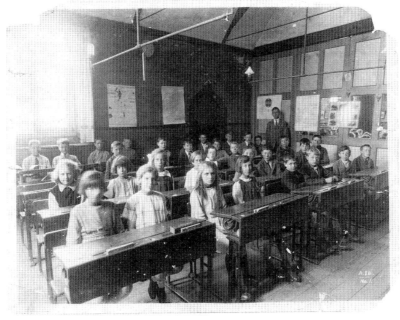

lifts up in one piece to enable things to be put on the shelf underneath. Two china inkwells can be seen and there is a slot at the front edge of the desk to hold a slate. This can be seen more clearly in the Middle School classroom where the children have used the slot for their exercise books *(see previous page)*. In the Seniors classroom the desks are of a more modern design, still seating two children but there are two lids and the shelf is boxed in.

Most of the girls are wearing pinafores, which now are quite plain and made in a variety of materials. A few of the girls are wearing a 'gym-slip'. This was a square-necked tunic

The Seniors' classroom with the headteacher Mr Blaxland standing at the back on the right. Standing on the left at the back is a student teacher, Dorothy Sale, later Mrs Challen. She was formerly a pupil at Send School.

Another class with the teacher Mrs Eugenie Goldsmith who taught at the schoo; from 1919 – 1924. the girl sitting in the back row on the right is Sybil Perrin, later Mrs Somerfield who became a teacher and taught in local schools.

with box pleats falling from a shoulder yoke and fastening on the shoulder. It was tied round the waist with a matching or coloured braid girdle. Some of the girls are wearing boots but most have shoes. The older boys are wearing jackets and ties, but the younger ones are wearing woollen shirts with collars.

Walls are hung with pictures and the children's paintings, and there are flowers on the window sills of two of the classrooms. The rooms are lit by overhanging gas mantles and heated by solid fuel stoves. One stove can be seen in the Infants classroom with a protective fireguard around it.

*****

In this Ripley class photograph of 1927, the children have been identified by Mrs Barbara Scott (née Gunner) a former pupil.

The teacher Miss Gladys Cosson is remembered because she rode her own motor-cycle to school.

Class at Ripley National school 1927 with Miss Cosson
Starting with the back row from the left are;
Sid Wyatt, Bert Freeman, Jack Richardson, Reg Tilett, Fred Wilkins, Sid Wright, Fred Samme, Alfred Hack, Miss Gladys Cosson (teacher), Barbara Gunner, Yvonne Baker, Irene Hutson, Hazel Plowman, Maudie Mills, Elsie Milton, Joyce Foster, Kathy Townsend, Rose Tickner, Doris Goodman, Ruth Gadd
Phyllis Pullen, Dorothy Sink, Winnie Charman, Alice Fenn, Eva Pullen, Millie Blakeman, Vi Foster,
Peter Giles, John Charman, Victor Weller, John Fruin, Bill Muir, Arthur Jelly, Alfred Martin,
George Best, John Perrin, Stan Perrin

Chapter 7

Sporting Activities

In the 1920s the nation had developed a passion for fresh air. This filtered down to the schools and as a result there was more participation in organised games, including football and netball. More time was allowed to be spent outside the classroom in the fresh air, and when the weather was fine then lessons too could be taken outdoors. The boys would go to Ripley Green for their football lessons and the school entered teams for the District events in Woking in the 1930s. They also had their own Sports Days, usually on Ripley Court Field by courtesy of one of the Managers.

Swimming was another activity now encouraged. The children were taken to the River Wey and were allowed to swim in a designated area near Walsham Lock. Girls and boys went there on different days.

In the District events, the children who learned to swim in canals and rivers competed against others who did the same. There was a separate event for those who learned to swim in public swimming baths.

Another sport was rifle shooting. Mr Blaxland had a keen interest in the sport and entered teams from the school in the National Rifle Shooting Competitions. The boys acquitted themselves well on these occasions, often carrying a trophy back to the school. Mr Blaxland was a member of the Ripley Rifle Club and was the winner of the Championship in 1926. His name appears on the Club board, which is now in the Send and Ripley History Society Museum.

Girls, too, were enjoying greater freedom

Ripley School 2nd XI (1931–32)
Peter Shinn, Stan Perrin, Mr George Hughes (teacher), Dennis Collyer, George Best, Peter Giles, John Stevens, George Burt, Fred Wilkins, Bill Muir, Frank Pullen, Bob Brewer.

Ripley School netball team 1934

Miss Kathleen Bullard(teacher), May Hersey, Freda Gunner, Olive Hatcher, Elsie Plumbridge, Elsie Milton, Eileen Hatcher, Trixie Martin, Audrey Chandler.

in outdoor activities. Drill had now been replaced by PT (physical training) and netball was a game that the girls were encouraged to play as it could be practised in the playground. They too were soon competing in the Woking District Sports and the girls of the school netball team can be seen in the photograph.

*****

In 1933 Mr Blaxland received a communication from Surrey County Council stating that the school would now be known as the Ripley Church of England School. It had unofficially been known as that since 1919 as one of the earlier photographs shows!

In 1935 and Mr and Mrs Blaxland were getting ready to retire. They had been at the school for 26 years and had seen many changes for the better for the children. The curriculum had expanded and some children were able to take up opportunities for higher education although most still left aged 14 to go out to work. More sporting activities were open to the children and Mr Blaxland's successor was a man who would continue to encourage sports and games.

On the next page are photographs, taken in 1934, of two school groups. One group is with a teacher, George Edward Hughes, and the other group is with William Blaxland, the Headmaster, in his last years at the school.

(Only some of the children have been named)

Bill Taylor, Stan Clarke, Harold Marsh, Norman Hill, Jimmy Potter, Bob Brewer, Richard Shorter, Roger Brown, Charlie Wanbon, Frank Hack, Winnie Farnfield, Kathy Chandler, Eileen Hatcher, Mary Morris, Peter Wood, Ken Freeman, Frank Pullen, Rob Hill, Audrey Chandler, Phoebe Sink, Audrey Sink, Albert Trussler, George Burt.

Class at Ripley Church of England School 1934, with George Edward Hughes, teacher

Back row: Albert Trussler, Walter Wood, George Burt, Len Yallop, Dennis Shoesmith, Dennis Collyer, Peter Giles, Alfred Hack, Frank Muir..

Next row: Violet Foster, Winnie Blakeman, Ruby Spooner, Irene Hutson, Elsie Milton, Ruth Gadd, May Hersey.

Seated row: Eileen Hatcher, Freda Gunner, Olive Hatcher, Mollie Wilkins, Trixie Martin, Elsie Plumbridge.

Front row: John Holt, Arthur Worsfold, Ronnie Knight, Stan Kellaway, Johnny Morris, Joe Burfield.

Class at Ripley Church of England School 1934, with William Blaxland, Headteacher

Chapter 8

Frederick Dixon

Fred Dixon started his work as Headmaster of Ripley School on 6th January 1936. He was to remain there for 25 years and he too saw changes in his time at the school, many of them brought about by his own efforts, and he too had to cope with a world war, albeit on the Home Front. His main concern always was the safety of the children in his care. After his retirement he spent many years writing his memoirs, in a book entitled *The Straight Furrow*. This book was first published by the Send and Ripley History Society, in 1986.

On his arrival in Ripley in 1936 Mr Dixon had found much that was feudal in the village. In his book he describes his battles with the School Managers to get essential repairs done to the school, and the efforts he had to make to get improvements in lighting and heating. Electric lighting and heating was not installed until 1938 and only then by the gift of a local benefactor, Mrs Hollingsworth. The gentry of the village, who formed the Managers and who were also the main financial subscribers to the school, were prepared to let the village children be educated under conditions that Mr Dixon found unacceptable. Having taught at other schools, including ten years in one in Woking, he was appalled at what he found at this Church school in rural Surrey.

The cleaning of the school, for example, was done under extreme difficulties and the toilets were a real cause for concern. Appeals to the Managers for action were ignored and Mr Dixon had to bring about changes through his own initiatives.

In 1939 Mr Dixon sadly reported the death of William Gunner who had been caretaker at the school for thirty years, He had been a great support to Mr Dixon in his initial efforts to improve conditions there in the three years that they had worked together.

Frederick Dixon, Headmaster

The first year of the Second World War brought problems for Mr Dixon and the staff at Ripley School. Children were being hastily evacuated from London and the south coast to Ripley and had to be accommodated in the school. Some were government evacuees, and some were independent evacuees with relatives in the village who took them in. Thirty-three children from London arrived in September 1939 and had to be found billets with families in the village, and another thirty-six children came during the following months before Christmas. Early in 1940 thirty more children came from Portsmouth and again the people of Ripley were asked to take them into their homes. Many did not stay very long and some children returned home within a few days of arrival! Life in a country village with only a few shops and no cinema must have seemed very alien to these displaced town children, so it was small wonder that they determined to return to their homes, bombs and all!

But some children stayed for the duration of the war and finished their education. Evacuees continued to come to Ripley school throughout the war years, the last one coming in August 1944. One evacuee will be remembered, Derek Holyoak, from Gipsy Road Senior Boys school, South Norwood. He was awarded the Parchment Testimonial of the Royal Humane Society for saving the life of a local boy, Dennis Hotson, at Walsham Lock bathing place in 1941. This was presented to him at the official opening of the new Send Central School in November 1941 where Derek was amongst the first pupils.

The beginning of the Second World War also brought about some radical changes to the school day. It had long been the wish of

social reformers to see hot meals served in schools at midday. Now the opportunity came to make this a reality. Mothers were needed to fill the jobs vacated by the men who had been called up for military service. The school no longer closed at midday for children to go home to dinner, and hot meals were cooked and served to the children at school at affordable prices, thus ensuring that children were properly fed during the war years. Teachers were expected to supervise the children during the dinner break, which they did until the war was over, and other helpers were recruited to be 'dinner ladies'. Local authorities subsidised the cost of the meals.

The School Meals Service continued after the war but the hope that all school meals would eventually be free was never realised, although children of parents with low incomes were entitled to free meals from the begin-

School meals being served in one of the classrooms

ning. The first school cook appointed at Ripley School was Mrs Victoria Surey. She was followed in 1945 by Mrs Dora Hockley, who was to stay until the school building closed in 1968. Mrs Hockley, née Surey, had been a former pupil at the school when Mr Blaxland was headmaster.

Despite the war there were educational changes ahead for the children. A new school

In the photograph (which is by courtesy of Mrs Dora Hockley) are, left to right, Mrs Hockley, Mrs Woods, Mrs Hotson, Mrs Marsh, Mrs Dart and Mrs Williams.

at Send opened its doors in September1941 offering free secondary education for all for the first time, and children were now transferred there from Ripley at the age of 11. The school leaving age was about to be raised to 15 and the new school offered subjects that couldn't be tackled at elementary level. These included commercial subjects such as shorthand and typing, and now children could be prepared for and take exams previously possible only from the grammar schools.

However, domestic science, woodwork and metalwork had been part of the curriculum for the senior boys and girls of Ripley school since the1920s. A hut in the playground of Send school had been built for this purpose and the children had travelled there and also to a centre at Cobham each week for these lessons. Now all this and more was available for them at the new secondary school. They were going to have better opportunities for sport too, as there were ample playing fields and large playgrounds, and there was a school canteen where the food was cooked on the premises.

The new secondary school started life as Send Central School. The name was later changed to St Bede's. It was a church-funded school for the children of Send, Ripley, East Clandon, West Clandon and Ockham and was supported financially by the five parochial church councils. Children could still leave school at the age of 14 but many chose to stay on until they were 15 or16.

*****

When the war was over Mr Dixon became concerned about the increased traffic on the road outside Ripley School. Cars that had been little used during the war years were now back on the roads, and more people were aspiring to owning a car or a motor-cycle. Mr Dixon again had to fight bureaucracy, this time to get pedestrian crossings on the busy road outside the school to help the children to cross safely. He decided then that the school bell should no longer be rung because he feared that children might run across the busy road in order not to be late for school. He observed that the bell had remained silent during the war years and was now no longer needed.

The post war years brought one improvement: the schools were allowed to appoint a School Secretary whereas previously the headteachers had had to cope with their own paperwork. At Ripley Primary School the first such secretary was Mrs Dorothy Gillett who was appointed in 1945.

The short times some children stayed at school have already been mentioned. There was one group of children who regularly made 'short stays' at the school. Their address was The Fair, Ripley Green, and they were children who travelled the country with their fairground parents, getting their education wherever they happened to be. Occasionally other

Children dancing on Ripley Green, June, 1953

Mr Dixon with Celia Baker, aged 10, who is practising reading a passage from the Bible in readiness for the service in Ripley church at which the Bible was to be blessed

families of children would arrive and be registered, only to disappear without notice during the year; or to go hop-picking with their parents! Their address would be The Caravans on the Green. The Headmaster referred to them as NOMADS, in the Admissions Register!

*****

In February 1952 King George VI died after a reign of 15 years. He had succeeded to

the throne in 1936 after the abdication of his brother, Edward VIII, who had become King on the death of their father George V. Now his daughter Elizabeth acceded to the throne to become Queen Elizabeth II.

The Coronation on 2nd June 1953 was celebrated in Ripley with country dancing *(see picture on previous page)*, maypole dancing and Morris dancing on Ripley Green and tea was provided for 260 children in the school.

Each of the children at Ripley School was given a New Testament to commemorate the Coronation. The school received a lectern bible from Surrey Education Committee as a permanent commemoration of the event.

Another child who was a pupil at Ripley School in the 1950s was Eric Clapton. He started school in January 1950 and moved on to St Bede's secondary school in 1956. As an adult he became famous in the world of music as a rock guitarist, a position he enjoys to this day. He is well remembered by his contemporaries and he still keeps in touch with Ripley and his old friends.

ADVERTISER AND COUNTY TIMES SATURDAY DECEMBER 19 1953

Celia is pictured here again with a group of other top-of-the-class prize-winners at Ripley Church of England School in December 1953

SCHOOL'S CORONATION BIBLE BLESSED

Schoolchildren and their parents filled Ripley Parish Church on Friday afternoon for the Blessing of a Holy Bible presented to Ripley County Primary School by Surrey County Council and the school managers in commemoration of the Coronation. The Bible was laid on the altar, where it was Blessed by the Vicar (the Rev. G. R. Wells). He carried it to the reading desk, where 10-year-old Celia Baker read the lesson from St. Luke's Gospel, chapter iv.

The black morocco-bound Bible will be used daily in school. An illuminated inscription recording the presentation on the inside of the cover is the work of Mr. B. Coward, a member of the teaching staff.

These children were "top of the class" prizewinners at Ripley C. of E. School this term. They are Corinne Mayhew, Celia Baker, Gillian Crane, Anthony Hill and Michael Beecham. Prizegiving was on Friday last week.

Here are some more photos of children taken in the 1950s.

From far left, Michael Lawrence, and Peter and Ann Nash.

Graham, Clive and Christopher Bowers

Julia and Paul Bowers

In the 1960s some families emigrated from Ripley to live in Australia and Canada. Very recently there has been some correspondence from David and Pat Bowers in Australia who, in seeking information for their family history, have added some about the later years of Ripley School. David Bowers was there in 1943, and his wife Pat (who was Pat Wood) was there in 1953 together with her sister Rosemary and brother Alan, both of whom are also in Australia. Pat remembers starting school in the old Church Hall in Ripley with Arnold Porter as her teacher, and later moving up to the primary school next to the church before going on to St Bede's School in Send. The church hall was brought into use as there was not enough accommodation for all the children at the school.

Above are some photographs of the children of Stanley (David's brother) and Joyce Bowers, who were at Ripley Primary School in the 1960s. Graham, Clive and Christopher Bowers are in the lower left picture, and Julia and Paul Bowers are in the lower right picture.

Mr Dixon retired in 1961, feeling confident that future education for the children of Ripley was now assured. A new primary school was being built in the Georgelands estate, away from the hazards of the main road, and with school accommodation more in keeping with the 20th Century. There were to be playing fields and playgrounds at the new school and a swimming pool was promised. Mr Dixon handed over the school to his successor, Jeffery John Reynolds, knowing that at long last Ripley children were going to be taught "under conditions worthy of them"(his own words).

Mr Dixon moved away from the village and settled in Christmas Pie near Normandy, to be near his daughter, Mrs Joan Wilkins. He died in his 99th year in 1995.

One of his former pupils, John Hutson, wrote of him that "... Fred instilled in us that the 'three Rs' were right for some, but to all of us there were the other three Rs of equal importance - responsibility, reputability and reliability. Our aims, he said, should be in both areas. He will long be remembered for this and for his fairness and counsel to all who sought it..."

There is of course a fuller account of Ripley C of E School during Mr Dixon's headmastership in his own story of those days, in his book *The Straight Furrow* already mentioned *(See next page)*.

THE STRAIGHT FURROW

by

Fred Dixon

SOME MEMOIRS OF
A SURREY VILLAGE SCHOOLMASTER
1936–61

Fred Dixon, Headmaster of Ripley Church of England School for a quarter of a century, vowed from the start to 'plough a straight furrow' in his determined efforts to improve the conditions in the school for his pupils. The memoirs give a vivid impression of his struggle, largely unaided, against established forces to achieve his goal. The war (1939–45) brought additional problems for the school, such as the billeting of evacuees and the air raids, all of which were overcome by Fred's resolute spirit.

This account of his experiences which could probably be told in many other places, is an absorbing and revealing piece of recent social history.

ISBN 09509961 1 4

Back cover of Mr Dixon's book,' The Straight Furrow'

Chapter 9
Farewell

Ripley C of E School was now in the care of Jeffery Jones Reynolds. A past pupil, Mrs Zelda Whittern, née O'Brien, described him as being in the same mould as Mr Dixon. He was a kindly headmaster to the children and his door was always open to the parents to discuss any problems and to offer advice.

But the days of the old school were numbered. It had outlived its usefulness, and the larger more modern premises now being built were needed urgently.

Mr Reynolds was involved in the organisation of the new school being built in Georgelands, and all the children and staff were transferred to the new site on 4th September 1968 at the start of the Autumn Term.

However, before the old school closed its doors for the last time there were parties; parties for the children, and parties for the parents, many of whom were past pupils, to celebrate the school building where for 120 years the children of the parish had been educated.

The old building continued to be used as a canteen, serving hot meals, until the new kitchen facilities in Georgelands were completed. So for a while, the children still had to cross the busy main road each day!

During his time at the old school Mr Reynolds had activated the Swimming Pool Fund and encouraged all fund-raising events to achieve this goal. Not long after the move to the new school this became a reality, to the joy of all the children. Mr Reynolds became the Headmaster of the new school and continued there for the next five years.

But what of the old school building? Without the children in daily occupation it soon began to look forlorn and neglected. Its future was undecided. The villagers wanted to keep it for village meetings and events, but the cost of essential repairs to make this possible proved to be too expensive. The old school was due for demolition, and in the 1980s it was pulled down and a group of small houses

Mr Reynolds with a group of children in 1968

Ripley School phtographed in the 1980s

Church Row built on the site of the old Ripley School. Note the church in the background

Ripley School Bell at the Symposium, 1983

named Church Row were built on the site, some of the bricks from the demolition being used to build the front garden walls. Now the only clue to where the school once stood is the name of a house, opposite Church Row, still called School View.

But that is not quite the end of the story. Let the school bell have the last word! During the time the school stood empty, one of the churchwardens, Gerald Hill, had found the bell tucked away in an outbuilding and, fearing that it might disappear in the demolition, he took it into his own safekeeping.

In 1983 Send and Ripley History Society took part in the Surrey Local History Symposium in Dorking. As the theme was 'Schools' Mr Hill offered the school bell to them for their display. Ted Goldup made a sturdy stand for it and the Society members were proud to ring the bell for the opening of the Symposium.

It still bore the clear inscription, RIPLEY 1847, and 150 years on, in 1997, the bell found its final resting place in the grounds of the present Ripley Church of England Primary School in Georgelands. A local architect,

Arthur Andrews, designed a roofed shelter of brick to house and display the bell, and the Ripley and Send Rotary Club financed the building of the shelter.

At an informal gathering at the school, amongst those present being John Hudson (who had started at the old school in 1934), the Diocesan Director of Education, the Rev. Canon A Chanter, officiated at the blessing of the bell in the school courtyard where it is rung every schoolday by pupils.

Two children, James Fluker and Alexander Lomax, had the honour of pulling the first chimes, and the custom is continued today, with every child in turn, having the honour of ringing the old school bell.

THE OLD SCHOOL BELL
DATING FROM 1847 WAS
RE-ERECTED BY THE
RIPLEY & SEND ROTARY
CLUB IN JANUARY 1997

Here is the bell in its shelter in the grounds of the
Ripley Church of England Primary School in Georgelands.

The inscription reads:
" THE OLD SCHOOL BELL DATING FROM 1847
RE-ERECTED BY THE RIPLEY & SEND ROTARY CLUB
IN JANUARY 1997 "

Pupil Lists for the School at Ripley

1847-1968

A

Year	Name
1939	John ABBOT
1914	Ernest ABBOTT
1922	Dorothy ADAMS
1954	Eugen ADAMS
1949	Christina ADES
1942	Donald ALDRIDGE
1964	Eileen ALDRIDGE
1952	Ian ALDRIDGE
1944	Margaret ALDRIDGE
1886	William ALEXANDER
1942	Joan ALGAR
1938	Leslie ALGAR
1938	Ronald ALGAR
1963	Ian ALLAWAY
1940	Beryl ALLEN
1938	David ALLEN
1867	Ada ALLWORK
1865	Agnes ALLWORK
1874	Benjamin ALLWORK
1876	Ebenezer ALLWORK
1863	Ellen ALLWORK
1869	Emmanuel ALLWORK
1871	John ALLWORK
1950	Colin ANCKORN
1853	Alfred ANDERSON
1853	Ellen ANDERSON
1852	Henry ANDERSON
1851	Mary Ann ANDERSON
1952	Roger ANDERSON
1850	Thomas ANDERSON
1854	Tryphena ANDERSON
1965	Janice ANGELL
1965	Tony ANGELL
1964	Beverley ANGUS
1965	Martin ANGUS
1964	Stephen ANGUS
1967	Heather ARMITAGE
1923	Harry ARMSTRONG
1903	Naomi ARMSTRONG
1968	Marye ARNETT
1962	Carole ASH
1962	Jeanette ASH
1933	Patricia ASHBY
1955	John ATKINS
1964	Angela ATTER
1966	Clifford ATTER
1964	Isabelle ATTER
1964	Richard ATTER
1964	Susan ATTER
1909	Helen AUTON
1880	Ada AVERY
1919	George AVERY
1961	Gillian AVERY
1908	Henry AVERY
1878	James AVERY
1909	Mary Ann AVERY
1960	Sandra AVERY
1912	Thomas AVERY
1965	Brian AYEARS
1955	Janet AYEARS
1958	Karen AYEARS
1962	Richard AYEARS
1961	Jeremy AYRES
1962	Penelope AYRES

B

Year	Name
1877	Amelia BACKHURST
1902	John BACKHURST
1904	Mary BACKHURST
1942	Douglas BAIGENT
1927	Joyce BAIGENT
1925	May BAIGENT
1905	Albert BAILEY
1894	Annie BAILEY
1953	David BAILEY
1871	Deborah BAILEY
1867	Edgar BAILEY
1864	Emma BAILEY
1901	Eveline BAILEY
1899	Maurice BAILEY
1894	Nellie BAILEY
1861	Walter BAILEY
1847	Abraham BAKER
1922	Audrey BAKER
1956	Brian BAKER
1968	Caroline BAKER
1948	Celia BAKER
1935	Daniel BAKER
1849	Eliza BAKER
1847	Emma BAKER
1863	Fanny BAKER
1919	Geoffrey BAKER
1935	Hilda BAKER
1857	James BAKER
1919	Joan BAKER
1924	Leslie BAKER
1968	Lynne BAKER
1852	MaryAnn BAKER
1940	Michael BAKER
1963	Nicholas BAKER
1963	Noel BAKER
1860	Sarah BAKER
1854	William BAKER
1927	Yvonne BAKER
1940	Alan BALDWIN
1965	Jill BALDWIN
1968	Carole BAMPTON
1968	Harry BAMPTON
1968	Shirley BAMPTON
1886	Martha BARDETT
1955	Tracey BARFORD
1957	John BARNES
1906	Hilda BARRATT
1955	Christopher BARRETT
1952	David BARRETT
1968	Geoffrey BARRETT
1940	June BARRETT
1962	Mary BARRETT
1889	John BARRON
1928	Geoffrey BARROW
1959	Alan BARTLETT
1962	Andrew BARTLETT
1968	Paul BARTLETT
1951	Dorothy BARTNIKOWSKI
1937	Audrey BASHALL
1934	Peggy BASHALL
1934	Talbot BASHALL

1965	Leslie	BASSETT	1894	William	BICKNELL	1963	Julia	BOWERS	1949	Beryl	BROWN
1964	Paul	BASSETT	1909	Mabel	BIGGS	1937	Margaret	BOWERS	1917	Cecil	BROWN
1966	Tina	BASSETT	1967	Alison	BIGWOOD	1923	Mary	BOWERS	1886	David	BROWN
1955	Christina	BATEMAN	1959	Cherrill	BIGWOOD	1885	Mary Ann	BOWERS	1917	David	BROWN
1965	Graham	BATEMAN	1952	Dawn	BIGWOOD	1927	Noah	BOWERS	1963	David	BROWN
1958	Judith	BATEMAN	1966	Deirdre	BIGWOOD	1944	Patricia	BOWERS	1893	Edith	BROWN
1966	Mark	BATEMAN	1955	Valerie	BIGWOOD	1966	Paul	BOWERS	1901	Ellen	BROWN
1963	Paul	BATEMAN	1910	Alice	BILLINGSHURST	1932	Rosie	BOWERS	1917	Ernest	BROWN
1941	Paul	BATTERSHILL	1909	Lallie	BILLINGSHURST	1929	Stanley	BOWERS	1886	Fanny	BROWN
1941	Yvette	BATTERSHILL	1919	Eric	BILLINGSLEY	1925	Violet	BOWERS	1905	Fanny	BROWN
1963	Peter	BAUGH	1919	George	BILLINGSLEY	1850	Caroline	BOXALL	1908	Frank	BROWN
1921	Iris	BAVISTER	1921	Sidney	BILLINGSLEY	1888	John	BOXALL	1947	Frank	BROWN
1960	Brian	BAXTER	1923	Stanley	BILLINGSLEY	1850	William	BOXALL	1906	Frederick	BROWN
1965	Wendy	BAYLEY	1847	Eliza	BIRD	1952	Paul	BOYCOTT	1911	George	BROWN
1937	Anthony	BEADLE	1847	Ellen	BIRD	1922	Winnie	BOYD	1899	Grace	BROWN
1936	John	BEARD	1938	Royden	BIRD	1955	John	BOYLETT	1966	Graham	BROWN
1936	Margaret	BEARD	1847	Ann	BIRMINGHAM	1955	Margaret	BOYLETT	1941	Jay	BROWN
1940	James	BEARNE	1883	Annie	BIRMINGHAM	1955	William	BOYLETT	1952	Jennifer	BROWN
1940	Robert	BEARNE	1890	Edward	BIRMINGHAM	1850	Ellen	BRACKLEY	1888	John	BROWN
1940	Wilfred	BEARNE	1849	Eli	BIRMINGHAM	1850	Emma	BRACKLEY	1904	Lily	BROWN
1949	Eric	BEASLEIGH	1886	Ellen	BIRMINGHAM	1848	Hannah	BRACKLEY	1949	Michael	BROWN
1952	Michael	BEAUCHAMP	1854	Emma	BIRMINGHAM	1847	Jemima	BRACKLEY	1896	Minnie	BROWN
1949	Violet	BECKETT	1886	John	BIRMINGHAM	1847	John	BRACKLEY	1912	Olive	BROWN
1889	Kate	BEDSER	1881	Lewis	BIRMINGHAM	1944	Elizabeth	BRADFORD	1937	Pamela	BROWN
1886	Leonard	BEDSER	1852	Mary	BIRMINGHAM	1869	Ellen	BRADLEY	1964	Roger	BROWN
1890	Mary	BEDSER	1896	Naomi	BIRMINGHAM	1860	Frederick	BRADLEY	1926	Roger	BROWN
1893	Thirza	BEDSER	1854	Sarah	BIRMINGHAM	1858	George	BRADLEY	1953	Rosemary	BROWN
1965	Barry	BEESON	1966	Anthony	BLACK	1866	Stephen	BRADLEY	1907	Rosie	BROWN
1966	Hazel	BEESON	1968	Cecil	BLACK	1887	William	BRADLEY	1922	Stanley	BROWN
1965	Maurice	BEESON	1965	Gavin	BLACKMAN	1961	Beverly	BRAITHWAITE	1884	Agnes	BROWNING
1965	Ruth	BEESON	1946	Charles	BLACKMORE	1963	Joanna	BRAITHWAITE	1886	Amos	BROWNING
1950	Anthony	BELL	1944	Donald	BLACKWELL	1959	Stephanie	BRAITHWAITE	1892	Ann	BROWNING
1957	Doreen	BELL	1940	Mavis	BLACKWELL	1959	Vanessa	BRAITHWAITE	1911	Arthur	BROWNING
1886	Annie	BELTON	1887	Percy	BLACKWELL	1942	Antoinette	BREGMAN	1889	Edith	BROWNING
1863	Caroline	BENSTEAD	1891	Alfred	BLAKE	1958	Gerda	BREITENFELD	1939	Ernest	BROWNING
1866	Eliza	BENSTEAD	1966	Caroline	BLAKE	1964	Sandra	BRENCHER	1910	George	BROWNING
1861	James	BENSTEAD	1964	Lesley	BLAKE	1919	Jessie	BREWER	1939	James	BROWNING
1967	Mark	BENSTEAD	1928	Frank	BLAKEMAN	1938	Margaret	BREWER	1952	Graham	BRUNNING
1859	William	BENSTEAD	1932	Jean	BLAKEMAN	1950	Maureen	BREWER	1957	Jean	BRUNNING
1911	Dorothy	BERE	1925	Millie	BLAKEMAN	1952	Norman	BREWER	1954	Susan	BRUNNING
1865	Charles	BERRIDGE	1923	Robert	BLAKEMAN	1933	Peter	BREWER	1967	Lynne	BRUTON
1866	Elizabeth	BERRIDGE	1957	June	BLANDFORD	1925	Robert	BREWER	1943	Althea	BRYANT
1863	Sarah Ann	BERRIDGE	1967	Richard	BLANDFORD	1885	Alice	BRIDGER	1927	Eveline	BUCK
1930	Edith	BERRY	1964	Pamela	BOGGETT	1889	Annie	BRIDGER	1909	Ivy	BUDD
1929	Ellen	BERRY	1968	Alison	BOLTON	1893	Caroline	BRIDGER	1960	Patricia	BULL
1929	Ernest	BERRY	1953	Terence	BOLTON	1895	Eliza	BRIDGER	1892	Annie	BURCHETT
1932	Jack	BERRY	1941	Audrey	BOND	1892	George	BRIDGER	1893	Edith	BURCHETT
1930	Norman	BERRY	1895	Archie	BONNER	1890	Harry	BRIDGER	1889	Elijah	BURCHETT
1929	Thomas	BERRY	1885	Harriet	BONNER	1894	Louisa	BRIDGER	1894	Ellen	BURCHETT
1856	Ellen Jane	BERRYMAN	1913	William	BONNER	1887	Rose	BRIDGER	1887	Mary	BURCHETT
1858	Harry	BERRYMAN	1964	Paul	BONSON	1894	Sidney	BRIDGER	1847	Ellen	BURDETT
1861	Hazlehurst	BERRYMAN	1939	Raymond	BOSSON	1900	William	BRIDLE	1847	Emma	BURDETT
1965	John	BESSANT	1964	Caroline	BOTTLE	1911	Ivy	BRIGINSHAW	1847	George	BURDETT
1965	Wyatt	BESSANT	1968	Alison	BOLTON	1945	Michael	BROCKWELL	1847	Jane	BURDETT
1900	Frank	BEST	1931	Gwendoline	BOUCHER	1945	Audrey	BROOKER	1854	Martha	BURDETT
1925	George	BEST	1931	Phyllis	BOUCHER	1941	Mary	BROOKER	1926	Joseph	BURDFIELD
1958	Janet	BEST	1965	Jacqueline	BOURNE	1966	Anita	BROOKS	1920	Bransby	BURGESS
1951	Keith	BEST	1965	Stuart	BOURNE	1888	James	BROOMFIELD	1961	Carole	BURGESS
1951	Vivian	BEST	1884	Alice	BOWERS	1958	John	BROOMFIELD	1967	Philip	BURGESS
1955	Anthony	BEVAN	1963	Christopher	BOWERS	1958	Richard	BROOMFIELD	1961	Stephen	BURGESS
1947	Phyllis	BEVIS	1962	Clive	BOWERS	1886	Willie	BROOMFIELD	1925	George	BURT
1960	John	BIARD	1952	Daniel	BOWERS	1963	Christine	BROTHWELL	1968	Jacqueline	BURT
1954	Michael	BIARD	1943	David	BOWERS	1915	Albert	BROWN	1964	Leslie	BURT
1894	Harold	BICKNELL	1960	Graham	BOWERS	1886	Annie	BROWN	1935	Philip	BURT
1894	Henry	BICKNELL	1934	Gwendoline	BOWERS	1908	Annie	BROWN	1929	Ronald	BURT
			1886	Isabella	BOWERS						

Year	Name	Surname
1958	Roy	BURT
1938	Jean	BUSBY
1950	Margaret	BUSH
1935	Frances	BUSHNELL
1932	Jessie	BUSHNELL
1963	Rodney	BUTCHER
1889	Ada	BUTLER
1881	Albert	BUTLER
1865	Alfred	BUTLER
1968	Alison	BUTLER
1879	Arthur	BUTLER
1900	Aubrey	BUTLER
1964	Carole	BUTLER
1872	Daniel	BUTLER
1863	Eliza	BUTLER
1883	Elizabeth	BUTLER
1894	Ella	BUTLER
1875	Frederick	BUTLER
1847	Alfred	BUTLER
1848	Eliza	BUTLER
1847	Emma	BUTLER
1848	George	BUTLER
1873	George	BUTLER
1903	Harry	BUTLER
1887	Henry	BUTLER
1850	James	BUTLER
1868	Jane	BUTLER
1837	John	BUTLER
1866	John	BUTLER
1885	Joshua	BUTLER
1903	Lucy	BUTLER
1885	Margaret	BUTLER
1890	Mark	BUTLER
1892	Minnie	BUTLER
1892	Robert	BUTLER
1884	Rose	BUTLER
1871	Sarah	BUTLER
1896	Sidney	BUTLER
1875	Thomas	BUTLER
1869	William	BUTLER

C

Year	Name	Surname
1876	Albert	CAFFIN
1867	Alfred	CAFFIN
1861	Edith	CAFFIN
1870	Frances	CAFFIN
1872	Mary	CAFFIN
1859	Sarah	CAFFIN
1864	Thomas	CAFFIN
1863	William	CAFFIN
1943	Bransby	CAFFYN
1914	Louis	CAFFYN
1913	Tommy	CAFFYN
1929	Thomas	CAIRNS
1968	Jacqueline	CALDERWOOD
1960	Margaret	CALDERWOOD
1956	Christina	CAMPBELL
1916	Martha	CAREY
1867	John	CARPENTER
1950	Lorraine	CARRUTHERS
1951	Maxine	CARRUTHERS
1960	Susan	CARRUTHERS
1940	Joan	CARSWELL
1957	Clive	CARTER

Year	Name	Surname
1852	Henry	CARTER
1927	Kenneth	CARTER
1964	Lorraine	CARTER
1852	Louisa	CARTER
1966	Maureen	CARTER
1847	Rachell	CARTER
1847	Rebecca	CARTER
1847	Samuel	CARTER
1847	Sarah	CARTER
1941	Shelagh	CARTER
1968	Susan	CARTER
1852	Thomas	CARTER
1938	Vanessa	CARTER
1933	Vernon	CARTER
1886	Walter	CARTER
1909	Ivy	CARTER
1911	Lily	CARTER
1965	Denise	CARTLEDGE
1967	Stephen	CARTLEDGE
1912	Douglas	CARTWRIGHT
1961	Raymond	CARTWRIGHT
1886	Annibel	CASEMORE
1878	Cassey	CASEMORE
1888	Colin	CASEMORE
1874	Dorothy	CASEMORE
1888	Fanny	CASEMORE
1880	Harriet	CASEMORE
1888	Jennie	CASEMORE
1892	Rose	CASEMORE
1968	Audrey	CATCHPOLE
1968	Bryan	CATCHPOLE
1959	Arostino	CEO
1959	Michele	CEO
1849	Amos	CHALCROFT
1847	Edmund	CHALCROFT
1847	Edward	CHALCROFT
1849	Jane	CHALCROFT
1911	Alfred	CHAMBERS
1910	Harry	CHAMBERS
1925	Joan	CHAMPNESS
1925	Olive	CHAMPNESS
1925	Phillip	CHAMPNESS
1925	Rhoda	CHAMPNESS
1917	Alfred	CHANDLER
1903	Annie	CHANDLER
1917	Arthur	CHANDLER
1926	Audrey	CHANDLER
1911	Doris	CHANDLER
1960	Eileen	CHANDLER
1909	Emily	CHANDLER
1899	George	CHANDLER
1940	Gerald	CHANDLER
1910	Jack	CHANDLER
1938	John	CHANDLER
1937	June	CHANDLER
1927	Kathleen	CHANDLER
1919	Lilian	CHANDLER
1910	Lily	CHANDLER
1952	Malcolm	CHANDLER
1952	Marlene	CHANDLER
1957	Maxine	CHANDLER
1950	Michael	CHANDLER
1933	Muriel	CHANDLER
1938	Patricia	CHANDLER
1900	Percy	CHANDLER

Year	Name	Surname
1940	Peter	CHANDLER
1917	Ralph	CHANDLER
1940	Robert	CHANDLER
1965	Sharon	CHANDLER
1955	Shirley	CHANDLER
1917	William	CHANDLER
1965	Heather	CHANNING
1967	Hilary	CHANNING
1919	Connie	CHAPLIN
1926	Olive	CHAPLIN
1938	Brenda	CHAPMAN
1910	Cyril	CHAPMAN
1938	David	CHAPMAN
1930	Doreen	CHAPMAN
1892	Albert	CHARMAN
1910	Alfred	CHARMAN
1910	Alfred	CHARMAN
1944	Alfreda	CHARMAN
1907	Annie	CHARMAN
1945	Anthony	CHARMAN
1943	Edna	CHARMAN
1928	Eileen	CHARMAN
1904	Ernest	CHARMAN
1903	Fanny	CHARMAN
1925	Fred	CHARMAN
1917	Gladys	CHARMAN
1919	Harry	CHARMAN
1952	Janet	CHARMAN
1965	Jennifer	CHARMAN
1890	John	CHARMAN
1924	John	CHARMAN
1951	John	CHARMAN
1949	Joyce	CHARMAN
1864	Martha	CHARMAN
1920	Mary	CHARMAN
1898	May	CHARMAN
1938	Patricia	CHARMAN
1963	Paul	CHARMAN
1894	Percy	CHARMAN
1925	Phillip	CHARMAN
1924	Raymond	CHARMAN
1917	Reginald	CHARMAN
1941	Ronald	CHARMAN
1915	Rose	CHARMAN
1847	Stephen	CHARMAN
1937	Victor	CHARMAN
1928	Violet	CHARMAN
1924	Winifred	CHARMAN
1965	Julie	CHATFIELD
1967	Philip	CHATFIELD
1967	Sandra	CHATFIELD
1967	Tony	CHATFIELD
1895	Bertha	CHEESEMAN
1889	Ellen	CHEESEMAN
1890	Frank	CHEESEMAN
1887	Richard	CHEESEMAN
1922	Dorothy	CHEESMAR
1945	Douglas	CHENNELL
1938	Pamela	CHERRY
1958	Kenneth	CHESTER
1847	Edward	CHILDS
1962	Malcolm	CHILDS
1951	Richard	CHILDS
1964	Stephen	CHILDS
1847	Ellen	CHITTY

Year	Name	Surname
1910	Harold	CHIVERS
1939	Arthur	CHUBB
1953	Dennis	CHUBB
1951	Roy	CHUBB
1912	Geoffrey	CHURCH
1960	Sherrell	CHUTER
1927	Audrey	CLAPP
1933	Daphne	CLAPP
1933	Joan	CLAPP
1917	John	CLAPP
1926	Ronald	CLAPP
1933	Adrian	CLAPTON
1950	Eric	CLAPTON
1934	Patricia	CLAPTON
1951	Michael	CLARGES
1951	Peter	CLARGES
1917	Alice	CLARK
1868	Anne	CLARK
1914	Edith	CLARK
1870	Emily	CLARK
1876	Fanny	CLARK
1885	Florence	CLARK
1881	Frederick	CLARK
1869	Henry	CLARK
1931	Mary	CLARK
1866	Sarah	CLARK
1873	William	CLARK
1893	William	CLARK
1915	Alfred	CLARKE
1952	Brian	CLARKE
1927	Connie	CLARKE
1946	Daniel	CLARKE
1915	Dick	CLARKE
1921	Florence	CLARKE
1938	Gladys	CLARKE
1943	John	CLARKE
1966	Robin	CLARKE
1928	Stanley	CLARKE
1959	David	CLAYTON
1957	John	CLAYTON
1966	Marit	CLAYTON
1956	Elizabeth	CLEW
1959	Alan	CLINTON
1959	Yvonne	CLINTON
1910	Lily	COBBALD
1936	Frederick	COCKCROFT
1920	Henry	COGAN
1958	Sally	COGBILL
1958	Susan	COGBILL
1885	Mary	COLBORNE
1913	Tom	COLBORNE
1875	Ada	COLBOURNE
1872	Alfred	COLBOURNE
1906	Dorothy	COLBOURNE
1865	Ellen	COLBOURNE
1868	Harry	COLBOURNE
1876	Mary	COLBOURNE
1870	Walter	COLBOURNE
1960	Barnaby	COLE
1960	Melanie	COLE
1916	Evelyn	COLLINS
1947	Margaret	COLLISON
1950	Ronald	COLLISON
1884	Ada	COLLYER
1962	Alan	COLLYER

1917	Alma	COLLYER
1935	Antony	COLLYER
1937	Barbara	COLLYER
1847	Cozbi	COLLYER
1926	Dennis	COLLYER
1918	Doris	COLLYER
1885	Edith	COLLYER
1886	Ethel	COLLYER
1849	Fanny	COLLYER
1885	Frank	COLLYER
1965	Geoffrey	COLLYER
1894	Harry	COLLYER
1851	James	COLLYER
1939	Joy	COLLYER
1939	Margaret	COLLYER
1932	Marjorie	COLLYER
1961	Michael	COLLYER
1938	Robert	COLLYER
1937	Rosemary	COLLYER
1852	Sarah	COLLYER
1888	Stephen	COLLYER
1941	Trevor	COLLYER
1966	Wendy	COLLYER
1937	Frederick	CONISBEE
1939	Jean	CONISBEE
1937	Peter	CONISBEE
1938	Catherine	CONSTANCE
1956	Lesley	CONSTANTINE
1968	Louise	CONWAY
1967	Susan	CONWAY
1918	Evelyn	COOK
1921	Ivy	COOK
1951	Shirley	COOK
1953	Ian	COOKE
1951	Kimberley	COOKE
1953	Margaret	COOMBES
1962	Alan	COOPER
1914	Albert	COOPER
1935	Alfred	COOPER
1894	Alice	COOPER
1847	Ann	COOPER
1865	Charles	COOPER
1928	Edward	COOPER
1914	Eva	COOPER
1869	Fanny	COOPER
1935	George	COOPER
1847	James	COOPER
1847	Jane	COOPER
1871	William	COOPER
1966	Veronica	CORBETT
1941	Jill	CORK
1968	Roger	CORKE
1965	Anita	CORNELIUS
1964	David	CORNELIUS
1964	Ian	CORNELIUS
1888	Robert	CORPES
1944	Alan	CORPS
1953	Derek	COTTINGTON
1953	Polly	COTTINGTON
1886	Albert	COX
1852	Anne	COX
1853	Arthur	COX
1881	Arthur	COX
1931	Betty	COX
1854	Caroline	COX

1939	Dorothy	COX
1878	Ellen	COX
1847	Emma	COX
1883	Frank	COX
1847	George	COX
1854	Harriett	COX
1852	James	COX
1968	Linda	COX
1850	Louisa	COX
1847	Robert	COX
1941	Thomas	COX
1929	Lawrence	COXON
1966	Robert	CRAIG
1963	Ann	CRANE
1925	Bertie	CRANE
1948	Carol	CRANE
1928	Ethel	CRANE
1950	Gillian	CRANE
1942	Gwendoline	CRANE
1906	Ivy	CRANE
1962	Janet	CRANE
1940	Jean	CRANE
1933	Leonard	CRANE
1950	Paul	CRANE
1966	Susan	CRANE
1929	William	CRANE
1943	Helen	CRAPPER
1968	Della	CRITCHLEY
1941	Joan	CROAD
1934	Laura	CROFT
1939	Angela	CROSS
1930	Rosemary	CROSS
1945	Doreen	CROUCH
1931	Maud	CROW
1913	Ivy	CUBBERT
1963	David	CUDDEN
1964	Suzanne	CUDDEN
1936	Jean	CURTIS
1936	Keith	CURTIS
1937	Pamela	CURTIS
1852	Ann	CUTT
1854	Edith	CUTT
1853	Edward	CUTT
1852	Emma	CUTT
1854	Frederick	CUTT
1850	Henry	CUTT

D

1941	Thomas	DALLAS
1905	Ada	DANCE
1852	Emma	DANCE
1903	Emma	DANCE
1887	Gertrude	DANCE
1902	Henry	DANCE
1847	James	DANCE
1907	James	DANCE
1847	Sarah	DANCE
1855	William	DANCE
1907	Winifred	DANCE
1853	Caroline	DANIELS
1853	Dinah	DANIELS
1957	Barry	DARLING
1955	Bruce	DARLING
1852	Joseph	DARLING

1957	Andrew	DART
1955	Christopher	DART
1951	Rosemary	DAVERN
1943	Frederick	DAVIES
1966	Janet	DAVIES
1957	Marilyn	DAVIES
1916	Matilda	DAVIES
1943	Michael	DAVIES
1914	Rose	DAVIES
1964	Wendy	DAVIES
1935	Annie	DAVIS
1935	Edward	DAVIS
1940	Jean	DAVIS
1935	Olive	DAVIS
1958	Paul	DAVIS
1935	Vera	DAVIS
1934	Dennis	DAVY
1934	Donald	DAVY
1950	Dianne	DAWES
1886	James	DAWES
1926	Margaret	DAWES
1948	Margaret	DAWES
1884	SarahAnn	DAWES
1847	Frances	DAWS
1847	Harriett	DAWS
1906	Albert	DAY
1948	Colin	DAY
1948	Doreen	DAY
1921	Edward	DAY
1918	John	DAY
1919	Kathleen	DAY
1915	Mabel	DAY
1954	Mary	DAY
1873	Alice	DEADMAN
1871	Caroline	DEADMAN
1968	Heather	DEAN
1966	Nicholas	DEAN
1956	Peter	DEAR
1956	Terence	DEAR
1958	Raymond	DEARDS
1882	Albert	DEDMAN
1879	Eliza	DEDMAN
1885	Ernest	DEDMAN
1877	John	DEDMAN
1895	Maurice	DEDMAN
1959	Margaret	DEERING
1894	Annie	DENBY
1890	Charles	DENBY
1885	Elizabeth	DENBY
1892	Ellen	DENBY
1880	Frances	DENBY
1886	Minnie	DENBY
1879	Sarah	DENBY
1883	William	DENBY
1953	Edward	DENTON
1847	Edmund	DENYER
1847	Henry	DENYER
1940	Joyce	DERBY
1964	Rosa	DESIMONE
1957	Marto	DI PLACEDO
1957	Vincenzo	DI PLACEDO
1891	Annie	DIBBLE
1887	Eveline	DIBBLE
1917	Joan	DIBBLE
1908	Maud	DIBBLE

1943	Robert	DIGGES
1885	Edith	DINES
1889	Emily	DINES
1889	Florrie	DINES
1893	Frederick	DINES
1924	Iris	DIVES
1955	Alan	DIXON
1939	Barry	DIXON
1955	Hilary	DIXON
1937	Joan	DIXON
1951	Judith	DIXON
1939	Raimon	DIXON
1924	Alfred	DOE
1914	Dorothy	DOE
1955	Lynda	DOE
1960	Peter	DOE
1924	William	DOE
1941	Brian	DORAN
1941	John	DORAN
1944	Peter	DORAN
1943	Yvonne	DORAN
1968	Christopher	DORRELL
1965	Elizabeth	DORRELL
1965	Susan	DORRELL
1941	Richard	DOWNS
1891	Isaac	DRAPER
1889	Alfred	DREW
1953	Brenda	DREW
1893	May	DREW
1955	Jennifer	DUNCTON
1886	Ernest	DUNSTAN
1966	Andrew	DURBRIDGE
1961	Colin	DURBRIDGE
1964	Ian	DURBRIDGE
1960	Carol	DYER
1965	Graham	DYER
1958	Pauline	DYER
1960	Susan	DYER
1952	Gwynneth	DYKES
1948	Richard	DYKES

E

1960	John	EARNSHAW
1960	Marion	EARNSHAW
1960	Michael	EARNSHAW
1908	Tyson	EAST
1961	Henry	EASTWOOD
1959	Rosey	EASTWOOD
1968	Nicholas	EBDON
1897	George	EDE
1905	Maurice	EDE
1883	William	EDE
1891	Ethel	EDES
1892	George	EDES
1891	Willie	EDES
1874	James	EDGELL
1876	Thomas	EDGELL
1914	Cecelia	EDIS
1918	Cissie	EDIS
1918	Henry	EDIS
1923	Jack	EDIS
1913	Sydney	EDIS
1918	Thomas	EDIS
1875	Anne	EDISON

Year	Name	Surname
1873	Mary	EDISON
1892	Annie	EDSER
1895	Bertha	EDSER
1893	Eleanor	EDSER
1907	Frederick	EDWARDS
1853	Joseph	EDWARDS
1851	Mary	EDWARDS
1945	Pamela	EDWARDS
1944	Patricia	EDWARDS
1945	Richard	EDWARDS
1851	William	EDWARDS
1934	John	EGGAR
1930	Philip	EGGAR
1949	Ian	ELDERFIELD
1967	David	ELLIS
1895	Ernest	ELLIS
1895	Frederick	ELLIS
1913	George	ELLIS
1949	David	ELLMORE
1847	Joseph	ELMS
1852	John	ELMS
1852	Luke	ELMS
1848	Mary	ELMS
1848	Peter	ELMS
1847	Emily	ELSTON
1940	Alfred	EMERY
1940	Jean	EMERY
1956	Sarah	EMERY
1941	Maud	EMESS
1889	Louisa	ENSOM
1963	Diane	ENTICKNAP
1957	Linda	ENTICKNAP
1912	Daniel	ETHERIDGE
1950	Geoffrey	ETHERIDGE
1886	John	ETHERINGTON
1888	William	ETHERINGTON
1940	Barbara	EVANS
1963	Brian	EVANS
1966	Carolyn	EVANS
1885	Isabella	EVANS
1968	Jean	EVANS
1935	Rowland	EVANS
1963	Sally	EVANS

F

Year	Name	Surname
1878	Henry	FAGENCE
1895	Frances	FAIGENCE
1955	Edward	FAIRFIELD
1941	Rita	FAIRFIELD
1873	Alice	FAITHFUL
1885	Catherine	FAITHFUL
1864	George	FAITHFUL
1853	Harriett	FAITHFUL
1865	John	FAITHFUL
1882	Robert	FAITHFUL
1871	William	FAITHFUL
1847	Henry	FALKNER
1847	Mary	FALKNER
1888	Charles	FARLEY
1887	Edgar	FARLEY
1923	Connie	FARMER
1920	John	FARMER
1885	Kate	FARMER
1917	Kathleen	FARMER

Year	Name	Surname
1965	Paul	FARMER
1968	Timothy	FARMER
1938	Betty	FARNFIELD
1939	John	FARNFIELD
1926	Violet	FARNFIELD
1928	Winnie	FARNFIELD
1891	Winifred	FARR
1904	Ella	FARR
1968	Alan	FARRANT
1968	Carol	FARRANT
1922	Maurice	FAULDS
1960	Dominic	FEELEY
1960	Mary	FEELEY
1924	Alice	FENN
1924	Dorothy	FENN
1924	Edith	FENN
1924	Ethel	FENN
1961	Anthony	FENNER
1958	Stephen	FENNER
1966	Stephen	FICE
1966	Susan	FICE
1850	Luke	FIELD
1964	Nigel	FIELD
1940	Albert	FINCH
1895	Ellen	FINCH
1890	Ethel	FINCH
1890	Maude	FINCH
1942	Patricia	FINCH
1940	Pauline	FINCH
1892	Percy	FINCH
1951	Richard	FINCH
1940	Robert	FINCH
1917	Lena	FIRTH
1920	Francis	FISHER
1920	Gilbert	FISHER
1920	Rosa	FISHER
1956	Wanda	FISHER
1959	Linda	FISZER
1962	Christopher	FITT
1963	Julie	FITZGERALD
1947	George	FIVEASH
1932	Alice	FLACK
1932	Herbert	FLACK
1966	Elizabeth	FLETCHER
1963	Susan	FOALE
1956	Christopher	FOLEY
1950	Beryl	FORD
1939	Ivor	FORD
1936	Phyllis	FORD
1956	David	FOREHEAD
1954	Raymond	FOREHEAD
1960	Carol	FORSDICK
1964	Patricia	FORSYTH
1952	Joy	FOSBERRY
1932	Dennis	FOSTER
1919	Frank	FOSTER
1919	Frederick	FOSTER
1921	Harold	FOSTER
1924	Joyce	FOSTER
1925	Violet	FOSTER
1931	John	FOWLER
1931	Ronald	FOWLER
1899	Albert	FOXLEY
1889	Annie	FOXLEY
1889	Edith	FOXLEY

Year	Name	Surname
1885	Francis	FOXLEY
1894	Isabel	FOXLEY
1937	Geoffrey	FRANCIS
1937	Joan	FRANKLIN
1952	Leslie	FRANKLIN
1939	Margaret	FRANKLIN
1953	Stephen	FRANKLIN
1890	Emily	FREELAND
1885	Hilda	FREELAND
1929	Cyril	FREEMAN
1924	Herbert	FREEMAN
1927	Kenneth	FREEMAN
1930	Margaret	FREEMAN
1920	Ernest	FREEZER
1920	Ivah	FREEZER
1932	Betty	FRENCH
1930	George	FRENCH
1928	Leslie	FRENCH
1936	Raymond	FRENCH
1968	Sharon	FRENCH
1958	Ann	FRESHWATER
1966	Hazel	FRESHWATER
1957	Ian	FRESHWATER
1957	Nigel	FRESHWATER
1968	Debra	FRICKER
1957	Agnes	FROST
1925	John	FRUIN
1923	Mary	FRUIN
1962	Lesley	FRYER
1905	Albert	FULLER
1874	Alfred	FULLER
1888	Arthur	FULLER
1908	Bessie	FULLER
1927	Betty	FULLER
1866	Elizabeth	FULLER
1876	Frank	FULLER
1872	George	FULLER
1907	George	FULLER
1908	Gertrude	FULLER
1868	Harriet	FULLER
1901	Henry	FULLER
1910	Ivy	FULLER
1930	Jean	FULLER
1884	Kate	FULLER
1904	Violet	FULLER
1870	William	FULLER
1919	George	FULLICK
1944	Lilian	FUOCO
1944	Norman	FUOCO
1908	Daisy	FURLONGER
1904	Edmond	FURLONGER
1848	Esther	FURLONGER
1903	Lilian	FURLONGER
1905	William	FURLONGER

G

Year	Name	Surname
1888	Arthur	GADD
1892	Bertram	GADD
1919	Dorothy	GADD
1934	Edwin	GADD
1896	Eleanor	GADD
1923	Elsie	GADD
1921	Evelyn	GADD
1920	Frances	GADD

Year	Name	Surname
1903	Frank	GADD
1891	Frederick	GADD
1889	George	GADD
1888	Hettie	GADD
1927	Irene	GADD
1917	Marjorie	GADD
1914	Mary	GADD
1906	Mildred	GADD
1945	Nicholas	GADD
1922	Norah	GADD
1925	Ruth	GADD
1885	Walter	GADD
1885	William	GADD
1905	Winifred	GADD
1968	Michelle	GAINES
1968	Nicholl	GAINES
1968	Paula	GAINES
1921	Joan	GALLOWAY
1921	Mabel	GALLOWAY
1889	Jessie	GAMBOLL
1889	Phillip	GAMBOLL
1847	George	GANDE
1847	Mary	GANDE
1920	Frederick	GARDINER
1920	Mabel	GARDINER
1920	William	GARDINER
1847	Abram	GARMENT
1847	Daniel	GARMENT
1862	Elizabeth	GARMENT
1853	Harriett	GARMENT
1850	Sarah	GARMENT
1852	Thomas	GARMENT
1852	William	GARMENT
1952	Ian	GARNER
1967	Sonia	GARNETT
1955	Margaret	GARRETT
1960	Richard	GARROOD
1933	Harold	GATES
1929	Albert	GENT
1929	Harold	GENT
1929	Kenneth	GENT
1961	Susan	GEORGE
1951	Jillian	GIBBINS
1957	Brian	GIBBS
1967	Dawn	GIBBS
1953	Mary	GIBBS
1951	Robert	GIBBS
1960	Hugh	GILBERT
1965	Robin	GILBERT
1963	Simon	GILBERT
1967	Andrew	GILCHRIST
1925	Albert	GILES
1847	Elizabeth	GILES
1930	Joyce	GILES
1918	Maria	GILES
1953	Peter	GILES
1963	Carole	GILESPIE
1946	Jenifer	GILLETT
1942	Mary	GILLETT
1940	Sheila	GILLETT
1968	Louise	GLAYSHER
1912	Alice	GODDARD
1912	Dorothy	GODDARD
1956	Gaye	GODDARD
1912	Nellie	GODDARD

1894	Ann	GODFREY
1881	Frederick	GODFREY
1882	James	GODFREY
1899	Walter	GODFREY
1906	George	GOERING
1963	Mark	GOHEGAN
1917	Agnes	GOLDSMITH
1886	Ethel	GOLDSMITH
1964	Anne	GOODCHILD
1966	Caroline	GOODCHILD
1921	Arthur	GOODIN
1934	Doris	GOODIN
1949	Shirley	GOODINOUGH
1961	Robert	GOODMAN
1939	Royston	GOODMAN
1888	Stella	GOSLING
1929	Evelyn	GOSTLING
1933	Winifred	GOSTLING
1964	John	GOUGH
1964	Mary	GOUGH
1953	Alan	GOULD
1949	Donald	GOULD
1960	Norma	GOULD
1913	Denis	GRACE
1899	Jack	GRACE
1910	Lois	GRACE
1847	Maria	GRAY
1941	Michael	GRAY
1892	Alma	GREEN
1895	Bessie	GREEN
1921	Ellen	GREEN
1894	Ernest	GREEN
1912	Reginald	GREEN
1891	Sydney	GREEN
1965	Alan	GREENER
1946	Michael	GREENHAIGH
1955	Richard	GREENING
1955	Kenneth	GREGORY
1956	Michael	GREGORY
1967	Barbara	GRIFFIN
1961	Denise	GRIFFIN
1958	Diane	GRIFFIN
1952	Jill	GROSSMITH
1953	Trevor	GROSSMITH
1919	Allan	GROVER
1922	Claude	GROVER
1966	Denize	GROVES
1850	James	GROVES
1927	Leonard	GROVES
1852	Sarah	GROVES
1906	Albert	GUNNER
1924	Barbara	GUNNER
1937	Douglas	GUNNER
1900	Edith	GUNNER
1882	Ellen	GUNNER
1901	Elsie	GUNNER
1942	Florence	GUNNER
1932	Freda	GUNNER
1917	Gladys	GUNNER
1875	Isaac	GUNNER
1885	James	GUNNER
1879	John	GUNNER
1907	Lilian	GUNNER
1934	Ronald	GUNNER
1878	Sarah	GUNNER
1905	Sylvia	GUNNER
1873	Thomas	GUNNER
1904	William	GUNNER
1912	Cecil	GUY
1960	David	GUY
1875	Eliza	GUY
1873	Ellen	GUY
1891	Emily	GUY
1870	Emma	GUY
1885	George	GUY
1869	James	GUY
1865	John	GUY
1905	Reginald	GUY

H

1925	Alfred	HACK
1928	Dorothy	HACK
1933	Frank	HACK
1933	Hilda	HACK
1940	Mary	HACK
1945	Michael	HACK
1950	Rowena	HACK
1926	Violet	HACK
1931	William	HACK
1911	Albert	HACKER
1911	Henry	HACKER
1937	Joy	HACKER
1950	Ann	HADEN-MORRIS
1937	Jean	HADWIN
1939	Peggy	HADWIN
1953	Carol	HAINES
1937	Cecil	HAINES
1967	David	HAINES
1929	Elsie	HAINES
1941	George	HAINES
1964	Gordon	HAINES
1939	John	HAINES
1930	Leonard	HAINES
1955	Linda	HAINES
1943	Margaret	HAINES
1945	Michael	HAINES
1933	Raymond	HAINES
1929	Sidney	HAINES
1949	Sandra	HALE
1943	Trevor	HALE
1944	Thomas	HALIDAY
1906	Edward	HALL
1862	Eliza	HALL
1876	Emily	HALL
1956	Janice	HALL
1940	Lily	HALL
1866	Sarah	HALL
1965	Susan	HALLIDAY
1962	Kathryn	HAM
1967	John	HAMILTON
1959	John	HAMMOND
1888	Frederick	HAMMONDS
1891	Thomas	HAMMONDS
1915	Florence	HAMPSHIRE
1913	Phoebe	HAMPSHIRE
1917	Alice	HAMPTON
1938	Beryl	HAMPTON
1950	Tony	HAMPTON
1955	Carol	HANDY
1955	David	HANDY
1950	Maureen	HANKIN
1929	Elsie	HANNAN
1956	Elizabeth	HANNIGAN
1918	Alexander	HARDING
1889	Alfred	HARDING
1891	Beatrice	HARDING
1918	Dorothy	HARDING
1927	Harold	HARDING
1895	Louisa	HARDING
1917	Maud	HARDING
1887	Oliver	HARDING
1953	Ann	HARGREAVES
1961	Alison	HARMAN
1964	Beverley	HARMAN
1895	James	HARMAN
1965	Lorraine	HARMAN
1889	Annie	HARMS
1852	Charlotte	HARMS
1850	Ellen	HARMS
1850	Louisa	HARMS
1847	Margaret	HARMS
1852	William	HARMS
1964	Robert	HARPER
1964	Susan	HARPER
1958	Colin	HARRIS
1966	David	HARRIS
1895	Ernest	HARRIS
1961	Peter	HARRIS
1958	Barbara	HARVEY
1959	Carol	HARVEY
1934	Joyce	HARVEY
1935	Kenneth	HARVEY
1940	Wilfred	HASKINS
1914	Alfred	HASTIE
1887	Henry	HASTIE
1887	Louisa	HASTIE
1917	Walter	HASTIE
1930	Arnold	HATCHER
1930	Edith	HATCHER
1925	Eileen	HATCHER
1936	Joan	HATCHER
1929	Joyce	HATCHER
1926	Lily	HATCHER
1929	Olive	HATCHER
1931	Patricia	HATCHER
1931	Patrick	HATCHER
1930	Stanley	HATCHER
1957	Vanessa	HATCHER
1954	Daniel	HAWKINS
1934	Dennis	HAYNES
1939	Sylvia	HAYNES
1924	Alice	HAYWARD
1924	Bessie	HAYWARD
1924	Charlie	HAYWARD
1924	Henry	HAYWARD
1924	Joseph	HAYWARD
1924	Louie	HAYWARD
1901	Blanche	HEAD
1967	Kevin	HEAD
1851	James	HEADY
1878	James	HEADY
1855	Martha	HEADY
1884	Mary	HEADY
1848	Thomas	HEADY
1882	William	HEADY
1916	Ina	HEARN
1900	Dolly	HEARTH
1918	Elizabeth	HEATH
1910	Frank	HEATH
1911	Jack	HEATH
1913	Nellie	HEATH
1968	Lorraine	HEATON
1847	Jane	HEDGCOCK
1847	John	HEDGCOCK
1851	Thomas	HEDGCOCK
1951	Allen	HENLEY
1947	Glenda	HEPBURN
1951	Rodney	HEPBURN
1889	Ernest	HERSEY
1888	George	HERSEY
1890	Henry	HERSEY
1925	May	HERSEY
1962	Alan	HESELWOOD
1962	Tony	HESELWOOD
1951	John	HEWITT
1904	Annie	HIGGINS
1895	Edith	HIGGINS
1885	Kate	HIGGINS
1876	Albert	HILL
1886	Alfred	HILL
1951	Alfred	HILL
1936	Alma	HILL
1965	Andrew	HILL
1951	Anthony	HILL
1912	Arthur	HILL
1943	Arthur	HILL
1886	Bert	HILL
1959	Beryl	HILL
1928	Betty	HILL
1935	Christine	HILL
1955	Christopher	HILL
1949	Clifford	HILL
1941	Doreen	HILL
1922	Doris	HILL
1945	Dorothy	HILL
1882	Edith	HILL
1932	Edith	HILL
1937	Edna	HILL
1883	Esther	HILL
1916	Ethel	HILL
1883	Frances	HILL
1906	Frank	HILL
1942	Frederick	HILL
1948	Geoffrey	HILL
1901	Gussie	HILL
1911	Hubert	HILL
1947	Hubert	HILL
1922	Joan	HILL
1938	Joan	HILL
1918	Kitty	HILL
1885	Laura	HILL
1916	Laura	HILL
1910	Lily	HILL
1877	Lydia	HILL
1888	Maggie	HILL
1926	Nancy	HILL
1926	Norman	HILL
1947	Paul	HILL
1929	Peggy	HILL

1899	Phyllis	HILL
1892	Robert	HILL
1918	Robert	HILL
1932	Robert	HILL
1886	Roland	HILL
1919	Ronald	HILL
1881	Samuel	HILL
1879	Sarah	HILL
1963	Simon	HILL
1961	Stephen	HILL
1949	Susan	HILL
1940	Tony	HILL
1931	William	HILL
1874	Bertha	HILLIER
1876	Margaret	HILLIER
1940	Sylvia	HILLS
1848	George	HITCHCOCK
1850	Lucy	HITCHCOCK
1848	Mary	HITCHCOCK
1919	Alice	HITCHMAN
1955	John	HOBBS
1923	Frank	HOCKLEY
1923	William	HOCKLEY
1965	Ian	HODGE
1965	Robert	HODGSON
1896	Bessie	HOLDEN
1896	Harvist	HOLDEN
1896	Thomas	HOLDEN
1968	Mary	HOLLAND
1968	Thomas	HOLLAND
1958	Angela	HOLLIS
1958	Carol	HOLLIS
1958	Lynda	HOLLIS
1923	Christene	HOLLOWAY
1908	Gertie	HOLLOWAY
1936	David	HOLT
1923	John	HOLT
1940	Stewart	HOLT
1912	Violet	HOLT
1940	Derek	HOLYOAKE
1943	Rita	HONOUR
1876	Albert	HOOK
1874	Elizabeth	HOOK
1936	Gladys	HOOK
1878	John	HOOK
1936	Margaret	HOOK
1868	Mary	HOOK
1939	Pansy	HOOK
1865	William	HOOK
1942	Adrian	HOOKER
1943	Barbara	HOOKER
1937	Molly	HOOKER
1911	Alfred	HOPCROFT
1911	Charles	HOPCROFT
1889	Beatrice	HOPKINS
1889	Bertha	HOPKINS
1847	Henry	HOPKINS
1847	Peter	HOPKINS
1921	Jack	HOPLEY
1921	Wilhelmina	HOPLEY
1948	John	HORNIBROOK
1948	Sylvia	HORNIBROOK
1959	Sally	HOSKINS
1956	Susan	HOSKINS
1933	Dennis	HOTSON

1952	Graham	HOTSON
1928	Kenneth	HOTSON
1959	Kenneth	HOTSON
1937	Leonard	HOTSON
1943	Penelope	HOTSON
1951	Peter	HOTSON
1954	Roy	HOTSON
1941	Stella	HOTSON
1920	Muriel	HOWARD
1912	Ivy	HOWELL
1912	Margaret	HOWELL
1928	Percy	HOWICK
1927	Sidney	HOWICK
1940	Derek	HUGGETT
1962	Deborah	HUGHES
1962	Paul	HUGHES
1964	Sarah	HUGHES
1943	Sheila	HUGHES
1955	Geoffrey	HULL
1955	Yvonne	HULL
1950	David	HUMPHREYS
1956	David	HUSSEY
1934	Albert	HUTSON
1953	Graeme	HUTSON
1926	Irene	HUTSON
1961	Jeremy	HUTSON
1958	Steven	HUTSON
1914	Frederick	HUTTON
1900	Ada	HYDE
1885	Agnes	HYDE
1869	Alice	HYDE
1890	Annie	HYDE
1890	Arthur	HYDE
1950	David	HYDE
1901	Dorothy	HYDE
1886	Edith	HYDE
1915	Hilda	HYDE
1958	Janet	HYDE
1946	Joan	HYDE
1868	John	HYDE
1866	Joseph	HYDE
1893	Laura	HYDE
1868	Lucy	HYDE
1892	Mary	HYDE
1896	May	HYDE
1886	Ralph	HYDE
1894	William	HYDE

I

1965	Umberto	IMPERATO
1865	Agnes	IMPEY
1863	Arthur	IMPEY
1867	Eleanor	IMPEY
1874	Florence	IMPEY
1888	Aden	INGRAM
1888	Helen	INGRAM
1948	Eric	INSLEY
1952	Yvonne	INSLEY
1967	Anne	IRELAND
1967	Peter	IRELAND
1866	Alfred	ISTEAD
1868	Sarah	ISTEAD
1940	Kenneth	IVEY

J

1966	Caroline	JACKMAN
1850	Daniel	JACKMAN
1968	Debra	JACKMAN
1847	Elizabeth	JACKMAN
1851	Fanny	JACKMAN
1853	George	JACKMAN
1851	Harriett	JACKMAN
1964	Michael	JACKMAN
1852	Stephen	JACKMAN
1851	William	JACKMAN
1952	Roger	JAMES
1916	Ethel	JARMAN
1968	Lorraine	JARVIS
1961	Martin	JARVIS
1964	Susan	JARVIS
1946	Patricia	JATER
1966	Nigel	JELLEY
1926	Arthur	JELLY
1944	Donald	JELLY
1847	Eliza	JELLY
1924	Ethel	JELLY
1932	Frederick	JELLY
1928	Norah	JELLY
1915	Percy	JELLY
1921	Reginald	JELLY
1944	Brian	JENKINS
1854	George	JENNINGS
1854	Robert	JENNINGS
1968	Charlotte	JEPSON
1966	Stephen	JEPSON
1960	Jennifer	JOHNS
1962	Heather	JOHNSON
1959	Marie	JOHNSON
1959	Mary	JOHNSON
1963	Paul	JOHNSON
1959	Sylvia	JOHNSON
1964	Wendy	JOHNSON
1967	Andrew	JONES
1935	Arthur	JONES
1891	Fanny	JONES
1891	George	JONES
1936	Hilda	JONES
1939	Jean	JONES
1964	Kevin	JONES
1939	Margaret	JONES
1950	Peter	JONES
1944	Sidney	JONES
1967	Susan	JONES
1967	Terence	JONES
1940	Eunice	JUDD
1940	Victor	JUDD

K

1938	Kathleen	KANSETT
1886	Amy	KEARSWELL
1886	Jane	KEARSWELL
1883	Ann	KEARVELL
1890	Horace	KEARVELL
1950	Margaret	KEENAN
1950	Morris	KEENAN
1950	Pamela	KEENAN
1939	David	KEENES
1931	Daisy	KELLAWAY

1931	Dora	KELLAWAY
1933	Edward	KELLAWAY
1931	Leslie	KELLAWAY
1931	Stan	KELLAWAY
1891	Albert	KENISTON
1932	Albert	KENISTON
1892	Annie	KENISTON
1888	Harry	KENISTON
1917	Harry	KENISTON
1895	Jane	KENISTON
1914	Kathleen	KENISTON
1895	Sidney	KENISTON
1959	Bryan	KENNARD
1953	Edie	KENNEDY
1953	Rosemary	KENNEDY
1934	Dawn	KENNETT
1936	Joy	KENNETT
1939	Kathleen	KENNETT
1886	Charles	KENT
1958	George	KENT
1895	Henry	KENT
1883	John	KENT
1890	George	KERSEY
1887	Alice	KEW
1886	Daniel	KEW
1883	George	KEW
1889	Harriet	KEW
1877	James	KEW
1880	Sarah	KEW
1953	Sylvia	KICK
1944	Barbara	KIDD
1968	Sarah	KIELY
1959	Anne	KILFORD
1847	Albert	KILLICK
1847	Jane	KILLICK
1888	Ethel	KIMBER
1884	Edmund	KING
1924	Edward	KING
1886	Emily	KING
1938	Gwendoline	KING
1885	Harry	KING
1927	Mary	KING
1883	William	KING
1924	William	KING
1963	Raymond	KINGSBURY
1946	Ian	KIRBY
1936	Joan	KIRBY
1913	Cecil	KNIGHT
1920	George	KNIGHT
1958	June	KNIGHT
1940	Phyllis	KNIGHT
1926	Ronald	KNIGHT
1920	Wilfred	KNIGHT
1955	Kelvin	KORSKOWSKI
1958	Gerald	KRUEGER
1957	Rosemary	KRUEGER
1959	Marjanna	KURKOWSKA
1932	David	KURN
1908	Alice	KYLE
1908	May	KYLE
1918	Sybil	KYLE

L

1965	Carol	LAIRD

1963	Sarah	LAIRD
1947	Betty	LAMB
1926	James	LAMB
1946	James	LAMB
1951	Jennifer	LAMB
1946	John	LAMB
1927	Leslie	LAMB
1951	Pauline	LAMB
1909	Rose	LAMB
1915	William	LAMB
1855	James	LAMBDEN
1847	Fanny	LAMBERT
1849	George	LAMDEN
1852	Walter	LAMDEN
1849	William	LAMDEN
1871	Harriett	LANGRISH
1927	Joan	LANGRISH
1873	Lydia	LANGRISH
1866	Mary	LANGRISH
1876	Sarah	LANGRISH
1868	Stephen	LANGRISH
1862	Thomas	LANGRISH
1946	Anne	LAWRENCE
1913	Forbes	LAWRENCE
1953	Michael	LAWRENCE
1913	Pat	LAWRENCE
1965	Andrew	LAYFIELD
1961	Susan	LAYFIELD
1886	George	LEE
1940	Peter	LEE
1957	Barrie	LEIGH
1968	David	LEIGH
1967	Heather	LEIGH
1957	Peter	LEIGH
1967	Stephanie	LEIGH
1921	Eric	LEVERMORE
1921	Phyllis	LEVERMORE
1948	Evelyn	LEWIS
1886	Kate	LEWIS
1886	Margaret	LEWIS
1888	MaryAnn	LEWIS
1948	Maureen	LEWIS
1885	SarahAnn	LEWIS`
1963	David	LEWORTHY
1945	Josephine	LEWORTHY
1966	Robert	LEWORTHY
1886	Edward	LIBBETER
1892	Emily	LIFFORD
1889	Jane	LIFFORD
1891	William	LIFFORD
1964	Darana	LIGUORI
1937	Alan	LILYWHITE
1967	Graham	LINDSEY
1888	Maggie	LING
1938	Joan	LINNEGAR
1943	Michael	LINNEGAR
1920	Louis	LINSEY
1914	Elsie	LITTLE
1921	Emily	LITTLECHILD
1921	Mona	LITTLECHILD
1921	Stephen	LITTLECHILD
1955	Frederick	LITTLEJOHN
1940	Derek	LLOYD
1941	Donald	LLOYD
1967	Jacqueline	LLOYD

1952	Victor	LODMELL
1967	Vincenzo	LOMASTRO
1951	Anthony	LOWE
1951	Christine	LOWE
1949	Jeffrey	LUCAS
1945	Richard	LUCAS
1944	Betty	LUCK
1940	Charles	LUCK
1949	John	LUCK
1942	Violet	LUCK
1968	Adele	LUNN
1963	Nigel	LUNN
1944	Elaine	LYGO
1885	Alfred	LYNN
1887	Charles	LYNN
1889	Frank	LYNN
1893	Frederick	LYNN
1911	May	LYNN
1899	Margaret	LYON

M

1944	Adrian	MABBS
1957	Barbara	MACCOWAN
1957	Catherine	MACCOWAN
1957	Hamish	MACCOWAN
1958	Margaret	MACCOWAN
1889	Louisa	MADDOX
1962	Caroline	MALBY
1854	Ann	MANDEVILLE
1851	Edmund	MANDEVILLE
1868	Edmund	MANDEVILLE
1847	Elizabeth	MANDEVILLE
1849	George	MANDEVILLE
1847	Martha	MANDEVILLE
1944	Anthony	MANESTER
1947	Nigel	MANESTER
1939	Peter	MANESTER
1941	Rodney	MANESTER
1940	Olive	MANSBRIDGE
1949	Michael	MARCHANT
1952	Ann	MARSH
1949	Anthony	MARSH
1921	Archibald	MARSH
1964	Carol	MARSH
1931	Eileen	MARSH
1966	Elaine	MARSH
1931	Frederick	MARSH
1956	Gordon	MARSH
1926	Harold	MARSH
1961	Jane	MARSH
1933	Kathleen	MARSH
1952	Leslie	MARSH
1962	Marion	MARSH
1955	Nicholas	MARSH
1959	Richard	MARSH
1928	Sidney	MARSH
1936	Stanley	MARSH
1935	Kenneth	MARSHALL
1941	Michael	MARSHALL
1947	Valerie	MARSHALL
1968	Ian	MARSHFIELD
1924	Alfred	MARTIN
1953	Anne	MARTIN
1923	Ernest	MARTIN

1936	Jean	MARTIN
1953	Mary	MARTIN
1951	Patrick	MARTIN
1968	Susan	MARTIN
1926	Trixie	MARTIN
1939	Eric	MARVELL
1939	Frank	MARVELL
1962	Daniel	MASKELL
1951	Gerald	MASKELL
1955	Julian	MASKELL
1957	Patricia	MASKELL
1959	Peter	MASKELL
1948	Rosemary	MASKELL
1957	Raymond	MASLING
1955	Thelma	MASLING
1952	Christine	MASON
1960	Keith	MASTERS
1966	Linda	MASTERS
1966	Peter	MASTERS
1966	Shirley	MASTERS
1966	Susan	MASTERS
1966	Vicky	MASTERS
1958	John	MATTHEWS
1894	Lily	MATTHEWS
1961	Richard	MATTHEWS
1892	Walter	MATTHEWS
1968	Steven	MATTINGLEY
1961	Ronald	MAULLIN
1964	Christopher	MAUNDER
1873	Levi	MAY
1871	William	MAY
1937	Kathleen	MAYES
1949	Corrine	MAYHEW
1919	Reginald	MAYNE
1955	Carol	MCBAIN
1963	Michael	MCCARTHY
1947	Patricia	MCCOY
1949	Rexina	MCCOY
1940	Wilfred	MCCOY
1954	Keith	MCDONALD
1942	Jean	MCKENZIE
1940	Jean	MCVITIE
1940	Cyril	MERCER
1938	Hilda	MEREFIELD
1933	Phyllis	MEREFIELD
1968	Carla	METZNER
1932	Albert	MILES
1930	Beatrice	MILES
1929	John	MILES
1967	Helen	MILLER
1919	James	MILLER
1912	Margaret	MILLER
1946	Roy	MILLER
1967	Jean	MILLIS
1967	Joan	MILLIS
1946	Michael	MILLIS
1967	Carol	MILLS
1926	Florence	MILLS
1922	Annie	MILTON
1952	Anthony	MILTON
1928	Arthur	MILTON
1915	Bill	MILTON
1926	Elsie	MILTON
1937	John	MILTON
1930	Joyce	MILTON

1958	Patricia	MILTON
1959	Paul	MILTON
1956	Peter	MILTON
1950	Rodney	MILTON
1939	Ronald	MILTON
1922	Kathleen	MITCHELL
1936	Margaret	MITCHELL
1919	Millie	MITCHELL
1947	Peter	MITCHELL
1906	Phyllis	MITCHELL
1923	Phyllis	MITCHELL
1932	Ruby	MITCHELL
1934	William	MITCHELL
1918	Anne	MOFFATT
1891	Frederick	MONEY
1871	Alfred	MONK
1872	Caroline	MONK
1900	Cecil	MONK
1869	Clara	MONK
1874	Gertrude	MONK
1847	Harriett	MONK
1873	Henry	MONK
1875	James	MONK
1888	John	MONK
1870	Louis	MONK
1847	Lydia	MONK
1870	Susan	MONK
1867	Walter	MONK
1875	William	MONK
1895	William	MONK
1888	Fred	MONNERY
1888	James	MONNERY
1921	Betty	MONTAGUE
1919	John	MONTAGUE
1943	Phyllis	MOORE
1953	William	MORELAND
1872	Charles	MOREY
1869	Elizabeth	MOREY
1876	Francis	MOREY
1904	Helen	MOREY
1874	Sarah	MOREY
1868	Thomas	MOREY
1870	William	MOREY
1901	William	MOREY
1936	Benjamin	MORRIS
1958	Carolyn	MORRIS
1923	Dora	MORRIS
1932	Duncan	MORRIS
1935	Edward	MORRIS
1928	Eileen	MORRIS
1930	Joan	MORRIS
1927	John	MORRIS
1925	Lilian	MORRIS
1937	Marie	MORRIS
1928	Mary	MORRIS
1941	Maureen	MORRIS
1933	Richard	MORRIS
1941	Sally	MORRIS
1947	Susan	MORRIS
1932	Sylvia	MORRIS
1944	Valerie	MORRIS
1947	David	MORSE
1965	Kenneth	MORTON
1919	Charles	MOTH
1919	Frank	MOTH

1920	Bertha	MOULSDALE
1919	Walter	MOULSDALE
1947	John	MUDDLE
1934	Frank	MUIR
1924	Jack	MUIR
1924	Myrtle	MUIR
1951	Rowland	MUIR
1924	Stanley	MUIR
1925	William	MUIR
1947	Douglas	MUMFORD
1962	Alan	MUNT
1962	Gillian	MUNT
1965	Philip	MUNT
1938	Alice	MURPHY
1938	Patrick	MURPHY
1952	Carol	MURRAY
1952	Christine	MURRAY
1957	Malcolm	MURRAY
1953	Susan	MURRAY
1957	Thomas	MURRAY
1941	Celia	MURRELL
1951	Heather	MURRELL
1948	Brian	MUSSEL
1940	Edward	MUSSEL
1925	Fred	MUSSEL
1915	Bessie	MUSSELL
1914	Edith	MUSSELL
1914	George	MUSSELL

N

1966	Ellen	NANN
1960	Maureen	NANN
1960	Patricia	NANN
1958	David	NAPPER
1958	Phillip	NAPPER
1965	Tina	NAPPER
1953	Ann	NASH
1913	Arthur	NASH
1953	Barbara	NASH
1908	Emily	NASH
1913	Leticia	NASH
1914	Lily	NASH
1908	Mabel	NASH
1908	Nellie	NASH
1950	Peter	NASH
1961	Phillip	NASH
1919	Vera	NASH
1938	Joyce	NEAL
1937	Edward	NEALON
1913	Albert	NEW
1910	Ellen	NEW
1914	Nellie	NEW
1905	Rose	NEW
1899	Walter	NEW
1950	Brian	NEWMAN
1937	Brian	NEWMAN
1927	Nancy	NEWMAN
1851	Charles	NIBBS
1853	William	NIBBS
1939	Alec	NICHOLAS
1939	Jessie	NICHOLAS
1939	Kathleen	NICHOLAS
1874	George	NICHOLS
1865	James	NICHOLS

1868	Sarah	NICHOLS
1871	William	NICHOLS
1847	Ann	NIGHTINGALE
1847	Charles	NIGHTINGALE
1847	Clara	NIGHTINGALE
1851	Elizabeth	NIGHTINGALE
1851	George	NIGHTINGALE
1847	James	NIGHTINGALE
1848	Lydia	NIGHTINGALE
1848	William	NIGHTINGALE
1956	Helen	NIX
1956	Patricia	NOBLE
1888	Agnes	NORMAN
1886	Constance	NORMAN
1886	Henrietta	NORMAN
1889	John	NORMAN
1850	Mary	NORMAN
1891	Ruth	NORMAN
1886	Shadrach	NORMAN
1961	Paula	NORRIDGE
1915	Alice	NUNN
1957	Christina	NUNN
1965	Colin	NUNN
1961	Gary	NUNN
1958	Sheila	NUNN
1962	Stephen	NUNN
1964	Alan	NYE
1964	Michael	NYE
1964	Theresa	NYE

O

1895	Mary	OAKLEY
1941	Brenda	O'BRIEN
1958	Denis	O'BRIEN
1943	Michael	O'BRIEN
1946	Zelda	O'BRIEN
1921	Albert	OCCOMORE
1921	Cecil	OCCOMORE
1922	Dorothy	OCCOMORE
1921	Regind	OCCOMORE
1921	William	OCCOMORE
1847	Edward	OFFORD
1847	William	OFFORD
1957	Susan	OLIVE
1949	Peter	O'NEILL
1953	Christopher	ORR
1949	Kathleen	ORR
1958	Steven	ORRELL
1951	Patricia	OSBORNE
1949	Sophie	OSBORNE
1958	Aprille	OWEN
1886	Ernest	OWEN
1956	Glyn	OWEN
1965	Mandy	OWEN
1956	Paul	OWEN
1966	Linda	OXLADE

P

1887	Louis	PAFFORD
1963	John	PAGET
1918	Phyllis	PANTLING
1896	William	PARFITT
1965	Amanda	PARKER

1955	Anne	PARKER
1965	Delia	PARKER
1886	George	PARKER
1886	Grace	PARKER
1965	Linus	PARKER
1913	Thomas	PARKER
1965	William	PARKER
1911	Frederick	PARROTT
1888	Arthur	PARSONS
1965	Graham	PARSONS
1967	Jacquelin	PARSONS
1946	John	PARSONS
1961	Stephen	PARSONS
1963	Alan	PATEMAN
1963	Anthony	PATEMAN
1963	Leslie	PATEMAN
1963	Robin	PATEMAN
1959	Alan	PAYNE
1939	John	PEACH
1947	Gordon	PEARCEY
1919	Kenneth	PEARSON
1919	Roy	PEARSON
1848	Harriett	PENDARY
1848	Mary	PENDARY
1847	Shadrach	PENDARY
1966	David	PENNY
1968	Lesley	PENNY
1960	Nigel	PERCIVAL
1930	Doreen	PERCY
1847	James	PERCY
1914	Ellen	PERRIER
1896	Albert	PERRIN
1905	Alice	PERRIN
1887	Annie	PERRIN
1926	Cecil	PERRIN
1920	Cicely	PERRIN
1928	Daphne	PERRIN
1931	Diana	PERRIN
1956	Diane	PERRIN
1887	Elizabeth	PERRIN
1931	Eric	PERRIN
1893	Frederick	PERRIN
1952	Gordon	PERRIN
1920	John	PERRIN
1924	Leslie	PERRIN
1891	Marion	PERRIN
1924	Marjorie	PERRIN
1895	May	PERRIN
1889	Sidney	PERRIN
1925	Stanley	PERRIN
1920	Stella	PERRIN
1921	Sybil	PERRIN
1886	Walter	PERRIN
1959	Dennis	PERRY
1920	James	PERRY
1958	Jean	PERRY
1938	Lionel	PERRY
1960	Ronald	PERRY
1964	Trevor	PERRY
1847	Ellen	PETER
1847	Rose	PETER
1847	William	PETER
1915	Alice	PETERS
1908	Doris	PETERS
1953	Ann	PETTY

1946	Joan	PHILLIPS
1963	Joseph	PICARIELLO
1889	Sidney	PIERCEY
1889	Willie	PIERCEY
1949	Graham	PIKE
1952	Maurice	PIKE
1940	Frederick	PILKINTON
1940	Robert	PILKINTON
1886	Alice	PINK
1869	Jane	PINNION
1872	Ruben	PINNION
1957	Christopher	PINNOCK
1908	Edith	PINNOCK
1870	Emily	PINNOCK
1864	Frank	PINNOCK
1918	Geoffrey	PINNOCK
1949	Jennifer	PINNOCK
1867	Kate	PINNOCK
1953	Linda	PINNOCK
1874	Rose	PINNOCK
1908	Sidney	PINNOCK
1908	Winnie	PINNOCK
1924	Hazel	PLOWMAN
1952	Sandra	PLOWMAN
1919	Stanley	PLOWMAN
1960	David	PLUMBRIDGE
1933	Donald	PLUMBRIDGE
1905	Edith	PLUMBRIDGE
1926	Elsie	PLUMBRIDGE
1914	May	PLUMBRIDGE
1920	Stanley	PLUMBRIDGE
1899	Sarah	PLUMRIDGE
1893	Winifred	PLYMEN
1910	Ethel	POOLEY
1950	David	PORTER
1949	Shirley	PORTER
1964	Amanda	POTTER
1885	Ellen	POTTER
1922	Fred	POTTER
1896	Frederick	POTTER
1869	George	POTTER
1922	Harry	POTTER
1872	James	POTTER
1927	James	POTTER
1890	John	POTTER
1942	Lilian	POTTER
1943	Margaret	POTTER
1953	Patricia	POTTER
1922	Rebecca	POTTER
1952	Shirley	POTTER
1923	William	POTTER
1929	Winifred	POTTER
1866	Harriett	POTTER
1873	Elizabeth	POTTERTON
1875	Ellen	POTTERTON
1847	Jesse	POTTERTON
1868	Louis	POTTERTON
1870	Rebecca	POTTERTON
1847	William	POTTERTON
1952	Leonie	POTTICARY
1953	Roy	POTTICARY
1963	Ashley	POULTER
1961	Dianne	POWELL
1945	Ivor	POWELL
1921	John	POWELL

1925	Alan	PRATT
1925	Eva	PRATT
1925	Mary	PRATT
1942	Dawn	PREDETH
1949	Jennifer	PRESTON
1949	John	PRESTON
1962	Lynn	PRICE-JONES
1950	Barry	PRING
1915	Daisy	PRYKE
1891	Alice	PUDDOCK
1928	Alfred	PULLEN
1853	Ann	PULLEN
1893	Annie	PULLEN
1894	Charlotte	PULLEN
1885	Edith	PULLEN
1900	Elizabeth	PULLEN
1892	Ethel	PULLEN
1924	Evelyn	PULLEN
1895	Florence	PULLEN
1926	Frank	PULLEN
1896	George	PULLEN
1891	Gertrude	PULLEN
1950	Guy	PULLEN
1894	Hannah	PULLEN
1921	Jack	PULLEN
1849	James	PULLEN
1959	Janet	PULLEN
1940	Jean	PULLEN
1892	John	PULLEN
1929	Leonard	PULLEN
1960	Linda	PULLEN
1847	Lucy	PULLEN
1931	Mabel	PULLEN
1934	Olive	PULLEN
1925	Phyllis	PULLEN
1957	Susan	PULLEN
1850	Thomas	PULLEN
1965	Trevor	PULLEN
1924	Walter	PULLEN
1947	Christopher	PULLINGER
1943	Mary	PULLINGER
1931	Reginald	PULLINGER
1847	Charles	PUNTER
1887	Ada	PUTTOCK
1890	Alice	PUTTOCK
1894	Amy	PUTTOCK
1892	Annie	PUTTOCK
1942	Barbara	PUTTOCK
1964	Barry	PUTTOCK
1933	David	PUTTOCK
1944	Dorothy	PUTTOCK
1964	Franklyn	PUTTOCK
1929	John	PUTTOCK
1907	Kathleen	PUTTOCK
1965	Michael	PUTTOCK
1935	Robert	PUTTOCK
1962	Stephen	PUTTOCK
1905	Wilfred	PUTTOCK
1898	William	PUTTOCK
1940	Pamela	PYMM
1940	Rosemary	PYMM

R

1968	Michael	RABIN

1847	Emma	RAGET
1852	Harriett	RAGGETT
1960	Jill	RAISTRICK
1957	John	RAISTRICK
1940	June	RANDALL
1940	Leslie	RANDALL
1940	Roy	RANDALL
1902	William	RANDALL
1888	Nellie	RAPLEY
1961	Sandra	RAPLEY
1964	Michael	RATCLIFFE
1936	Dinah	READ
1962	David	REDDICK
1876	Emily	REDMAN
1868	Fanny	REDMAN
1870	Henry	REDMAN
1872	Robert	REDMAN
1912	George	REEVES
1851	Caroline	REIGATE
1851	Eliza	REIGATE
1847	Emma	REIGATE
1851	Thomas	REIGATE
1928	John	REMMENT
1926	Winifred	REMMENT
1876	Constance	REYNOLDS
1874	George	REYNOLDS
1872	Mary	REYNOLDS
1914	Arthur	RHODES
1920	Herbert	RHODES
1928	John	RHODES
1951	Joan	RICHARDS
1940	Robert	RICHARDS
1958	Geoffrey	RICHARDSON
1925	John	RICHARDSON
1951	Raymonde	RICHARDSON
1949	Thomas	RICHARDSON
1940	Eric	RIDES
1956	Linda	RIDES
1958	Peter	RIDES
1918	Evelyn	RILEY
1918	William	RILEY
1919	Jack	RINGWOOD
1936	Albert	RIXON
1870	Augustus	ROBERTS
1956	Dennis	ROBERTS
1943	Eileen	ROBERTS
1876	Emma	ROBERTS
1946	John	ROBERTS
1948	Margaret	ROBERTS
1951	Richard	ROBERTS
1869	William	ROBERTS
1952	John	ROBERTSON
1958	Charmaine	ROBINS
1962	Elizabeth	ROBINS
1955	Ian	ROBINS
1956	Penelope	ROBINS
1950	Peter	ROBINS
1951	Terence	ROBINS
1952	David	ROBINSON
1947	Lily	ROBINSON
1947	Mary	ROBINSON
1949	Michael	ROBINSON
1886	Annie	ROKER
1885	Arthur	ROKER
1887	Ellen	ROKER

1893	Florence	ROKER
1888	George	ROKER
1892	Harriet	ROKER
1890	Jane	ROKER
1890	Sarah	ROKER
1895	Sophia	ROKER
1886	William	ROKER
1900	Daisy	ROLLINSON
1905	Ernest	ROLLINSON
1934	Arnold	RONALD
1864	Elizabeth	ROSE
1869	Patience	ROSE
1864	Sarah	ROSE
1952	Ann	ROTHERY
1952	Dennis	ROWLAND
1949	Sallie	ROWLAND
1964	Julie	ROWLATT
1966	Terence	ROWLATT
1959	Stephen	ROWLEY
1961	Susan	ROWLEY
1960	Marius	RUDNICK
1938	Hazel	RUFF
1949	Angela	RUFFLES
1951	Colin	RUFFLES
1949	Derek	RUFFLES
1959	Lynn	RUFFLES
1852	Mary Ann	RUGMAN
1852	Thomas	RUGMAN
1961	Graham	RUSSELL
1956	Rosemary	RUSSELL
1952	Trevor	RUSSELL
1956	Brian	RUTHERFORD
1954	Caroline	RUTHERFORD
1944	Maureen	RYAN
1921	Alice	RYDER

S

1847	Hannah	SALE
1847	Reuben	SALE
1847	John	SALMON
1919	Eric	SAMME
1919	Evelyn	SAMME
1920	Fred	SAMME
1921	Ronald	SAMME
1927	Sylvia	SAMME
1922	Connie	SANDERS
1847	Margaret	SANDERSON
1963	Ruth	SAPSFORD
1968	Sharon	SAPSFORD
1964	Terry	SAPSFORD
1960	Andrew	SAUNDERS
1960	Ian	SAUNDERS
1945	Irene	SAUNDERS
1866	Caroline	SAVAGE
1870	Emma	SAVAGE
1868	John	SAVAGE
1909	Ada	SAYERS
1927	Caroline	SAYERS
1963	Janice	SAYERS
1927	John	SAYERS
1927	Margaret	SAYERS
1943	Norma	SAYERS
1968	Richard	SAYERS
1962	Susan	SAYERS

1965	Terry	SAYERS
1961	Susan	SCAMP
1921	Arthur	SCARLET
1930	Charles	SCHMID
1932	Louis	SCHMID
1932	Paul	SCHMID
1956	Christina	SCHMIEDER
1957	Heather	SCHMIEDER
1967	Paul	SCHOLES
1918	Albert	SCOTT
1943	Elizabeth	SCOTT
1939	Jacqueline	SCOTT
1945	Rosalyn	SCOTT
1939	William	SCOTT
1927	Stanley	SELFE
1918	Dorothy	SELMES
1964	Anne	SETRIGHT
1961	Michael	SETRIGHT
1957	Patricia	SETRIGHT
1964	Robin	SETTERFIELD
1945	Alan	SEWELL
1945	Elsie	SEWELL
1940	Beryl	SEXTON
1959	Linda	SEYMOUR
1954	Robert	SHACKLETON
1954	Sally	SHACKLETON
1954	Arthur	SHEARING
1947	Barry	SHEPPARD
1951	Gloria	SHEPPARD
1929	Lily	SHINN
1929	Thomas	SHINN
1929	William	SHINN
1928	Dennis	SHOESMITH
1962	Jane	SHOESMITH
1946	Paula	SHOESMITH
1957	Peter	SHOESMITH
1932	Rita	SHOESMITH
1952	Stuart	SHOESMITH
1928	Victor	SHOESMITH
1921	Alice	SHORTER
1923	Arthur	SHORTER
1925	Richard	SHORTER
1938	Joyce	SHRIMPTON
1938	Patricia	SHRIMPTON
1926	Owen	SHUTTLE
1939	Miriam	SILVESTER
1892	Albert	SIMMONDS
1890	Alfred	SIMMONDS
1849	Ann	SIMMONDS
1898	Annie	SIMMONDS
1847	Charlotte	SIMMONDS
1849	Daniel	SIMMONDS
1925	Doris	SIMMONDS
1847	Emma	SIMMONDS
1890	Frederick	SIMMONDS
1894	George	SIMMONDS
1888	James	SIMMONDS
1900	Maurice	SIMMONDS
1886	William	SIMMONDS
1847	Francis	SIMMONS
1847	Sarah	SIMMONS
1953	George	SIMPSON
1947	Janet	SIMPSON
1967	Charles	SINES
1940	Sheila	SINES

Year	Name	Surname		Year	Name	Surname		Year	Name	Surname		Year	Name	Surname
1886	Annie	SINK		1912	Dolly	SMITHERS		1942	Shirley	STEDMAN		1921	Bertram	SUREY
1927	Audrey	SINK		1910	Doris	SMITHERS		1964	Amanda	STEEL		1953	Catherine	SUREY
1924	Dorothy	SINK		1919	Edith	SMITHERS		1962	Rebecca	STEEL		1921	Dora	SUREY
1869	Elizabeth	SINK		1849	George	SMITHERS		1960	Sally	STEEL		1921	Frank	SUREY
1865	Emma	SINK		1913	George	SMITHERS		1959	Pauline	STEELE		1928	Leonard	SUREY
1865	Florence	SINK		1954	Godfrey	SMITHERS		1847	Abraham	STEER		1923	Robert	SUREY
1903	Herbert	SINK		1944	Graham	SMITHERS		1908	Alice	STEER		1938	Robin	SUREY
1884	Hollis	SINK		1920	Ivy	SMITHERS		1847	Eliza	STEER		1955	Raymond	SUTHERLAND
1899	James	SINK		1949	Janice	SMITHERS		1847	John	STEER		1951	Francis	SUTTON
1922	James	SINK		1940	John	SMITHERS		1847	Mary	STEER		1958	Anthony	SYKES
1863	Jane	SINK		1920	Kitty	SMITHERS		1949	Norma	STEER		1956	Brenda	SYKES
1859	Jessie	SINK		1849	Lydia	SMITHERS		1947	Pamela	STEER		1959	David	SYKES
1862	Joshua	SINK		1914	Margaret	SMITHERS		1947	Roger	STEER		1957	Peter	SYKES
1900	Leonard	SINK		1947	Margaret	SMITHERS		1884	Ellen	STENNING				
1930	Leonard	SINK		1853	Mary Ann	SMITHERS		1865	John	STENNING				
1888	Lily	SINK		1968	Michael	SMITHERS		1847	Mary	STENNING			**T**	
1872	Lizzie	SINK		1941	Roy	SMITHERS		1859	Mary	STENNING				
1927	Phoebe	SINK		1947	Sylvia	SMITHERS		1861	Richard	STENNING		1955	Tania	TAILOR
1912	Queenie	SINK		1966	Terence	SMITHERS		1847	William	STENNING		1887	Gertrude	TALBOT
1929	Rhona	SINK		1912	Thomas	SMITHERS		1933	Alice	STEVENS		1887	Willie	TALBOT
1903	Walter	SINK		1912	William	SMITHERS		1921	Annie	STEVENS		1948	Felicity	TAMBLYN
1885	William	SINK		1912	Willis	SMITHERS		1894	Arthur	STEVENS		1906	Lily	TAPLIN
1890	Grace	SKELTON		1890	Alice	SNELLING		1919	Edith	STEVENS		1886	Edith	TAPPIN
1911	Walter	SKINNER		1887	Annie	SNELLING		1915	Elizabeth	STEVENS		1888	Eva	TAPPIN
1953	Leon	SLATER		1870	Catherine	SNELLING		1924	Frances	STEVENS		1904	Grace	TAPPIN
1852	John	SMALE		1854	David	SNELLING		1923	John	STEVENS		1886	Herbert	TAPPIN
1855	Mary	SMALE		1851	Edward	SNELLING		1952	Leslie	STEVENS		1888	Olive	TAPPIN
1968	Sharon	SMILERY		1885	George	SNELLING		1929	Lilian	STEVENS		1895	Frank	TAPPLIN
1910	Albert	SMITH		1868	Henry	SNELLING		1927	Margaret	STEVENS		1911	John	TARDIFF
1918	Amy	SMITH		1885	Lavinia	SNELLING		1926	Stella	STEWART		1964	Gillian	TASKER
1966	Angela	SMITH		1868	Lizzie	SNELLING		1962	Theresa	STILL		1962	Jayne	TASKER
1951	Barbara	SMITH		1874	Nellie	SNELLING		1941	Bryan	STILWELL		1937	Beryl	TAYLOR
1955	Barry	SMITH		1872	Sarah	SNELLING		1935	David	STOCKER		1926	Charles	TAYLOR
1871	Calib	SMITH		1926	Marjorie	SOAL		1947	Mary	STOCKER		1950	Colin	TAYLOR
1967	Christopher	SMITH		1921	Ellen	SOANES		1965	Paul	STOCKER		1922	Florence	TAYLOR
1966	Cynthia	SMITH		1921	Winifred	SOANES		1935	Walter	STOCKER		1852	Mary	TAYLOR
1952	David	SMITH		1921	Alfred	SOPP		1936	David	STOKES		1888	Willie	TAYLOR
1868	Ebenezer	SMITH		1923	Wilfred	SOPP		1936	Mary	STOKES		1943	Ann	TEASDALE
1853	Elizabeth	SMITH		1929	Cyril	SPANNER		1937	Freda	STONE		1947	Janet	TEASDALE
1847	Ellen	SMITH		1934	Richard	SPAVIN		1967	David	STRANGE		1848	Emma	TEGG
1886	Frank	SMITH		1947	David	SPEAR		1939	Edward	STRANGE		1956	Andrew	TERRY
1910	Frank	SMITH		1947	Margaret	SPEAR		1933	Joan	STRANGE		1962	Ann	THACKERY
1911	Fred	SMITH		1946	Patricia	SPEAR		1965	Michelle	STRANGE		1962	Elaine	THACKERY
1854	George	SMITH		1953	John	SPICKETT		1933	Ronald	STRANGE		1962	Eric	THACKERY
1847	Henry	SMITH		1957	Gillian	SPIRES		1961	Sally	STRANGE		1929	Walter	THELWELL
1956	Henry	SMITH		1957	Susan	SPIRES		1964	Andrew	STRONG		1946	Diana	THIRTLE
1847	James	SMITH		1883	Albert	SPOONER		1945	Brian	STRONG		1956	Norman	THIRTLE
1944	James	SMITH		1885	Alfred	SPOONER		1964	Graham	STRONG		1947	Geraldine	THOMAS
1951	Janet	SMITH		1931	Anthony	SPOONER		1964	Philippa	STRONG		1948	Jacqueline	THOMAS
1847	John	SMITH		1960	Carolynne	SPOONER		1947	Sylvia	STRONG		1949	Elizabeth	THOMPSON
1958	Linda	SMITH		1954	Christine	SPOONER		1964	Susan	STROUD		1952	Terence	THOMPSON
1942	Mary	SMITH		1886	Ellen	SPOONER		1851	Eliza	STRUDWICK		1953	Dennis	THORNDALE
1961	Patricia	SMITH		1886	Frank	SPOONER		1854	Emily	STRUDWICK		1920	Fred	THORNDALE
1942	Peter	SMITH		1888	Hubert	SPOONER		1947	Susan	STRUDWICK		1887	Amelia	TICE
1959	Sarah	SMITH		1918	Maurice	SPOONER		1951	John	STUART		1891	Annie	TICE
1960	Sheila	SMITH		1915	Phyllis	SPOONER		1919	Beryl	STYLES		1886	Ethel	TICE
1914	Sidney	SMITH		1914	Ronald	SPOONER		1962	Donna	STYLES		1847	Mary	TICE
1966	Susan	SMITH		1933	Roy	SPOONER		1958	Edward	STYLES		1885	Mary	TICE
1910	Violet	SMITH		1931	Ruby	SPOONER		1965	Kim	STYLES		1895	Rose	TICE
1850	Walter	SMITH		1919	Gwendoline	STANBRIDGE		1964	Vanessa	STYLES		1882	Albert	TICKNER
1849	William	SMITH		1924	Horace	STANBRIDGE		1960	Wanita	STYLES		1927	Albert	TICKNER
1886	William	SMITH		1930	Olive	STANLEY		1919	William	STYLES		1966	Alison	TICKNER
1911	Albert	SMITHERS		1872	Elizabeth	STANSFIELD		1963	Danny	SUMMERSCALES		1885	Arthur	TICKNER
1966	Christine	SMITHERS		1886	Joseph	STEDMAN		1960	Peter	SUMMERSCALES		1861	Arthur	TICKNER
1954	Clive	SMITHERS		1946	Leon	STEDMAN		1959	Ann	SUREY		1966	Christopher	TICKNER
												1964	Debra	TICKNER

1927	Edith	TICKNER
1881	Eliza	TICKNER
1903	Elizabeth	TICKNER
1927	Elsie	TICKNER
1847	Emma	TICKNER
1854	Fanny	TICKNER
1848	George	TICKNER
1871	George	TICKNER
1883	Harriet	TICKNER
1946	Janet	TICKNER
1885	Jesse	TICKNER
1876	John	TICKNER
1878	Kate	TICKNER
1851	Lydia	TICKNER
1962	Mark	TICKNER
1914	Maud	TICKNER
1927	Rosie	TICKNER
1940	Sheila	TICKNER
1894	Walter	TICKNER
1917	Walter	TICKNER
1855	William	TICKNER
1873	William	TICKNER
1878	Willis	TICKNER
1917	Bernard	TIGWELL
1937	Jean	TIGWELL
1945	Kenneth	TIGWELL
1958	Richard	TIGWELL
1940	Robert	TIGWELL
1935	Stanley	TIGWELL
1951	Bernard	TITCOMBE
1952	Anthony	TOBIAS
1962	Alan	TOWNSEND
1936	Audrey	TOWNSEND
1929	Dennis	TOWNSEND
1917	Dorothy	TOWNSEND
1914	Elsie	TOWNSEND
1947	Jaqueline	TOWNSEND
1923	Kathleen	TOWNSEND
1909	Lily	TOWNSEND
1921	Mollie	TOWNSEND
1936	Pamela	TOWNSEND
1956	Raymond	TOWNSEND
1913	Reggie	TOWNSEND
1891	Robert	TOWNSEND
1910	Rose	TOWNSEND
1928	Roy	TOWNSEND
1891	Sarah	TOWNSEND
1957	Susan	TOWNSEND
1925	Terry	TOWNSEND
1895	Winifred	TOWNSEND
1948	Anita	TRESSIDER
1951	Clive	TRESSIDER
1946	David	TRESSIDER
1959	Dennis	TRESSIDER
1956	Mark	TRESSIDER
1872	Fanny	TRUELOVE
1865	Georgina	TRUELOVE
1875	Richard	TRUELOVE
1870	William	TRUELOVE
1929	Albert	TRUSSLER
1876	Elizabeth	TUBB
1867	James	TUBB
1873	Martha	TUBB
1870	Richard	TUBB
1868	William	TUBB

1886	Agnes	TUBBS
1910	Annie	TUBBS
1847	Eliza	TUBBS
1890	Fanny	TUBBS
1847	Henry	TUBBS
1851	Mary	TUBBS
1851	Sarah	TUBBS
1908	Agnes	TUCKER
1904	Elizabeth	TUCKER
1951	Jean	TUCKER
1908	Lily	TUCKER
1952	Wendy	TUCKER
1919	Elsie	TULETT
1922	Reggie	TULETT
1940	Roy	TULETT
1918	Stanley	TULETT
1914	Violet	TULETT
1950	Wendy	TULETT
1915	William	TULETT
1942	Anthony	TUNNELL
1911	Adeline	TURNER
1874	Albert	TURNER
1901	Albert	TURNER
1911	Eva	TURNER
1870	Mary	TURNER
1967	Nigel	TURNER
1957	Susan	TURNER
1910	Win	TURNER
1914	Tom	TURPIN
1949	Donald	TYLER
1949	Doreen	TYLER
1950	June	TYLER
1946	Rodney	TYRRELL

U

1900	Lily	UPFOLD
1941	Joan	UPTON
1938	Ronald	UPTON

V

1965	Victor	VASILUS
1957	Teresa	VINE
1940	Alfred	VOST
1940	Ronald	VOST

W

1847	Elizabeth	WADE
1849	Emma	WADE
1849	George	WADE
1847	Jane	WADE
1964	Joan	WADE
1852	John	WADE
1851	Louisa	WADE
1851	Ritchard	WADE
1965	Susan	WADE
1852	William	WADE
1847	John	WAKEFORD
1957	Stella	WALDEN
1959	Ceridwen	WALKER
1918	Gwendoline	WALKER
1948	Hilary	WALKER
1847	James	WALKER

1950	Jennifer	WALKER
1959	Sheila	WALKER
1952	Stuart	WALKER
1914	Eunice	WALKLEY
1944	Jenny	WALLBRIDGE
1939	Victor	WALLER
1966	Bryan	WALLIS
1944	James	WALLIS
1941	Ronald	WALLIS
1953	David	WALTERS
1946	Gillian	WALTERS
1951	Jean	WALTERS
1931	Charles	WANBON
1936	Constance	WANBON
1931	Richard	WANBON
1852	George	WAPSHOTT
1854	Helen	WAPSHOTT
1965	Ornagh	WARD
1923	Arthur	WARNER
1952	Brian	WARNER
1947	Gerald	WARNER
1923	Ruth	WARNER
1962	Julie	WARREN
1953	Patricia	WATERS
1893	Agnes	WATSON
1914	Alan	WATSON
1939	Betty	WATSON
1934	Elizabeth	WATSON
1847	Emma	WATSON
1900	Emma	WATSON
1935	Janet	WATSON
1909	Maggie	WATSON
1847	Mary	WATSON
1853	Mary-Sophia	WATSON
1894	Robert	WATSON
1896	Thomas	WATSON
1847	William	WATSON
1913	Elsie	WATTS
1962	Gary	WATTS
1913	Harry	WATTS
1966	Maxine	WATTS
1968	Vanessa	WATTS
1961	Debora	WEBB
1967	Jacqueline	WEBB
1847	James	WEBB
1965	Karen	WEBB
1964	Vincent	WEBB
1947	Anthony	WEEDON
1951	Janet	WEEDON
1947	John	WEEDON
1852	Isabella	WEIGHT
1850	Lydia	WEIGHT
1848	Rosa	WEIGHT
1959	Marie-Ann	WELKER
1915	Alice	WELLER
1945	Edward	WELLER
1952	Jennifer	WELLER
1957	Kathleen	WELLER
1947	Leslie	WELLER
1925	Norman	WELLER
1946	Peter	WELLER
1922	Roland	WELLER
1923	Victor	WELLER
1890	Alice	WELLS
1953	Anna	WELLS

1953	Gillian	WELLS
1956	Stephen	WELLS
1948	John	WELTON
1868	Annie	WEST
1876	Caroline	WEST
1866	Eleanor	WEST
1864	John	WEST
1871	Kate	WEST
1870	William	WEST
1942	David	WESTON
1943	Derek	WESTON
1863	Olive	WHAPSHOT
1856	Edith	WHAPSHOTT
1891	Edith	WHAPSHOTT
1848	Ellen	WHAPSHOTT
1850	Emma	WHAPSHOTT
1886	Kate	WHAPSHOTT
1931	Margery	WHAPSHOTT
1855	Mary	WHAPSHOTT
1920	Robert	WHAPSHOTT
1929	Winifred	WHAPSHOTT
1847	Charles	WHEELER
1953	Ann	WHITE
1913	Arthur	WHITE
1910	Cynthia	WHITE
1945	Elisabeth	WHITE
1866	Frederick	WHITE
1891	George	WHITE
1900	Hugh	WHITE
1916	Irene	WHITE
1847	James	WHITE
1940	Janet	WHITE
1888	Lily	WHITE
1886	Lizzie	WHITE
1945	Margaret	WHITE
1945	Pamela	WHITE
1940	Pauline	WHITE
1901	Percy	WHITE
1900	Tommy	WHITE
1965	Julie	WHITMAN
1962	Susan	WHITMAN
1968	Tania	WHITTERN
1947	Alfred	WICKHAM
1958	Julie	WICKHAM
1853	Ann	WIGMAN
1896	Annie	WIGMAN
1949	Barry	WIGMAN
1855	Celia	WIGMAN
1914	Dorothy	WIGMAN
1896	Edith	WIGMAN
1928	Irene	WIGMAN
1930	Joyce	WIGMAN
1906	Leonard	WIGMAN
1931	Lilian	WIGMAN
1908	Mildred	WIGMAN
1890	Thomas	WIGMAN
1892	William	WIGMAN
1953	Margaret	WIGMORE
1923	Fred	WILKINS
1926	Mollie	WILKINS
1936	Dennis	WILKINSON
1952	Janet	WILKINSON
1939	Jeffrey	WILKINSON
1946	Susan	WILKINSON
1885	Alice	WILLIAMS

1958	Anne	WILLIAMS	1930	Walter	WOOD	1869	Ruth	WOOLGAR	1940	Edward WRIGHT
1941	Donald	WILLIAMS	1888	Ada	WOODGER	1899	Ruth	WOOLGAR	1910	George WRIGHT
1966	Gary	WILLIAMS	1920	Evelyn	WOODGER	1854	Sarah	WOOLGAR	1914	Gladys WRIGHT
1918	Luther	WILLIAMS	1861	Harriett	WOODGER	1854	William	WOOLGAR	1909	Harry WRIGHT
1963	Rosalind	WILLIAMS	1860	William	WOODGER	1873	Winifred	WOOLGAR	1957	Ian WRIGHT
1940	Stuart	WILLIAMS	1908	Charles	WOODHAM	1965	Susan	WOOSTER	1923	Sydney WRIGHT
1963	Timothy	WILLIAMS	1896	Archibald	WOODHAMS	1962	Susan	WORKMAN	1914	William WRIGHT
1946	Andrew	WILSON	1896	Fanny	WOODHAMS	1876	Ada	WORSFOLD	1920	Arthur WYATT
1968	Nigel	WILSON	1896	Minnie	WOODHAMS	1867	Ann	WORSFOLD	1967	David WYATT
1967	Wendy	WILSON	1951	Patricia	WOODHAMS	1927	Arthur	WORSFOLD	1937	Doreen WYATT
1961	Dawn	WINSON	1892	Sidney	WOODHAMS	1926	Betty	WORSFOLD	1944	Frederick WYATT
1965	Karen	WINSTANLEY	1885	Ellen	WOODS	1913	Cecil	WORSFOLD	1944	Irene WYATT
1941	Christine	WINTER	1956	Julie	WOODS	1891	Edmund	WORSFOLD	1937	Joan WYATT
1965	Cherry	WINTERBOURNE	1951	Eileen	WOODWARD	1888	Ernest	WORSFOLD	1938	Laura WYATT
1917	Albert	WISDOM	1885	Alice	WOOLGAR	1872	Fanny	WORSFOLD	1937	Reginald WYATT
1899	Annie	WISDOM	1860	Ann	WOOLGAR	1886	Florence	WORSFOLD	1921	Sidney WYATT
1904	James	WISDOM	1905	Beatrice	WOOLGAR	1870	George	WORSFOLD		
1912	Louisa	WISDOM	1871	Edmund	WOOLGAR	1883	Herbert	WORSFOLD		**Y**
1903	Mary	WISDOM	1860	Eliza	WOOLGAR	1911	Iris	WORSFOLD		
1913	Olive	WISDOM	1880	Elizabeth	WOOLGAR	1849	Jane	WORSFOLD	1960	Gary YALLOP
1909	Rhoda	WISDOM	1862	George	WOOLGAR	1862	John	WORSFOLD	1933	Kenneth YALLOP
1901	William	WISDOM	1856	Harriet	WOOLGAR	1930	Joyce	WORSFOLD	1931	Leonard YALLOP
1888	Ellen	WISE	1891	Harriet	WOOLGAR	1882	Louisa	WORSFOLD	1931	Philip YALLOP
1888	Jessie	WISE	1864	Henry	WOOLGAR	1873	Martha	WORSFOLD	1965	Marion YATES
1952	Alan	WOOD	1852	James	WOOLGAR	1852	Mary	WORSFOLD	1963	Ruth YATES
1896	Ellen	WOOD	1894	James	WOOLGAR	1871	Montague	WORSFOLD	1956	William YEATES
1930	Florence	WOOD	1850	Jane	WOOLGAR	1880	Percy	WORSFOLD	1963	Alison YOUNG
1957	Gillian	WOOD	1865	John	WOOLGAR	1864	William	WORSFOLD	1917	James YOUNG
1952	Joan	WOOD	1911	Lily	WOOLGAR	1968	Jonathon	WREN	1949	Jane YOUNG
1951	Maralyn	WOOD	1884	Louise	WOOLGAR	1960	Denise	WRIGHT	1966	Janette YOUNG
1930	Peter	WOOD	1868	Mary	WOOLGAR	1940	Dennis	WRIGHT	1949	John YOUNG
1945	Vernon	WOOD	1866	Rose	WOOLGAR	1940	Derek	WRIGHT	1961	Patricia YOUNG

The *Masters* and *Mistresses* of the *School* at *Ripley*

1847-1968

1847   Master (unknown)
Mistress - Miss Catherine BARTLETT

1851   Master - John WEIGHT
Mistress - Miss Catherine BARTLETT

1852   Master - Thomas Marriott BERRIDGE
Mistress - Miss Catherine BARTLETT

1859   Master - Thomas Marriott BERRIDGE
Mistress - Mrs Ann FORDER

1863   Master - Gabriel McCONNOCHIE
Mistress - Mrs Ann FORDER

1867   Master - Thomas OSBORNE
Mistress - Mrs Jane OSBORNE

1868   Master - James STRICKLAND
Mistress - Miss Harriett STRICKLAND (sister)

1872   Master - Lomax James PLYMAN
Mistress - Mrs Mary PLYMAN

1878   Master - Arthur TURNER
Mistress - Miss Emma TURNER (sister)

1882   Master - Joseph LEWIS
Mistress - Mrs Ann LEWIS

1893   Master - James H ROACH
Mistress - Mrs Mary ROACH

1896   Master - Ernest John Cosier YOUNG

1900   Headmaster - G W WARD
Assistant Mistress - Mrs WARD

1901   Headmaster - Harry TILBURY
Assistant Mistress - Mrs TILBURY

1903   Headmaster - H J BEST
Assistant Mistress - Mrs Caroline BEST

1910   Headmaster - William BLAXLAND
Assistant Mistress - Mrs Kate BLAXLAND

(1917-1919 Temporary War Appointment - R H GREEN)

1936   Headmaster - Frederick DIXON

1961-1968   Headmaster - Jeffery Jones REYNOLDS

September 1968. The school moved to new premises in Georgelands with Mr Reynolds as Headmaster.

And so to Send...

Watercolour of Send National School and schoolhouse painted by P Jenner, 1924

Photographed by K H Bourne MSc 2000

Chapter 10

The New School at Send

Send National School opened in October 1854 so the children of Send now had a school of their own! They had previously gone to Ripley where the Send and Ripley National School had been the only school for the children of both villages since 1847.

There had been much fund-raising in the parish before a new school at Send could be built. Half the cost of the school building had to be raised locally before a grant could be applied for. The Reverend Charles Richmond Tate, Vicar of Send and Ripley, had applied to the National Society in 1853 for aid to help build a school, with schoolhouse, to accommodate 100 children. *(See next pages.)*

See also Chapter One for details about 'The National Society for Promoting the Education of the Poor in the Principles of the Established Church'.

The land on which it was proposed to build the new school belonged to the Lord of the Manor, the Earl of Onslow, who resided at Clandon Park on the eastern boundary of Send. Most of Send and Ripley formed part of his estate. The land for the school was at Send Hill and had been in use as sand and gravel pits *(see page 78)*. It was conveyed to the minister and the churchwardens, and their successors, under the authority of the School Sites Act of 1841, which allowed the land to be used for education, albeit with a clause that, should the land cease to be used for that pur-

pose, it would revert to the former owner. This Act enabled a future Earl of Onslow to reclaim the site once the school had closed. But more of that later.

Plans for the school and the schoolhouse were drawn up by Henry Peak, a young architect from Guildford. Mr Peak went on to become the first Borough Surveyor of Guildford and was made Mayor of Guildford in 1899.

The Rev. Tate had set up a Send School Committee which included local dignitaries, among them the Hon. Francis Scott who lived at Sendhurst Grange a large house on Fell Hill, Send; he was also Member of Parliament for Berwick. The Minute book of the Send School Committee 1854-60 gives details of the meetings for the first few years of the school. It also shows that a Ladies Visiting Committee was selected from among the wives of the School Committee; their task was to visit the school regularly to see that it was being run properly.

There were still two Dame schools in Send and it was expected that they would be absorbed into the proposed new school.

The population was rising and plenty of children were waiting to come to school when they were of age. Also some of the Send children at the Ripley school would have been transferred to the new school. Final cost for the school and residence was £508 16s 8d and the school opened free of debt, as was required by the National Society, for all grant schools at this time had to be self supporting. Although the National Society had contributed only a small part of the money, the school was 'in union' with them and was conducted along their guidelines as was the school in Ripley, now the Ripley National School, as already covered.

The schoolhouse attached to the school was large, comprising parlour, kitchen, scullery and three bedrooms, and the first people to occupy it were Frederick Thomas North and his wife Sarah, the new Master and Mistress.

There were two schoolrooms, each of which had a 'gallery'. This was a tiered wooden structure where the children sat on benches so that

NATIONAL SOCIETY

FOR

PROMOTING THE EDUCATION OF THE POOR IN THE PRINCIPLES OF THE ESTABLISHED CHURCH.

Application for Aid towards building School-rooms, to accommodate *100* children, *for the*

Parish of
or
District of *Send*

} **Post Town.**
Ripley, Surrey

The Schools will be (*according to the conditions stated by the* Committee) *united to the* SOCIETY *by the terms of the Trust-Deed, when completed.*

QUESTIONS.	ANSWERS.
1. Amount of population at the last Census of the parish or district for which the Schools are intended.	The whole Parish numbered 1852 *[illegible]* which Send comprised nearly *[illegible]*
2. What provision already exists in the parish or district for educating the children of the poor in Church principles? Will this provision be superseded either in whole or in part by the proposed new Schools?	Two Dame Schools, held in *[illegible]* of which has 30, the other 20 Scholars One will certainly the other *[illegible]* be superseded by the proposed new School
3. What is understood to be the existing provision for education, gratuitously or at a very small charge, in Schools *not connected with the Church?*	None
4. Is it proposed to erect *Boys', Girls',* and *Infant* Schools, or which of them?	Mixed — Boys & Girls
If it is intended to *purchase* a house to be converted into a School-room, instead of *building* a new one, the circumstance must be clearly stated, and a Surveyor's Certificate be forwarded, which may show the actual present condition of the building, and what its state will be when the undertaking is accomplished. The date of erection must be also mentioned, and the purpose to which the building was originally applied.	

5. What are the proposed dimensions of the School-rooms?	FEET LONG.	FEET WIDE.	HEIGHT TO THE WALL PLATE.
Boys (internally).	35 5/ × 1 7		
Girls.	34 / × 1 /		11
Infants.			

The plans of the building must be submitted to the Committee for approval.

6. Does a residence for the Teacher form part of the plan? if so, state the number and size of the rooms.	Parlor 12 × 12	8
	Kitchen 12 × 11	
	Scullery	
	3 Rooms over	8

Application for Aid form, 1853

7. At what rate of payment is the instruction to be afforded, and what prospect is there that the Schools will be permanently continued?

[handwritten] 1½ a week ... and children's pence with for the means of permanent support

8. What extent of accommodation will be provided for the children in the parish or district church?

[handwritten] For all

9. What is the legal tenure of the proposed School-site? and who are the Trustees to whom it is to be conveyed?

N.B. A *Draft* of the conveyance is required to be sent to the National Society *before the deed is engrossed.*

[handwritten] Freehold by grant from Lord of the Manor, conveyed to the Vicar & Churchwardens

10. What is the estimated cost of the undertaking, including ground, labour, materials, conveyance, &c. &c.?

Cost of School-site.	*Given*	
,, ,, School-rooms.	—	214 - 0 - 0
,, ,, Teacher's Residence.	—	185 - 0 - 0
,, ,, Fittings, Fencing, &c.	—	39 - 13 - 6
,, ,, Legal Expenses.	—	10 - 0 - 0
	TOTAL	£ 448 - 13 - 6

11. Means to meet the Cost :—

	RAISED.	EXPECTED.	TOTAL.
Local Funds.	187 . 10 .. 6	10	197 . 10 . 6
Diocesan or Local Board.			
Committee of Council.*	*[handwritten]*	/ 197-10-6	
Other sources.			39 . 5 . 10 .. 6

* State particularly whether it is intended to apply or not to the Committee of Council on Education.

12. Of what materials are the School-premises to be built?

Walls of *brick,* and 14 inches thick; roof of, *Tiles,* floor of, *Memel deal*

13. State any peculiar circumstances, on the fly-sheet of this paper, upon which you ground a claim to assistance from this Society.

To be signed by the Incumbent, as well as the Applicant or Secretary of the School Committee.

(Signed)

[signature] Charles R. Tate, Vicar, Secretary of School Committee

In case the School is intended for a district including several parishes, the Incumbents or other persons must sign the application; or the applicants must state that he is empowered to do so in their behalf.

This *thirteenth* day of *December* 1853

To be transmitted through the Bishop of the Diocese, for his Lordship's approval and counter-signature.

Approved by me,

[signature]

N.B.—It is particularly requested that a copy may be preserved of the Application, and also a copy of any further correspondence that may take place relating to it.

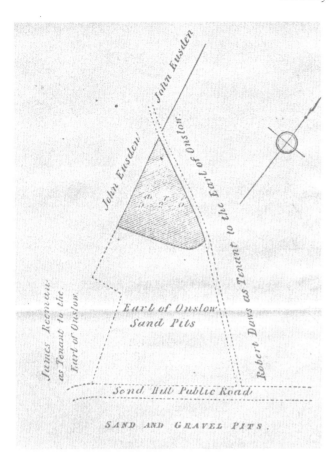

Plan of school site from the Trust Deed 1854

Children's Pence, was payable at the Send National School by the parents, and this money went towards paying the salary of the Master and Mistress, and equipment for the school. These receipts show that Mr North was paid £10 a quarter and his wife £2 a quarter. They lived rent-free in the schoolhouse.

"Received April 5th 1859 of the Revd Coles the sum of £4 8s 11d by School Pence and Cash £5 11s 1d for a Quarter's Stipend due Lady Day. £10 0s 0d" and signed by Frederick North

"Received April 5th 1859 of the Revd J B Coles the sum of £2 0s 0d, one Quarter's Salary and signed by Sarah North

the teacher could easily see the whole group he was addressing. The school was approached from Send Hill by a footpath known as School Lane, which was never more than a well-trodden path liable to the vagaries of the weather. Playgrounds were constructed in the sunken area that was previously the sand and gravel pits, and were reached by a flight of steps.

Send National School opened with nearly a hundred children. From the very beginning a Sunday School was held at the school and all the children were obliged to attend; this explains why the school is sometimes referred to as ' the schools'. Names of children in Send who were of an age in 1854 to attend the school (and probably did) appear in the Pupil lists at the end of Chapter 20.

Education was not free for the children. A sum of 1d per child per week, called

The monitorial system was in place at the school, as it was still regarded as the most effective and inexpensive way of teaching a large number of children; the monitors, older boys and girls, would help the Master with the teaching of the younger children. They would be paid a small wage for being a monitor, and this could lead on to them taking an apprenticeship as a Pupil Teacher on reaching the age of 13. Lessons and the methods of teaching have been described in earlier chapters.

William Daniels, Harriett Faithful, John Nightingale, Mary Ann Raggett, James Steer, Mary Tickner and Rhoda Watson were thought to be monitors in 1861, and Elizabeth Daniels and Richard Jackman were known to be Pupil Teachers that same year.

All schools had to submit to a Government Inspection and Send National School had its first inspection by Her Majesty's Inspector (HMI) in April 1858. There were 75 children at the examination and the HMI wrote the following report: "**A nice orderly school but not yet having much to show in way of attainment ... the Master should direct his attention to awakening and exercising the children's minds ...**".

The Send School Committee had been expressing dissatisfaction with Mr North, mainly because he had failed to gain the required teaching certificates. This report possibly added to their opinion that Mr North should be replaced, and he and his wife left the school in 1861, Arthur R Marshall and his wife Mary becoming the school's Master and Mistress.

By 1861 the government was showing concern that, although more children throughout the country were receiving elementary education, they were not satisfied that standards were consistent. Attendance was poor and many children left school before the age of ten. The cost of elementary education was rising and the country felt it was not getting value for money.

A Revised Code for the financing of elementary schools therefore came into practice in 1862. Every child over the age of six was to be examined annually and a grant was given per child, dependent on his success in passing the examination. This was further graduated by the child's record of attendance. This system of inspection became known as 'Payment by Results'. Whilst it did cut the cost of education and improve attendance generally, it had a disastrous effect on the teachers who, knowing their salaries were dependent on the grants earned by their pupils' results, taught only the examinable subjects. A school's

finances fluctuated according to the children's efforts and their attendance record. The grant paid for each child was 12 shillings and a failure in any of the three Rs reduced this by 2/8d. A grant of 6/6d per head for the under

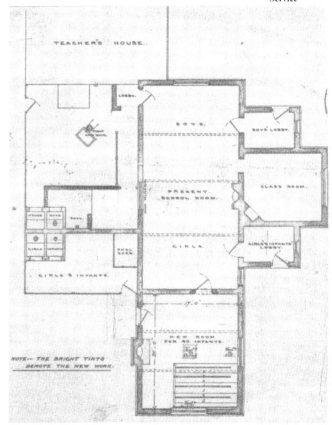

sixes would be paid only if a satisfactory report was made by the HMI. The day of the Inspection was dreaded by teachers and pupils alike, and many deceptions were practised to help children pass their tests; this did not go unnoticed by the Inspectors, who deplored the mechanical methods of instruction and rote learning. However, this system was to last many more years.

The government wanted to make elementary education compulsory for all children. Hence in 1870 an **Educational Census** was taken throughout the land to see if this was a viability, the intention being to take over inefficient voluntary schools, and also the building

The plan of the school shows the position of the classrooms and the separate entrances for the boys and girls. It also shows the toilets which were outside in a yard and were just buckets in cubicles!

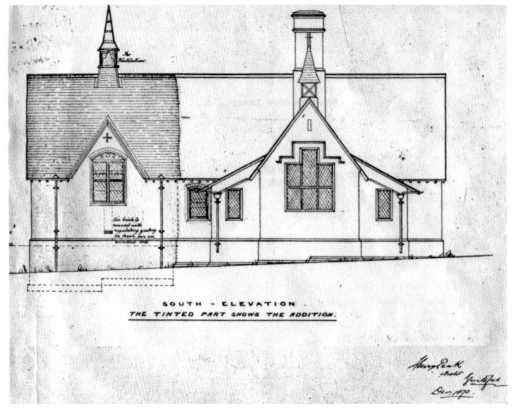

SOUTH - ELEVATION.
THE TINTED PART SHOWS THE ADDITION.

The south elevation of the school showing the new addition. Note the signature of Henry Peak, the architect, in the bottom right-hand corner, dated Dec. 1870.

Copyright of Surrey History Service

of new ones called Board Schools in areas where no schools existed.

Send National School was considered efficient, and remained as a church school, to the relief of the parishioners who wanted to keep it under the control of the church.

Following this seal of approval, the Send School Committee decided to build an Infants Room to separate the younger children, since it was considered that they took up too much of the Master's time to the detriment of the older children. There was more fund-raising amongst the parishioners and more applications by the Rev. Tate for grants from the government and the National Society, to meet the required sum of £198 15s 6d. The plans drawn up by Henry Peak in 1870 show that the new room had a gallery, the wooden tiered structure as in the original schoolrooms built in 1854. Although many HMIs had expressed a dislike for this arrangement and often recommended their removal, the gallery

remained firmly in place in most church schools until the turn of the century. The new Infants Room opened in 1873 with 42 infants.

Mr and Mrs Marshall left the school in 1873, and Thomas and Mrs Howick came in their place, with Miss Howick as Infants Mistress for the newly built room.

*****

Education became compulsory in 1876 together with new rules about the ages that a child could leave school to go to work. Now the child had to be ten years old and have reached Standard 1V, with a good record of attendance, and a Certificate had to be obtained from the newly formed Schools Attendance Committee. There was one in Guildford for the area, set up by the Board of Guardians.

A Schools Attendance Officer, Charles C Frye, was appointed and he was responsible for four schools including Send and Ripley.

His story has been told in earlier chapters and he served his schools faithfully for 14 years before coming to an unfortunate end.

Above is a certificate awarded to Florence May in 1887. She has passed the Fourth Standard and if her attendance record is good enough she can now leave school provided she is ten years old.

The certificate is signed by Thomas L Vincent, Schoolmaster. Thomas Lewis Vincent and his wife Mary Ellen came to the school in 1880 as Master and Mistress, replacing the Howicks who had been there since 1873. The new Infants teacher, who replaced Miss Howick in 1880, was Miss Emma Diddams aged 21. She was to stay at the school for another forty years and was a well-loved, and well-remembered teacher.

There were four changes of Masters and their wives during the first 35 years of Send National School. Little is known of them or their effect on the life of the school. Mr North's presence is confirmed by the receipts he and his wife signed for their salaries; Arthur and Mary Marshall were in the 1871 Census, living in the Schoolhouse at Send as Master and Mistress; the presence of Mr and Mrs Howick and Miss Howick is confirmed only by an entry in Kelly's Post Office Directory for 1874. Mr and Mrs Vincent are in the 1881 Census for Send as Master and Mistress of Send National School, and Mr Vincent acted as Enumerator for the 1881 Census. The Vincents left the school in 1889.

Chapter 11

Lancelot and Jessie Rawes

In March 1889 Lancelot Rawes and his wife came to Send National School. The school was about to embark on a period of great stability, for Mr and Mrs Rawes were to remain as Master and Mistress for 34 years, the longest period of service of any of the school's head teachers.

Lance, as he was known, and Jessie Rawes were a young couple, and in December 1889 their first child, a daughter, Winifred Newling, was born at the schoolhouse. Their joint salary in 1891 was £125, with a rent free house.

The population of Send was increasing and by 1892 there were 190 children at the school and another room was added, which was opened in 1893. Attendance figures were always a concern and incentives were offered to encourage children to attend more regularly.

Send Parish Magazine reported in 1892 that a medal had been given to George James for having made full attendance for a year. In 1893 nine scholars made full attendance and were presented with small purses containing a florin (two shillings), and George James, 'the regular' for the second year in succession, was awarded a purse containing half-a-crown (two shillings and sixpence). The following year he headed the list of five who made full attendance, and in 1895 nine children made full attendance - including one boy who had made full attendance for the fourth year (surely our George!). His effort and rewards must have inspired others to follow his lead, but also he must have been a very healthy lad.

Jim French, who started at Send School in 1894, recalled in his later years several events worth recording "... in 1897 we were given a school break to see the first motor cars pass along the main road through Send ... also in the late 1890s we again had a break to see the Duke and Duchess of York arrive at Clandon Station and Park ...". (Later, of course, they were King George V and Queen Mary.).

Mr French recalled too that in 1897, to celebrate the Diamond Jubilee of Queen Victoria, Arthur Lancaster, who had recently come to Send, gave a fete at 'Sendholme', his home in Potters Lane (then known as Guildford Road.) The school children were all given a cup to mark the occasion.

Following an inspection by the HMI in 1898, the Managers were required "to remove the present brick partition which divides the large schoolroom and to put up a lighter one with glass so that the Master can better superintend".

No Children's Pence now had to be paid as the school was being supported by a voluntary rate of 5d in the £ by parishioners. Although the government was giving more grants to help schools, and paying some of the teachers salaries, voluntary and church schools such as Send would still have to rely for a few more years on funding from the local parishioners to run the school

Then in 1902 a new Education Act was passed. Local Education Authorities (LEAs) were set up and they gradually took over the maintenance of the schools in their areas. Voluntary schools such as Send had to make changes to their running. They had to have six Foundation Managers, two of whom were to be appointed by the LEA; other Foundation Managers were appointed by the religious body to whom the building belonged, in this case the church.

The first Foundation Managers to be appointed at Send National School were Arthur Lancaster of Sendholme, the Vicar the Reverend H O'Rorke, and John A Oliver and Walter Grove both of whom had property in the area. Staines Boorman and Henry J Hill were appointed by the Local Authorities. Arthur Lancaster became School Correspondent and he and his family were to have a long association with the school.

Under the new Education Act of 1902 the Master was required to pay an annual rent for his house. This was fixed at £30 a year but at the same time the house was enlarged and another room was added, making it a double-fronted house. Mr and Mrs Rawes by now had a large family and were no doubt glad of the extra space. They had six children, two girls and four boys, the last child being born in 1902. Their first child, Winifred, born in 1889, had been followed by Lancelot in 1893, Alan in 1896, Victor in 1897, Marjorie in 1899 and Roy in 1902. The children all had the same middle name of Newling, which was Jessie Rawes's maiden name.

*****

Evening Classes

During Mr Rawes's first years at the school, evening classes for adults were introduced there. Surrey County Council had set up a Technical Instruction Committee in 1891, funded by money released by the government, and Send Evening School was started soon after. Mr Rawes encouraged the adults to improve their skills at classes in woodworking, cookery, dressmaking and nursing. Other subjects were added after a few years and by 1906 there were classes in commercial arithmetic, commercial geography, elementary drawing and elementary science. The Managers watched the development of these classes with interest, but gave the greatest credit for their success to Mr Rawes " for his skill, tact and sympathy ", stating, that with him "it has been a labour of love".

In 1910 the Evening School presented Mr Rawes with a handsome marble clock to mark the 21st anniversary of his coming to live in Send, together with a framed address containing the names of past and present members. The evening classes were well attended and continued all the years that he was at the school, and for years afterwards.

*****

The Day School had flourished under Mr and Mrs Rawes and the reports of the HMIs reflect the tone and progress of the school during their time. Here are some extracts from the reports of 1902 through to 1912:

"Creditable work is being done in this school ..."

"The tone and discipline is good and the teaching is intelligent and successful ..."

"The order is good and the teachers work with zeal and assiduity ... The children are in good order and some very satisfactory work is being done ..."

"This is a well conducted school ... the curriculum is exceptionally wide ..."

And the reports continued to reflect favourably on the way the school was run and the quality of the teaching.

Mr Rawes's own children all attended the school. Winifred, was working in the school as a Pupil Teacher in 1903, and Lancelot, won a County scholarship from Send National in 1904. Alan, Victor, Marjorie and Roy followed in their turn and can be seen in some of the photographs.

Further improvements were made in the school in 1905. They included toilets in the playground (still of the bucket variety), built at the rear of the large open-fronted shelter at the far end of the playground for use by the children in inclement weather. There was now a railing to segregate the boys from the girls as was required by the local authorities. The Managers objected to the playgrounds being separated but their objections were overruled and the railing remained and was never removed.

Lance Rawes had always taken a strong interest in the wider aspect of education. He was a contemporary of Chuter Ede, a Surrey man who went on to be Secretary of State for Home Affairs and they formed a friendship based on mutual respect. Chuter Ede had met Mr Rawes when they were both members of the Surrey County Teachers Association; Mr Rawes was President of the Association in 1906 and Chuter Ede regarded him as "the most outstanding man to be an officer of the Association ... his capacity for handling difficult situations proved adequate to every demand that was made on it ...". Mr Rawes and Chuter Ede were in frequent contact during the following years and further reference will be made to this later in the chapter.

*****

Mr and Mrs Rawes now had two Assistant Teachers to help run the school as well as their daughter Winifred as a Pupil Teacher, and Ethel Read as a monitress.

Annual rates of pay in 1903 were as follows;

Joint salary for Mr and Mrs Rawes ...	£150
Infants Teacher, Miss Diddams	£65
Uncertificated Assistant Teacher	£52
Pupil Teacher, Winifred Rawes	£15 12s
Monitress, Ethel Read	£10

Salaries improved slightly each year and in 1908 Ethel Read became a Pupil Teacher and was paid £20 a year; Winifred Rawes was engaged as an Uncertificated Assistant Teacher at £55 a year; and Mr and Mrs Rawes joint salary was now £261 a year.

In 1911, Miss Rawes, having completed her teacher training, was appointed as Principal Certificated Assistant Teacher with an annual salary of £116.

Miss Read was now a Supplementary Teacher at the school, in charge of a class of 31 gipsy children. She was paid £39 a year plus £6 10s 0d for dinner-time supervision of these children - a very low salary. The gipsy children, many of whom had never been to school before, were all in one class; their classroom was the Technical Room in the playground, isolated from the rest of the school. Miss Read was highly praised by the Managers for her work with these children.

The technical room in the playground

Miss Read had tried several times to pass exams to be a Certificated Teacher but was never successful. However, she was valued for the quality of her work and stayed on at the school for many more years. She can be seen in one of the photographs.

The photograph at the top of the next page of Mr Rawes with some of the school was taken around 1908. The back two rows are the Senior School and the front two rows are the Infants. The Middle School is missing. The children had just performed in a school play and three of the girls were allowed to

Left to right, back row: ---? Victor Rawes, Dick Lilywhite, Victor Strudwick, Bernard Strudwick, Arthur Sex.
Third row: Mr Lance Rawes, Mrs Winifred Dolbear, Florrie Lilywhite, Marjorie Rawes, Violet Wilcox, Connie Hobby, Cissie Burns, Miss Ethel Read.
Second row: Roy Rawes, Ivy Fuller, Violet Whapshot, Olive Sirman, Nellie Gadd, ---? Ethel Humphries, Dolly Sale, ---?
Front row: Harriet Saul, Percy Saul, Ernest Mathis, Reginald Mathis, --? --? --?
Information kindly supplied by Mrs D Challen, née Sale.

| SURREY EDUCATION COMMITTEE. | | | | | | | [CARD S.A. 1] |

Mixed. department.
Send. school.
Summary of the attendance during the week ended on the Oct 15th 1915

	No. on registers.	No. admitted.	No. withdrawn.	No. of times open.	Total No. of Attendances.	Average Attendance.	Percentage.
BOYS	65				597	60	92
GIRLS	100			10	918	92	92
TOTAL	165				1515	152	92
INFANTS	37			10	195	20	53

No. in each Standard.

	I.	II.	III.	IV.	V.	VI.	VII.	EX.VII.	
Boys									Signed,
Girls									*Lance Rawes*
Infants									Head Teacher.

Head Teacher's remarks as to attendance *Infants. Whooping Cough & seclusions*

He had a printed prepaid post card for this purpose and this one is for 1915 and signed by him.

This photograph, taken in 1915,
is of a group of children described as "Perfect Attenders"
Mr and Mrs Rawes are in the photograph with them

hold the dolls in the photograph. Dolly (Dorothy) Challen, née Sale, in the second row, is almost hidden by the 'Queen Doll'!

The Great War started in 1914. Air raids were anticipated and plans had to be made for the safety of the children. The Managers decided that in the event of an air raid the school should be closed and all the children sent home.

Young men from Send were responding to Kitchener's 'call to arms', and Mr Rawes's sons, and his son-in-law 'Dick' Dolbear (he and Winifred were married in 1914) volunteered their services and were soon in uniform. The youngest son Roy, was not old enough to go to war but later joined the Woking OTC, and so was also in uniform. Mr Rawes joined the Woking VTC and Mrs Rawes joined the British Red Cross, and they gave their services outside school hours.

School life continued as normally as was possible for the sake of the children. Attendance figures always dominated the school week and the Headmaster had to send weekly returns to the Superintendent of School Attendance in Woking.

Surrey Education Committee had for some years awarded picture postcards as incentives to children for being **'Never Absent Never Late.'** One of these is reproduced below.

SURREY EDUCATION COMMITTEE.

ABBOTS HOSPITAL, GUILDFORD. E.S.A. LONDON. Copyright.
Never Absent, Never Late ....

Medals were also awarded for continued good attendance, as had been going on the past 20 or more years. They were usually presented to the children on Empire Day, 24th May, when a ceremony took place at the school to celebrate the British Empire; that date was also Queen Victoria's birthday and was chosen in memory of her long reign. See Chapter 4.

Children from Send School made their contribution to the war too. In 1914 Arthur Lancaster had sent crates of khaki and grey wool to the school, and the girls knitted socks, gloves and helmets, in lesson time, for local men fighting in the war. Perhaps these went as Christmas presents to them in 1915, since a certificate below shows that gifts were sent.

In 1917 they, like the children of Ripley, went out to collect blackberries at the request of the Ministry of Food. They also collected money for sick and wounded horses, and in 1918 they made a collection for the children of blinded soldiers.

There must have been plenty of hardship in the village. In 1918 when the war was drawing to a close the Managers received permission from Guildford Rural Food Control " ... to obtain bones without expense to enable soup to be provided for the children and staff at the school ... 70 children wished to avail themselves of this opportunity ... the pence paid by the children should cover the cost ... the soup to be made by the older girls under the supervision of Mrs Rawes".

The war did not stop the children's educational progress. In 1917 Send Parish Magazine

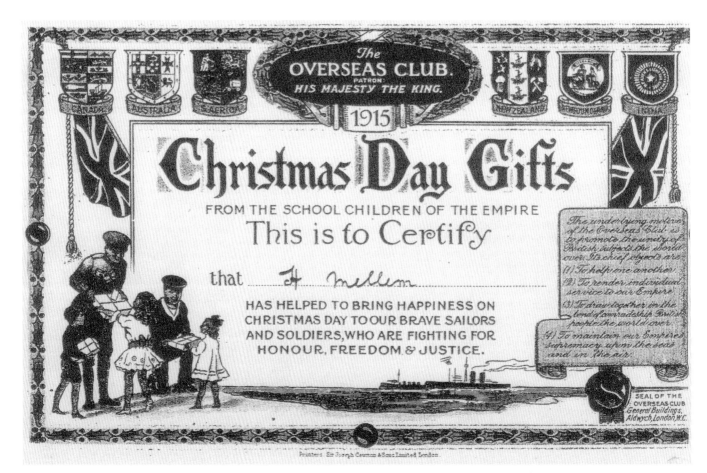

proudly announced that Frank Baker and Ruby Simmonds had both won County Scholarships. As only eight scholarships were awarded in the rural districts of Surrey, this was regarded as "highly satisfactory", and a year later in 1918, Marjorie Baigent and Flossie Molesey also won County Scholarships.

*****

Fourteen young men from the village did not return from the war and their names are recorded on the War Memorial in Send Road, in a quiet location next to the Church Rooms. They are remembered each November on Armistice (Remembrance) Day when poppy wreaths are placed on the Memorial by the local community. The children from Send School always attended the occasion. The men that did return were welcomed back with parties to celebrate their homecoming.

On 13th August 1919 Mr Lancaster, one of the school Managers, unveiled a Memorial at the school " ...erected to those who had been educated in the school and at the call of duty laid down their lives for their country ..."

William Collins,
Albert Giles,
William Giles,
David Millard,
Ernest Tickner,
Jack Tickner,
Herbert Wallis,
Edward Whapshott.

Jimmy Nunn who was at Send School in 1932 recalls seeing this memorial in one of the class rooms, above a fireplace. He described it as being a black wooden shield, about 2ft by 2ft 6ins with the names painted on in gold letters.

*****

When the war was over in 1919 there were celebrations throughout the land and schools were granted an extra week's holiday for the return of Peace. A new recreation ground was being prepared in Send for the use of the people of the village, as a practical memorial to those who had died in the war.

*****

In 1920 Mrs Dolbear, née Rawes, asked the Managers to re-employ her and she continued to teach at the school until three years after her parents retired. Miss Diddams also announced her intention of retiring in 1920. She had taught in the school for 40 years, and was entitled to a full pension. She offered to stay on until another teacher was appointed and finally left in 1921. She was presented with an armchair and a clock on her retirement. It was decided by the Managers that Miss Read could succeed Miss Diddams as Head of the Infants Room.

Successes by two pupils who had previously won scholarship places to schools in Guildford were reported in 1921. Marjorie Strudwick had gained a London School Certificate with credits in French and Arithmetic, and had been awarded a County Teaching Scholarship, which enabled her to go to Goldsmiths College and train as a teacher; and Frank Baker had gained a London Matriculation with distinctions in History, and credits in six other subjects. The school was obviously very proud of its former pupils.

Mr Rawes continued with his work outside the school. By 1921 he had been Hon. Secretary of the Surrey County Teachers Association for 16 years and the members of the Association presented him with a leather-bound book in which was a beautifully decorated citation commending him as a " ...fearless champion of their cause and a successful leader of their campaigns" *(see next page)*. He continued to serve the cause of teachers as Hon. Secretary for another 29 years making a total of 45 years in the post.

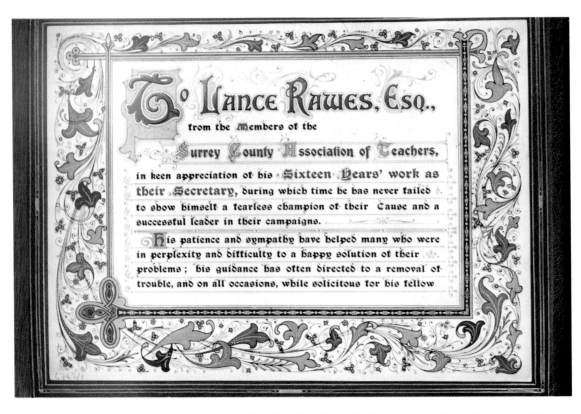

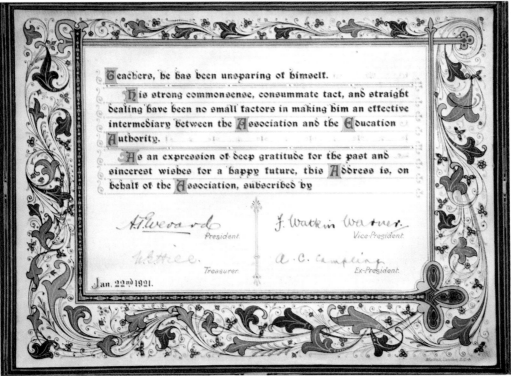

Copyright of Surrey History Service

School group with Mr Rawes 1922. In the photograph are : Alan Pink, Steve Smith, Fred Piercey, Clive Smith, Jack Ford, Ernest Pullinger, Olive Craddock, Beatrice Norman, Edie Hack, Winnie Perrier, Dorothy Pantlin, Vic Smith, Freddy Hack, May Gale, Olive Pantlin, Phyllis Giles, Edie Gadd, Marjorie Charman, Nora Perrier, Winnie Tizzard, John Gale, Basil Leper and Frank Gale. Note the children standing behind and above the group, showing the drop into the playground.

Above is one of the last photographs of Mr Rawes with the children at Send School taken in 1922 in the school playground.

The photograph below, taken inside the school in 1923, shows how the classrooms were separated by wooden frame panels with glass to let in the light.

Children are sitting three to a desk, possibly for the purpose of the photograph. The desk-tops lift up to reveal a shelf underneath, and the slots between the inkwells were originally for slates.

In the photograph are, left to right and starting at the back: Sarah Martin, Cis Carpenter, Monica Simpson, Jack Parrot, Alice Nunn, Bert Gent, Basil Lepper, Edie Turner. John Gale, Peggy Hepburn, Winnie Tizzard, Ken Cable, Bill Parrott, Vic Smith, Sybil Fullick, Kath Hampshire, Ernie Hack, Bob Wright, Norah Spooner, Pat Roake, Jack Ford, Elsie Sewell, Reg Charman, Keith Cable, Fred Bowers, Bobby Pullen, Harry Springett, Desmond Tice, Daphne Styles, Dorothy O'Brien, Vera Pink, Maisie Springett.

In 1923 Mr Rawes had not been in the best of health and in April of that year he wrote to the Managers tending his resignation with regret, on his doctor's advice.

Mr and Mrs Rawes retired in December 1923 and their last day at the school is recorded in this page of the logbook of Send National School.

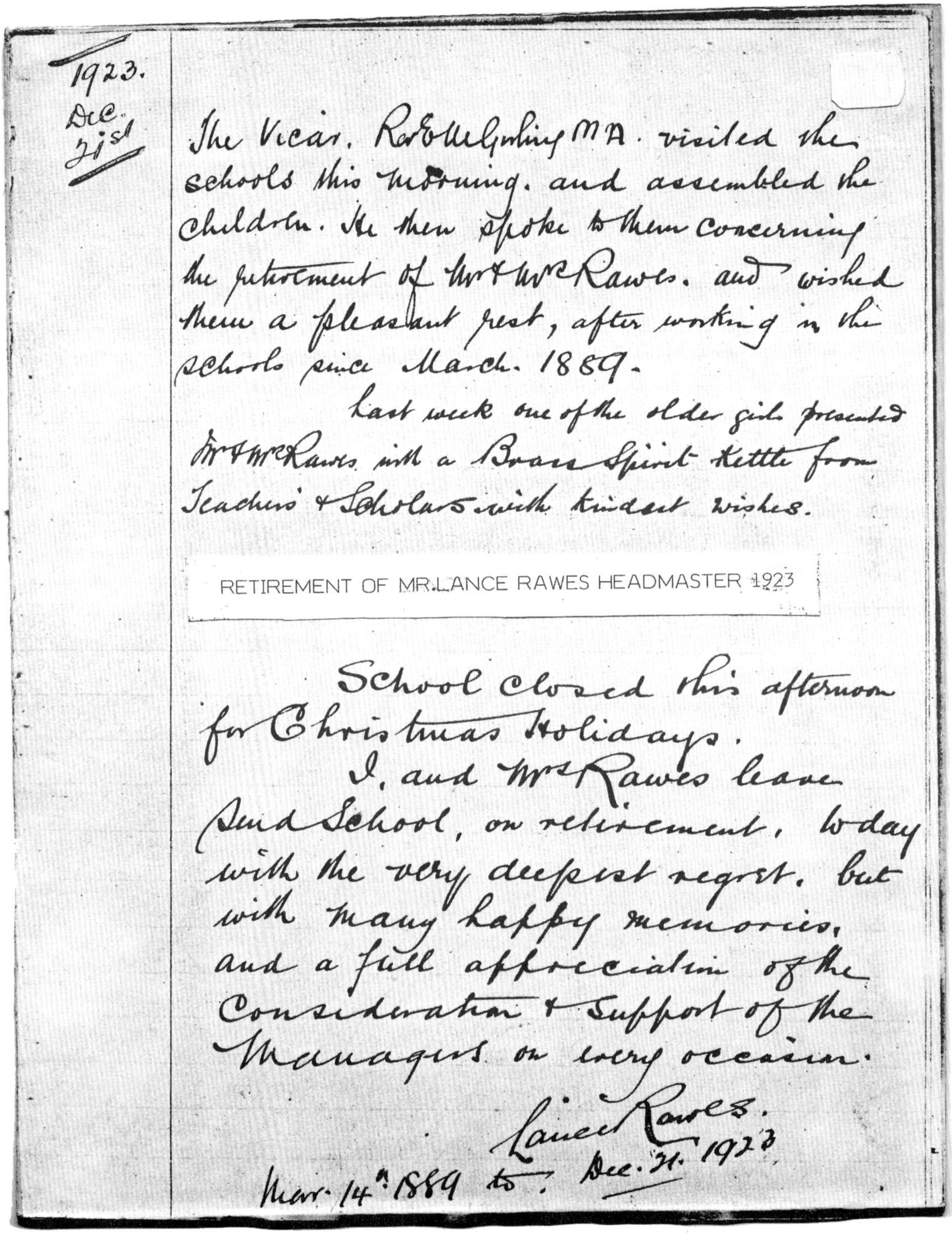

1923.
Dec.
21st

The Vicar. Rev. W. Gosling M.A. visited the schools this morning. and assembled the children. He then spoke to them concerning the retirement of Mr & Mrs Rawes. and wished them a pleasant rest, after working in the schools since March. 1889.

Last week one of the older girls presented Mr & Mrs Rawes. with a Brass Spirit Kettle from Teachers & Scholars with kindest wishes.

RETIREMENT OF MR. LANCE RAWES HEADMASTER 1923

School closed this afternoon for Christmas Holidays.

I. and Mrs Rawes leave Send School, on retirement, today with the very deepest regret. but with many happy memories, and a full appreciation of the Consideration & Support of the Managers on every occasion.

Lance Rawes.
Dec. 31. 1923

Mar. 14th 1889 to Dec. 31. 1923

Early in 1924 a presentation was made to Mr and Mrs Rawes to mark their years at the school, and an 'illuminated manuscript' was given to them by old scholars and the many friends they had in the village. This is a work of art, lovingly executed, and was treasured by Lance and Jessie Rawes and their children; beautifully inscribed in the manuscript were the names of all their old scholars and friends.

The manuscript is now in the Surrey History Centre at Woking, where it was deposited by their grand-daughter Mrs Susan Weighton (daughter of Roy Rawes) in 1999, along with the 1921 citation from the Surrey County Association of Teachers. Her generosity in making this gift is much appreciated.

Lance and Jessie Rawes did not move away from Send. They made their home on Send

Copyright of Surrey History Service

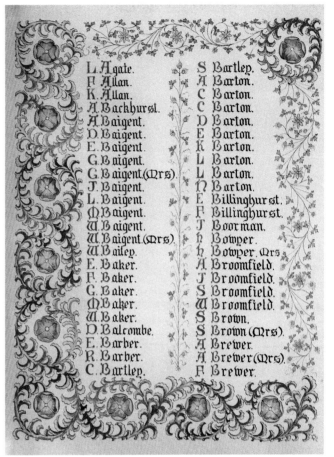

Copyright of Surrey History Service

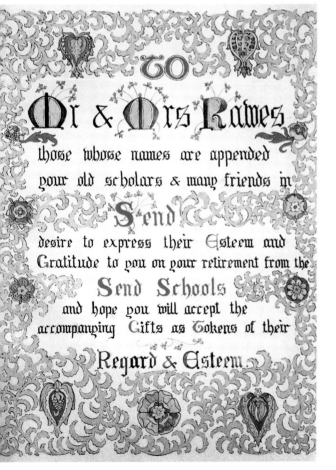

Hill close to the school in 'The Bungalow' (now renamed) with a garden that overlooked the school playground, so that they could watch the children at play. Their daughter Winifred and her husband Dick Dolbear also lived on Send Hill, just a few houses away at 'Bryn Derwyn' (also now renamed). The Dolbears did not have any children, but Lance and Jessie had ten grandchildren who were frequent visitors at 'The Bungalow' and who always went up the road to visit Auntie Winnie and Uncle Dick as well.

Mr Rawes continued to be involved with village affairs, especially with the cricket club. Arthur Lancaster had encouraged village cricket and had made a cricket pitch on his estate at 'Sendholme'. Cricket matches were played there every weekend in the summer

Lance Rawes also enjoyed an active association with the Send Football Club, the Send Institute and the Send Flower Show. In his retirement he continued to serve on several Education Committees, often mediating between the authorities and the teachers to ensure that a professional relationship was maintained. Also he was widely esteemed for his work as Hon. Secretary of the National Union of Teachers in Surrey. He opened the Henley Fort School Camp on the outskirts of Guildford and was Chairman of the committee from its inception. Mr Rawes was indeed a very busy man, but he was never too busy to help local people with problems. His friends and neighbours knew that they could always count on him for advice and support in difficult times. In this he was helped by his wife Jessie who offered a warm welcome to anyone who called at their home.

In June 1934 his services to education and the community were recognised when he was awarded the MBE in the Kings Birthday Honours List. Congratulations flowed into his home from friends and public from all parts of the county.

Chuter Ede paid a personal tribute, acknowledging that Lance Rawes's taking on so many duties had enabled he himself to devote much more of his time to county and national affairs, becoming a Member of Parliament and then Parliamentary Secretary to the Board and the Ministry of Education.

Lance and Jessie Rawes outside 'The Bungalow' in 1940. Photograph by courtesy of their granddaughter, Mrs Rosalie Cheeseman (daughter of Alan Rawes).

ELECTED HON. MEMBER OF S.C.T.A. COUNCIL

MR. LANCE RAWES, M.B.E.

Hon. Secretary, Surrey County Teachers' Association, 1906-1940.

[From the portrait at County Hall, Kingston-on-Thames.

In 1940 this portrait of Lance Rawes MBE was hung in County Hall, Kingston-upon-Thames, to mark his service as Hon. Secretary of the Surrey County Teachers Association from 1906 to 1940.
Copyright of Surrey History Service

Lance Rawes died suddenly at home in March 1942 aged 81. A memorial service held in the Cathedral Church, Guildford, was attended by an impressive list of dignitaries from local and national education authorities. Head teachers came from other schools in the area to pay their last respects, also many local people from all walks of life. Also attending was Chuter Ede who, speaking in his last tribute to his old friend, said of him "His unostentatious but unfailing attainment of the highest standard of personal and social conduct marked him out in any assembly of men.

When asked by the authorities to take charge of a bigger school, Lance Rawes had replied, 'There is no promotion from Send'…".

Chapter 12

Jimmy Rogers

In January 1924, A. James Rogers, aged 43, was appointed Headmaster of Send School and moved into the schoolhouse with his wife, although Mrs Rogers was not on the teaching strength. Another male teacher, Sidney Kenneth Penn, was appointed at the same time.

Mr Rogers was obviously dissatisfied with the conditions in the schoolhouse for when he paid his first quarterly rent he also enclosed a request for a flush toilet to be installed in the house. "At present we only have a bucket and the smell is quite offensive. My wife has never used anything so primitive and feels embarrassed when she has to show her friends there ...". The Managers quickly granted this request as they did not want to lose Mr Rogers whom they regarded as a good man.

Mr Rogers was concerned for the children in his care and reported to the Managers, in the summer of 1924, that attendance was low as children were going to the strawberry fields with their parents. Mr Boorman, one of the Managers and also owner of the fruit farm in Send, pointed out that during the fruit picking season the parents came bringing their children with them, although the latter were not employed. He agreed it was detrimental to school attendance but could not be helped.

Holidays had in the past been arranged during fruit-picking and harvest times but now they were not so flexible. Parents had traditionally relied on this seasonal work to add to their low incomes and, as they had to start picking at 4.30am, the children went too. This situation was always a problem.

The school leaving age had been raised to 14 in 1918, and all early leaving and half-time work had been stopped. More secondary education was being made available with some free places for children from elementary schools. There is evidence that some children from Send School won places through examinations; but very few parents could afford to allow their children to take advantage of higher education. Send was still a rural community, many parents being farm labourers on low wages.

One girl who was fortunate enough to benefit from higher education was Marjorie Strudwick who returned as a trained teacher in later years to teach in Send School with Mr Rogers. Marjorie had started at Send School in 1908 and had won a Scholarship to the

Ron and Marjorie Sex outside their bungalow. Photograph by courtesy of their son, Mike.

Guildford County School for Girls in 1913. She thought she was the first girl to achieve that distinction. She later went to Goldsmiths College in London and trained to be a teacher. She married Ronald Sex, also a former pupil of Send school, who had followed in his father's trade of village blacksmith. They settled in Send in a bungalow called St Anne, on Send Hill, near the school and opposite to 'The Bungalow' where Lance and Jessie Rawes, their former Headmaster and teacher, still lived!

During the first few years under Mr Rogers, more opportunities for sports became available for the children at the school. Organised Games (OG) for the older boys were approved by the Managers but there were no playing fields at Send School. In previous years, outside activities had been limited to nature walks in the area close to the school, and Drill in the playground.

But now the village had a recreation ground which could be used for games lessons. Football was played and Mr Penn was in charge of Send School Football Team.

Permission was given also for swimming lessons, with Mr Penn in charge. Swimming took place in the canal, at High Bridge at the end of Wharf Lane, Send, which was considered a safe place to bathe. The canal was part of the Wey Navigation, and other schools in the area also had their designated places to bathe in the canal.

This certificate, for swimming 50 yards was awarded to George Masters when he was eight years old. The 50 yard course was from High Bridge to the first bend in the canal, and the certificate was signed by Mr Rogers.

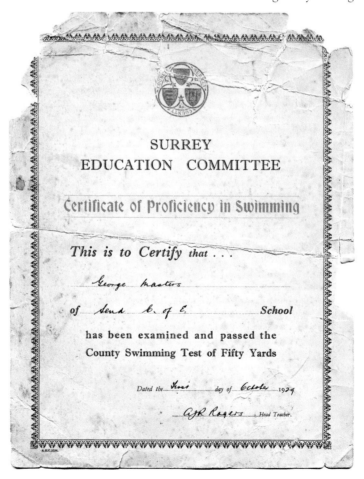

Certificate by courtesy of George Masters.

SURREY EDUCATION COMMITTEE

Certificate of Proficiency in Swimming

This is to Certify that . . .

George Masters

of Send C. of E. School

has been examined and passed the County Swimming Test of Fifty Yards

Dated the first day of October 1929

A.J.R. Rogers, Head Teacher.

Soon the girls were asking for swimming lessons too, and the Managers agreed but demanded that a screen be made for use by the girls for changing purposes, although boys and girls had their swimming lessons on separate days.

It was now compulsorary for the older girls and boys to be separated for PE (physical education) lessons, which took place outside in the playground, weather permitting. There was no hall for such purposes at the school.

There were Organised Games too for the older girls, and the photograph is of the Send School Netball team, with Mr Rogers, taken in 1924 or 1925.

Send School netball team with Elsie Jackman, Elsie Darling, Beatrice Norman, Ruby Garment, Irene Gale, Phyllis Giles, Phyllis Pantling, Hilda Charman, and Olive Craddock.

Already mentioned, George Masters who started his school days at Send School in 1926 is the second boy from the left in the front row of this school photograph, taken in 1928 or 1929. A young teacher, Miss Palmer, is in the back row, far right. Also in the photograph are George Springett, Les Bigwood, Jack Parrott, Dorothy Barnes, Betty Lepper, Rene Hepburn, Phyllis Smith, Kathy Hampshire, Arthur Charman, Kathy Brewer, Joan Stedman, Molly Turner, Winnie Crane, Freddy Dunn, Jack Ford and Stan Taylor. Photograph is by courtesy of George Masters.

In 1925 a Boy Scout Troop was started for the boys of Send School with Sidney Penn as Scoutmaster, but under the supervision of the headmaster.

Permission was given for Mr Penn to take the boys to camp that year at Friday Street, near Dorking, about 10 miles away.

George Masters remembers playing in the Send School football team. The team won the Woking League Cup for the 1933-34 season and in this photograph George can be seen at the centre of the group holding the Cup. Sidney Penn, the teacher who took the boys for football lessons, is also in the photograph which is reproduced by courtesy of George himself.

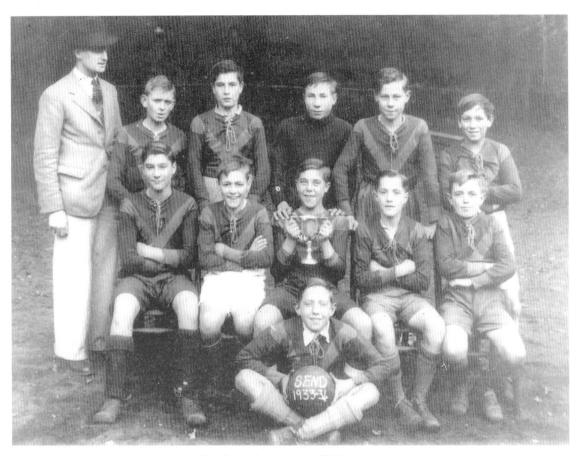

Send School football team 1933-34 season.

From left to right:
Back row - Stan Taylor, Albert Bowers, Dennis Doe, Jack Pink
Front Row - Ronnie Pullen, Sam Friend, Les Huggins, George Masters, Jack Weller, Sonnie Pullen.

Ernie Dunn is holding the ball.

Chapter 13

Events and Changes

Arthur Lancaster died in 1928 at the age of 82. He had been a School Manager since 1896 and the School Correspondent since 1902. His home Sendholme in Potters Lane, Send, was a large Victorian house set in extensive grounds. He employed over 30 staff to take care of the family, house and grounds, and many youngsters went into service there when they left school. He had two daughters, Elsie and Evelyn, who were both involved with the school.

Elsie Lancaster became a School Manager in place of her father, and the school benefited from her generosity. The oil lamps at the school were replaced by electric light in 1928, and Elsie and her sister contributed towards the cost. They also paid for a gramophone for the children's drill and for country dancing at the school.

In May 1930 Elsie presented football medals to the school, paid for out of her own pocket, and in June that year she made it possible for the children to go to the Aldershot Tattoo by subsidising the fares.

*****

Miss Ethel Read, a teacher at the school for many years, became seriously ill in 1932. The proceeds of the school Christmas concert were given as a benefit to her, but she died in May 1933. Mr Rogers wrote in the logbook "she was much loved by the children and was a valued member of staff".

Miss Annie Kathleen Palmer became Infants Mistress in 1932. She had joined the school in December 1926 and was a teacher who endeared herself to the children by her kindly manner. She was to stay at the school for many years. Mrs Marjorie Sex applied to be a Supply Teacher in 1932 and she too was to have a long teaching association with the school.

Several past pupils have recalled that in the 1930s the Headmaster's wife, Mrs Rogers, made cocoa for the children who had sandwiches at mid-day, until Horlicks sponsored a scheme for schools, supplying a large plunger mixer, small paraffin stove, storage cabinet for trays of cups, and large jugs, together with a 7lb tin of Horlicks. The children were obviously impressed by this generosity, being charged only a half-penny a cup. Later on, the local dairy at Boughton Hall Farm supplied one third of a pint bottles of milk for a half-penny. The school took advantage of this during the summer but continued with the Horlicks in the winter. This was prior to an officially sponsored milk scheme which eventually gave every child a free bottle of milk daily.

Mr Rogers was as concerned as his predecessors about the level of school attendance. Children would be absent for a variety of reasons, not the least being the weather. Lack of suitable clothes would keep some of them at home during bad weather, and another factor was that during wet weather and after heavy snow falls, the children living in low-lying areas of Send (that is Cartbridge, Papercourt and Newark) would find roads impassable as ditches and streams filled up and overflowed, and the canal and the river broke their banks. Illness in the family would keep the older girls at home to look after the rest of the family, and contagious diseases at school would cause parents to keep their children away, influenza, diphtheria, impetigo and scabies being prevalent in the 1920s and 30s.

Sometimes there would be no coal for the fires in the school due to the miners' strikes, and in 1929, it was so cold that the ink froze in the inkwells.

Central heating was installed in 1934, thanks to a generous contribution from the Misses Lancaster, making the school much more comfortable.

Weekly attendance figures still had to be sent to the authorities and were also recorded in the school logbook. The School Attendance Officer would be sent after missing children if there appeared to be no reason for absence. Clarence Walter Jarman was appointed to this post in 1925. He had lost a leg in 1916, in the Battle of the Somme, but despite this disability he cycled on his specially adapted bicycle around the schools in his area, and sorted out the offenders with firmness and humour. He was School Attendance Officer for 33 years and then lived another 35 years in retirement until his death in 1996 at the great age of 100 years.

Genuine days off were allowed for special events such as royal weddings, Sunday school treats, and General Elections when the school was used as a polling station. The school was allowed to close for the local flower show,

held at Sendholme, and one year a whole marquee was reserved for schools' exhibits. There were school treats, too, when children were taken to the seaside, the zoo or to London; the expenses of these outings were often underwritten by the Misses Lancaster. The annual Sports Day was also held at Sendholme.

There continued to be annual government inspections by HMIs but the school finance was no longer governed by the results and a half-day holiday would still be given once the inspection was over. Every Ascension Day the children would be marched to Send Church for a special service which would be followed by a half-day holiday.

An event to be remembered was the Silver Jubilee of the King and Queen on 6th May 1935. Miss Elsie Lancaster invited all the children to Sendholme,(where they celebrated with sports and tea in the grounds) and gave each child a medal to commemorate the occasion.

Photographs of the medal belonging to Sid Stanley,
which he has kindly donated to the Send and Ripley Hstory Society.

Sadly this event was overshadowed a few months later by the death of the King, and the school was closed all day on 28th January 1936 for his funeral.

It was an exceptional year for the nation since three kings reigned in that year: King George V, his eldest son who became Edward VIII for a short time before abdicating, and George VI, Edward's brother, who then acceded to the throne in his place.

The Coronation of George VI and Queen Elizabeth was held in May 1937 and Elsie Lancaster presented Coronation mugs to the children. Extra holidays were given to the school in honour of the occasion.

One of the regular lessons throughout the life of the school was gardening. Sid Stanley who was at school in the 1930s, remembers the school gardens at the end of the playgrounds behind the toilets. They were in a wooded area known as the 'plantation'. There were five plots; each class had its own plot and the children moved to a different plot as they

progressed through the school. Practical gardening lessons were given here and the children grew vegetables and flowers. The produce was shared out between the school and the families of the pupils themselves.

Sid's parents were the caretakers at the school and one of his father's duties was to empty the cesspit with a hand-pump located at the end of the plantation. Water from the cesspit was allowed to flow freely over the area of the plantation, where it was quickly absorbed into the sandy soil, thus watering and nourishing the soil at the same time!

A triangular area of land beside the boys' playground was the Headmaster's garden and the children would work there during lesson time under his watchful eye.

Gardening lessons were always popular, being the chance to be outdoors and away from the blackboard! They were to play an important role in the years ahead during wartime.

Pat Clack, née Gibbons, was a pupil at

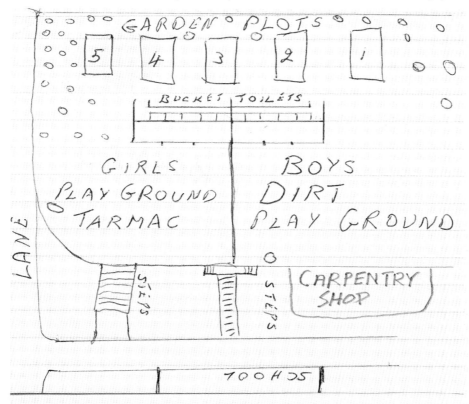

This plan of the playground showing the garden plots and carpentry shop was hand-drawn by Peter Rixon, an old pupil of the school.

Send School during the 1930s. She lived in Send Road, only a short distance from the school, but her mother Mrs Gibbons always walked with her to and from school. Pat's mother was well known to the other children and she was on hand when any mishaps fell, which included dealing with a boy who regularly had fits!

Pat recalls celebrating Empire Day, 24th May, at Send School. The children would perform country and maypole dancing, and often Sir Arthur Glynn, a member of Surrey County Council, would be there to watch and he would invite a team of dancers to a country dance party at his country house in Ewell.

Mrs Marjorie Sex was one of Pat's teachers, as was Mr Penn. Examination of the children's progress was now taking place within the school and reports were sent home to the parents at the end of the year. A typical example is Pat's report which shows her attainment

marks and attendance, and is signed by her teacher Mr Penn. It also has the stamped name of Mr Rogers the Headmaster.

Another girl who attended Send school in the late 1930s was Jean Turner, née Smallbone. She remembers Sidney Penn as a class teacher and as the Headmaster after Mr Rogers died. Jean had three head teachers in her stay at the school as she was also there when Miss Perrin came in 1941.

Mr Penn was remembered also as a good pianist who often entertained the children with his renderings on the piano. Jean also recalls the generosity of the Misses Lancaster who provided the sweets that were kept in the classrooms as rewards for good work, and also eggs for all the children at Easter She remembers the chocolate eggs as being graded according to the child's place in the school; small eggs for the little infants; medium size eggs for the middle school children; and big eggs for the oldest boys and girls.

Jean's mother, Edith Smallbone, née Faithfull, was also at Send school when Mr Rawes was the Headmaster. Seven other members of the same Faithfull family were at the school in Mr Rawes's time.

The photographs show Jean Smallbone, on the left, and Pat Gibbons on the right, taken at Send School in the 1930s.

SURREY EDUCATION COMMITTEE.

Send C of E School. M Senior Department.

Report on Pat Gibbons

for the Term ending July 31st, 1935.

Class II   Number on Roll 42   Position in Class 7

Subject	Possible	Obtained	Remarks	Subject	Possible	Obtained	Remarks
Scripture	10	9		Handwriting	10	7x	
Reading		10		G.K. Drawing		3t	
Recitation		8		Needlework		6	
Composition		8		Handwork		7	
English Spelling		9		Physical Training		7	
Geography		7					
History		7					
Nature Study		5					
M.A. Science		6					
Arithmetic		10					

General Report: *Progress very satisfactory. Pat is certainly a worker & deserves her share of credit for all her work. Her behaviour is excellent & is a decided example to others in her class.*

S.R.Penn
Class Teacher.

A.J.R. Rogers.
Head Teacher.

A diphtheria epidemic was sweeping the country in 1938 taking its toll of young lives. A programme of immunisation of children against the disease was carried out in the schools. The health of the children of the nation had been given priority in the 1930s and medical inspections were carried out as children started school. The Schools Medical Service sent doctors and nurses into the schools to give dental and eye examinations, and clinics were set up to enable parents to follow the recommendations made. Children were given treatment free of charge, or at low cost, at these clinics.

Elsie Lancaster died in 1938 and all the children in the top class walked to Send Church to attend her funeral service. They were each given a commemorative prayer book to mark the occasion.

Evelyn Lancaster set up a memorial at the school, for her sister, in the form of the Elsie Lancaster Memorial Prize which consisted of a book awarded each year to one girl and one boy in the top class for good work and good conduct.

Pat Clack, received one of the first of these prizes in 1939 in her last year at the school. Her prize was the Complete Works of William Shakespeare, handsomely bound in leather.

*****

Evelyn Lancaster became a School Manager after her sister's death and she continued the family's benevolence, sending sweets and oranges for the children at Christmas time.

In Loving Remembrance

of

ELSIE LANCASTER

Born 2nd. July, 1881.

Died at Sendholme,

14th. April, 1938.

THE ORDER

FOR

The Burial of the Dead.

¶ Here is to be noted, that the Office ensuing is not to be used for any that die unbaptized, or excommunicate, or have laid violent hands upon themselves.

¶ The Priest and Clerks meeting the Corpse at the entrance of the Church-yard, and going before it, either into the Church, or towards the Grave, shall say, or sing:

I AM the Resurrection and the Life, saith the Lord: he that believeth in Me, though he were dead, yet shall he live: and whosoever liveth and believeth in Me shall never die.

S. John xi. 25, 26.

I KNOW that my Redeemer liveth, and that He shall stand at the latter day upon the earth. And though after my skin worms destroy this body, yet in my flesh shall I see GOD: Whom I shall see for myself, and mine eyes shall behold, and not another.

Job xix. 25, 26, 27.

3

Chapter 14

Send School in Wartime

Another World War was looking **inevitable** and the country made contingency plans well ahead. When war was declared on 3rd September 1939, a government evacuation scheme, code-word PIED PIPER, went into action. Due to the well-laid plans of the London County Council, 1,473,000 evacuees, mainly children, were moved in three days away from London to previously arranged reception areas in the country. All the teachers were recalled from their summer holiday to help with the evacuation.

RIVERDALE School from south London was evacuated to Send. The children shared Send School premises and were billeted in the village. Each school kept its identity, but the Headmaster, Mr Rogers, had overall charge. Times of attendance were changed so that each school had alternate morning and afternoon sessions. The Drill Hall and the Church Rooms, in Send Road, were brought into use and eye-witnesses remember crocodiles of children being moved around the village throughout the day, as the schools changed places.

BEULAH School from Croydon was also evacuated to Send and shared the Drill Hall and the Church Rooms. There were also 24 London children privately evacuated to Send and they were combined with the Send children, making the numbers high.

During the summer holidays in the war years all teachers had to do some holiday duties. The schools were kept open since many mothers were on war-work. Teachers supervised free play and organised some activities, and hot dinners and milk were available to those who wanted them. Miss Palmer remembered that the teachers at Send School had only two weeks summer holiday because they took over the evacuee schools to allow their staff a break.

The photograph below shows three evacuees from one family. The two girls, Christine and Doreen Scoles, were billeted with Mr and Mrs Gibbons at Mays Corner, and they attended Send school. Their brother, Geoff, was billeted with another family at Kingfield and he went to school there.

Dig for Victory

Wartime restrictions meant food rationing, and posters like these reminded the public of the need to produce food on every available piece of land. Gardens were dug up and planted with vegetables to help feed the family. Gardening and cooking advice was given on the radio, in pamphlets and in the newspapers.

In September 1939 the Board of Education issued memoranda to schools about how those with school gardens could play their part by growing vegetables and fruit on these plots, and on any other land that could be secured.

Mr Rogers noted in the school logbook in October 1939 that he had obtained the use of a large piece of land near the school for the boys to work on during the time that Riverdale School was using the school build-ing. This was the land on the opposite side of School Lane known as the Sandfields. The village was given the use of this land as war-time allotments; after the war the council built houses there and kept the name Sandfields for them.

A memorandum came from the Board of Education in 1939 asking schoolchildren to collect the "harvest in the woodlands" this being acorns and beech mast that could be useful to the farmers to feed their pigs. It also pointed out that in areas to which children had been evacuated "it will be a useful part-time occupation for the next few weeks". Here was an opportunity, it suggested, for town and country children to come together in a healthy outdoor activity. In reality the evacuee and the village boys were often in fights (from verbal reports!).

In 1940 another memorandum asked schools to organise salvage collections. Salvage included waste paper, woollen and cotton rags, metal, and bones, all of which was recycled to help with the war effort. The children from the top classes were allowed to do this and Peter Rixon recalled that they pushed and pulled a trailer, normally towed by a car, around the village on Saturday mornings. The salvage collected was unloaded and sorted at the school.

The next memorandum came in the autumn of 1941 and concerned the wild fruit crop. Not only the children but the general public too were asked to go out and gather the blackberries, elderberries, crab apples and other wild fruit. They were asked to take these to their local fruit preservation centre where they would be paid on a scale, for example, of 3d a pound for blackberries and 2d a pound for crab apples. The Send Women's Institute had set up a Fruit Preserving Centre in the Drill Hall, and throughout the early war years the ladies of the Send WI made hundreds of pounds of jam, and bottled a similar amount of fruit to add to the national larder. Other Women's Institutes throughout the country were doing this too. Jam was rationed during the war and the Ministry of Food relied on these contributions to ensure that everyone had a fair share. The schools could choose to make their own jam by getting extra sugar rations from the local Food Office and retaining the jam for consumption in the school, outside the ration.

However none of this was noted in the logbook. The strain of running the school under severe difficulties was too much for Mr Rogers. In January 1940 he wrote to the Managers stating that he was ill, and requesting some weeks of absence to recover. His entry in the log book reads "I was suddenly taken ill, almost nervous collapse, in other words overwork. The last few months have been very hard in a full school and with extra work added. I may be away some weeks…". This was his last entry, for a few weeks later, on 18th March, whilst recuperating at Bournemouth, Mr Rogers died. He had been Headmaster for 16 years and the Managers stood for a one-minute silence at their next meeting in his memory, for he was a man they had held in high regard.

Mr Rogers's death prompted the Managers to take action, and a few weeks later the evacuees and their teachers took themselves and their school stock to the Drill Hall.

Send School then returned to a full time curriculum.

Mr Penn was asked to take over the school as Acting Headmaster, and he remained in charge for over a year.

The Managers wanted to know his arrangements for the safety of the children in the event of air-raids as there were no shelters at the school. Mr Penn thought the children would be safer under cover and should be kept at school, sheltering under their desks or in the woodwork room in the playground. Some past pupils recall lying down behind a wall at the end of the playground behind the toilets. A loud siren in the village gave a wailing sound as a warning that enemy planes were heading for the area, and another siren sounded a one-note 'All Clear' when the danger had passed.

Every adult and child was issued with a gas mask to put on in the event of a gas raid by the enemy; this was in a square cardboard box and had to be carried at all times. The Air Raid Warden, Mr Paice, would come to the school once a week to check them and to practise gas mask drill so that the children knew how to use them. Fortunately there was never a need to do so.

The windows in the school had to be covered with strips of sticky brown paper, neatly criss-crossed onto the panes, sometimes forming the pattern of the Union Jack as several children recalled! The older children helped with this task. In the event of bomb blast, this would reduce the risk of injury from flying glass. Later on, the windows were fitted with expanding wire-mesh to give further protection.

More evacuees came to Send School, this time from Portsmouth, and Mr Penn wrote in the logbook in November 1940 that " … This will be eight weeks that I have had to manage nearly 80 children this term …".

The school day was shortened in the winter months to enable the children to travel to and from school in the daylight, and the younger children were always accompanied home by older children.

Although the country was considered a safer place for children than London or Portsmouth, Send had several air-raids, during which bombs were dropped on the village. The school escaped with only slight damage when a large land-mine fell at May's Corner.

Despite the war, reorganisation of elementary schools was due to take place in September 1941. A new secondary school opened in the village, in Bush Lane off Send Hill, offering free secondary education for all children. (This school had been ready for use in 1939 but the military had kept it empty in case it was needed for a war emergency.)

All the senior children, aged 11 years and above were to be transferred to the new school. The school leaving age was about to be raised to 15. Children could still leave at 14 but it was hoped that they would stay on after that. Better opportunities were offered at the new school including commercial subjects, and exams could be taken that were previously possible only at grammar schools. There were extensive playing fields providing wider sporting facilities and large playgrounds; there was also a canteen where meals were cooked and served.

Send Central School, as it was first called (the name was later changed to St Bede's), was a church school funded by grants from the government, the church, the National Society and local donations. Pupils came from Ripley, Ockham, East Clandon and West Clandon as well as Send, and the five parochial councils helped to support the school.

Sid Stanley, who went for a short while to the new secondary school in 1941 as one of its first pupils, also received one of the last book prizes awarded from the Elsie Lancaster Memorial Fund as he left the old school.

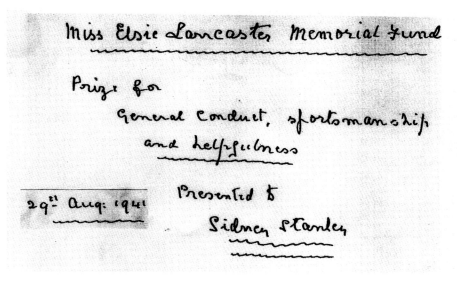

Miss Elsie Lancaster Memorial Fund

Prize for General Conduct, sportsmanship and helpfulness

29th Aug: 1941   Presented to Sidney Stanley

Mr Penn, who had been Acting Headmaster since the death of Mr Rogers, left Send school at the end of the 1941 summer term. He had been at the school since 1924 and was well respected. He was a bachelor and lived on in Send in his retirement, lodging with a family on Send Hill. In his later years he moved away and lived by himself in a caravan on a site by 'The Victoria', a public house at Byfleet, and he was over 90 when he died. Several former colleagues and friends always kept in touch with him.

*****

A new head-teacher, a woman, had been appointed to start in the Autumn Term of 1941. She was to stay at the school for the next 30 years.

Chapter 15

Miss Stella Eugenie Perrin

Miss Perrin was born in Ripley in 1911. She started school as a pupil at Ryde House School, a private school in Ripley, and then at the age of nine she moved to Ripley National School with her sister, Cicely. (See entry below from Ripley School Admission Register.) Another sister, Sybil, joined them in 1921.

Stella Perrin was one of the first pupils to win a scholarship to the new Woking Girls Grammar School when it opened in 1923. She trained at Homerton College, Cambridge and had taught at several schools, including Ripley C of E, before coming to Send as the new Headmistress.

Miss Perrin moved into the schoolhouse with her mother, Mrs Annie Perrin, on 1st September 1941. The name of the school had been changed, with the reorganisation, and Miss Perrin took over her duties as the first Headmistress of Send C of E Junior Mixed and Infants School.

There were 151 children on roll which included officially evacuated children from Croydon and London. One of Miss Perrin's first entries in the logbook reads "A senior group of Croydon and LCC officially evacuated children in charge of Mr Vivian and Miss P N Barber have from today the use of one classroom in the school. They are working as an entirely separate group...". This was not a happy arrangement and there were times of conflict when one group encroached on the other's space, according to several verbal reports!

60	12	4	20	Gardiner	William	William	Geo.		Roborrow Cott.
61	19	4	20	Perrin	Stella Eugenie	Arthur	Leonard		High St Ripley
62	19	4	20	Perrin	Cicely Madeline	"			" "
63	19	4	20	Gardiner	Frederick	William	Geo.		Roborrow Cott.

Mr R B Roberts, the Headmaster of St Bede's, the new secondary school in Bush Lane, came and introduced himself to all the classes and staff in September 1941. The children were now using the canteen facilities at his new school; they had the first sitting there for dinner at midday and were escorted to and from the school by their teachers. The primary school no longer closed at midday and teachers were expected to supervise their classes both in the canteen and before afternoon school started. They continued to do so until after the war when 'dinner-ladies' were engaged to do this work,

Although some children still went home at midday, many mothers were now not at home since they were engaged in temporary war-work, filling the jobs that had been left vacant by the men called up for war service. The School Meals Service made sure that children were adequately fed, despite food rationing, and the local authorities subsidised the meals. The hope that all school meals would eventually be free was never realised, although families with low incomes were given free dinners from the beginning.

*****

In the Autumn Term of 1942, all the junior evacuees from the Drill Hall were admitted to Send School and a third junior class had to be formed as the numbers rose to 180. Miss Perrin recommended her sister, Mrs Sybil Somerfield, as a Supply Teacher (coming in at a moment's notice when other teachers were absent.)

Mrs Somerfield continued as a Supply Teacher, with a few breaks when her children were young, until the school closed. She was one of several teachers living in the village whose services were called on frequently during the years of teacher shortages.

Air raids continued to disrupt the school time-table. With no air raid shelters at the school there was concern for the safety of the children, and attendance figures were often low because some parents kept their children at home at these times.

During the war there were continual fund-raising events to help the war effort, and more salvage drives.

Concerts were given by the school children to raise funds for the services; **Warship Week in 1942; Wings for Victory Week in 1943; Salute the Soldier Week in 1944.**

Also in 1944 there was a Book Salvage Drive and the children collected over 6,400 books. Thirteen of the children qualified for the rank of 'Field Marshal' for collecting more than 250 books each and certificates were presented to them by the Mayor of Guildford.

*****

Throughout the war years people were urged to put money into National Savings to help pay for the war effort. National Savings Groups were set up in offices, factories and schools and there was competition amongst these groups to see how much they could save.

The Send School Group was in the charge of Miss Palmer and she reported in 1942 that the school children had raised £743 6s.6d for National Savings, as well as £14 3s.4d for Red Cross funds and £5 7s.6d for Poppy Day. Children could save by buying National Savings Stamps for 6d or 2/6d and would stick the stamps into savings booklets which when full could be used to buy National Savings Certificates.

After the war the King and Queen gave a garden party at Buckingham Palace for all the leaders of National Savings Groups, and Miss Palmer received an invitation to attend *(see next page)*.

GRE

The Lord Chamberlain is

commanded by Their Majesties to invite

Miss A. K. Palmer

to an Afternoon Party in the Garden of Buckingham Palace,

on Thursday, 6th June, 1946, from 3 to 5 p.m.

(Weather permitting).

Day Dress.

Chapter 16

The Post-War Years

On May 8th 1945 Miss Perrin wrote in the logbook "The school is closed today and tomorrow owing to the war in Europe having come to an end. Thus today is to be known as VE Day (Victory in Europe) ...". There were celebrations throughout the land; the evacuees prepared to go home; and families looked forward to their menfolk returning.

Fourteen Send men did not return, having lost their lives fighting in the war, and their names were added to the war memorial in Send Road in due course.

*****

The departure of Riverdale school was not mentioned in the logbook, but amongst the old and tattered books being thrown out when cupboards were emptied at the end of the last term of Send School in 1972 was one that was stamped Riverdale School, Merton SW18 - further evidence of that school's stay in Send.

School life gradually returned to normal and the Managers presented their report to the Subscribers for the five years 1941-46 *(see next page)*. Note the names of the Managers at the bottom of the page. Elsie Lancaster should read Evelyn Lancaster, since Elsie had died in 1938. *(See Chapter 13.)*

Picture of Riverdale book and stamp

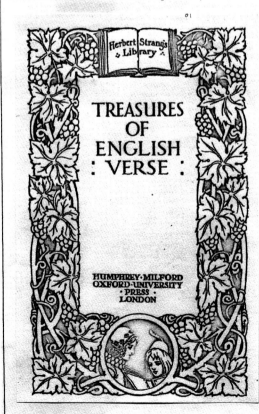

teacher in 1947, and Miss Ann Rhodes, a teacher who had been at the school since 1922, retired in 1950. Miss Rhodes had taught needlework of a very high standard to the girls, but was also remembered by her former pupils for reading delightful stories to them from the "Milly-Molly-Mandy" books.

In the photograph are:
Back row left to right – Student teacher (name unknown), Mrs Docherty, Mrs Somerfield.
Front row left to right – Miss Palmer, Miss Perrin, Miss Rhodes.

To the Subscribers of the Send Church of England Primary School.

We have pleasure in sending you the Managers' Account for the Quinquennial period 1st April 1941—31st March, 1946.

Owing to your continued support the School Buildings and School House have been kept in proper repair. The retaining walls to the Playground have been rebuilt and a new Fuel Store constructed. A new heating boiler has also been installed in the School. The main roofs of the School are, however, in a poor condition and considerable expenditure will be necessary in retiling these in the near future. The School buildings and House received superficial damage from a flying bomb in June 1944 and the temporary repairs have been carried out.

Upon the reorganisation of Elementary Schools in September 1941 the School became a 'Primary School' for children under 11 years of age, and all children above that age were transferred to St. Bede's Secondary School.

It was at this period that Miss S. E. Perrin commenced her duties as Headmistress. During the period under review conditions have been difficult owing to the War, but the work of the School has gone steadily forward and has been considered very satisfactory by H.M. Inspectors. Thirteen pupils have been given entrance awards to Secondary and Grammar Schools. Good work has been done in Social Training, in connection with Red Cross work and several special efforts have been made for the National Savings Campaigns.

Canteen meals have been in operation since October 1941 and some 130–140 children are taken daily to St. Bede's School for these. The Hut in the Playground is at present being converted into a Canteen and it is hoped that this will be in use by the autumn. The numbers on the School Roll remain fairly constant between 170–185.

A meeting of the Subscribers will be held at the Church Room on Tuesday, 1st October, 1946, at 6 p.m., for the purpose of passing the accounts, and it is hoped that all subscribers will endeavour to attend.

C. E. SYLVESTER, Chairman.
ELSIE LANCASTER ⎫
W. E. GROVE   ⎬ Foundation Managers.
R. S. DIXON   ⎭
R. S. BOORMAN, County Council Representative.
W. BLAXLAND, Parish Council Representative.

Managers'
Report
for the years
1941-1946

*Copyright of
Surrey History
Service*

In 1945 Mrs Docherty was appointed School Secretary. This was a new appointment as previously head teachers had had to cope with their own paperwork. Her 'office' was in a corner of the Infants' cloakroom! A telephone had been installed in the schoolhouse just before the war and the secretary had to rush to answer it when Miss Perrin was busy; the phone had often stopped ringing by the time she got to it! Mrs Docherty is in the staff photograph taken in 1946 in the school playground.

There was a change of staff around this time. Miss Kathleen Baigent, (later Mrs Jones) a former pupil, returned to the school as a

Frederick William Donaldson was appointed to the teaching staff in May 1950, and his wife Ivy, also a teacher, joined him in 1952. They lived in a flat in 'Sandmore', a big house at the Send Road end of Send Hill and close to the school. They were a young couple, in their 20s, and they stayed at Send Primary School for ten years before moving on to teach at another school.

The school was now competing in the Woking Schools Music Festival, the Woking Schools Sports, the Woking Football League and the Woking Schools Swimming Gala, all events previously curtailed during the war years. The whole school was closed for these events so that the children could attend and cheer on their teams.

In 1950 Send Primary was the first school to win a trophy for schools with less than 200 children on the roll. By 1953 the numbers on the roll were rising and there

"The 'Rose Queen" and it was roses all the way for Jean Marsh who was chosen to be the Rose Queen. Wearing a crown and surrounded by her Rosebud attendants she sat on a rose-strewn throne and won second prize for the school.

Photograph by courtesy of Mrs Jean Weller (née Marsh)

The Send School football team taken at West Byfleet in 1949.

Back row – left to right: Ken Batten, ? Imery, Denis Williams, Bobby Godfrey, Dennis Nolan, Peter Smithers.

Front row – left to right Alan Salisbury, Alan Stanford, Ted Smith, Roy Masters, David Whittern.

Photograph by courtesy of Peter Smithers.

were now well over 200 children in the school. The former woodwork room, which had been renamed the Canteen as meals were now served there, was brought into use as an extra classroom. All classes used it in turn and the children had to vacate it each day in time for the canteen staff to lay-up for school dinners! Weather permitting they had a PE or Games lesson in the playground at that time.

Queen Elizabeth II's Coronation in June 1953 was a time of rejoicing for the nation. Send village was en-fête for the event and a procession of decorated vehicles led the way into the recreation ground for a day of coronation celebrations.

Send Primary School entered a float called

Send Parish presented each child in the village with a Coronation mug as a souvenir of the occasion and to finish the celebrations, the whole school had a special outing to Chessington Zoo.

In 1953 the school said farewell to Mr and Mrs Stanley, the school caretakers, who retired after many years service; they had looked after the school since the late 1930s.

In that year the school was given £10 by Surrey County Council to purchase something to commemorate the Coronation. It was decided to buy a garden seat and place it in the girls' playground. Mrs Ansell, who had taken over from Mrs Docherty and was School Secretary from 1947-1954, is pictured on the next page sitting on the seat with some of the children.

MRS. ANSELL on The Coronation Seat - -

primary and secondary education for all, provided by the state. A hundred years before, children could leave school at the age of ten, and now they were in full time education to the age of 15 with higher education on offer; all state funded. It was a far cry from the Children's Pence and the patronage of the landed gentry!

There were Centenary Celebrations at the school and a special fund-raising concert was held at St Bede's School. Some of the proceeds went towards the purchase of a large climbing frame which was sited in the girls' playground and was used by the children, under supervision at playtime, and in PE lessons.

Lionel Tice, a former pupil of the school, made an oak lectern and presented it to the school to mark the Centenary Year. The lectern was suitably inscribed and used at morning assembly. A large Bible was purchased from the funds raised at the concert to use with it. Miss Palmer took special photographs of the whole school, class by class, and they are shown here and on the following pages.

The School Centenary

There was a very special occasion in 1954 when the school celebrated its Centenary Year. One hundred years had passed since the Parish of Send and Ripley (as it was then) had built the new school for the children of Send. The country had accepted that the children of the labouring classes should be educated, and during those 100 years children had moved from part-time elementary education to full-time

Included in this photograph are: Doreen Morris, Jennifer Hobbs, Valerie Upstone, Michael Doe, Rodney Charman, Alan Kimber, Bob Stonard, Brian Carpenter, Brian Pullen, Eileen Cooper, June Sines, Peter Smith, David Exall, Annette Oliver, Michael Denyer, Jane Bowers, Sarah Hall, Janet Franklin, Janice Smithers, Maureen Norman, Pamela Smith, Frances Collyer, Alan Leese, John Willis and Trevor Tice.

MR. DONALDSON WITH CLASS I JUNIOR.

MRS. BROWN WITH CLASS II JUNIOR.

Included in the photograph (left) are:
Graham Rudkin, Clive Woodhams, Malcolm Isted, Brian Brough, Jackie Laking, Linda Gadd, Ray Williams, Lucille Tickner, Janet Baker, John Wade, Keith Irvine, Terry Irvine, Steve Docherty, Jean Marsh, Carole Woodhams, Maureen Tickner, Jimmy Brewer, David Marshall, Malcolm Haines. Patrick Young, Roland Searle, Patsy Whelan, Helen Pound, Georgina Wells, Audrey Smithers, Rosemary Boit, Roy Collyer, Janet Munday, Joyce Hobbs, Linda Jackson, Jean Masters and Jean Marsh.

MRS. DONALDSON WITH CLASS III JUNIOR.

Included in the photograph on the right are:

Linda Hoare, Jeffrey Bowers, Ronnie Smith, Jenny Harris, Desmond Carter, Barry Taylor, Michael Tice, Beryl Williams, Evelyn Green, Doreen Sharp, Mary Challen, Brenda Perryer, David Roake, Elizabeth Elliot, Jimmy Sines, Joan Charman, Christine Brown, Jeanne Bowers, Wendy Bowers, Valerie Caswell and Beryl Hobbs.

MRS. GODWIN WITH CLASS IV. JUNIOR.

Included in the photograph above are: David Leper, Malcolm Shuttleworth, Wendy Spooner, Jill Marsh, Rosemary Warren and Christine Hook.

MRS. BIRJAC WITH CLASS II INFANTS.

In the photograph above are: William Mayer, Cathy Collyer and John Baines.

This photograph shows Miss Palmer with Class I Infants also in 1954. This was her own class and she named all the children including the absentees! Left to right starting with the back row: Bill Swaffield, Michael Newman, Allen Mead, Kenneth Sutton, Richard Bowditch, Caroline Corps, David Pullen, Sally White, Pat Brown, Mervyn Wallace. Susan Hook, George Taylor, Michael Hampshire, Brian Street, Kathleen Green, Robert Sivyer, Richard Tickner, Michael Silver, Stephen Noakes, Howard Bates. Carol Jones, Jennifer Kent, Christina Kent, Geraldine Boycott, Dawn Amos, Sydney Stone, David Wells, Brian White, Michael Sweeney. Christine Warren, Linda Jones, Jill Oliver, Wendy Darling, Maureen Temple, Andrea Bromage, Shirley Marshall, Billy Shinn. Absentees - Raymond Burt, Ian Sims, Alan Gold, Lawrence Wright, Susan Hepburn, Robert Neeve, Sandra Pullen, Richard Anscombe.

THE SCHOOL STAFF - taken by - MRS. ANSELL. - SCHOOL HELPER.

MRS. UPSTONE   MISS PERRIN.   A.K. PALMER   MRS. BROWN.
MRS. SMITH   - CANTEEN -   - HEADMISTRESS -   I INFANTS.   II JUNIOR.   MR DONALDSON.
CANTEEN.   I JUNIOR.
MRS. DONALDSON   MRS. BIRSAC   MRS. WALTERS.   MRS GODWIN.
III JUNIOR.   II INFANTS.   MRS. PERRIN   - CANTEEN -   IV JUNIOR.

Staff photograph including Miss Palmer in the Centenary Year 1954

. THE 'CENTENARY' CLIMBING FRAME .

Photograph of children on the Centenary climbing frame, 1954

Chapter 17
A Small Boy Remembers

David Porter remembers with clarity his first day at Send School. It was a cold, drizzly January morning in 1955 when five-year-old David set out from his home in Send Barns Lane, with his mother, to start his first term. As they approached Mays Corner they were joined by other mothers and children making their way to the school. But David was looking out especially for his friend Roland Doe who was also starting school that day. Roland and he had known each other almost from birth as their mothers had become friends when the boys were babies. David was glad and relieved to see his friend coming into view as they reached Mays Corner.

The two boys and their mothers greeted each other and made their way up Send Hill and then into School Lane, At the entrance to the lane was a wooden signpost painted white with black lettering. It read SEND PRIMARY SCHOOL ENTRANCE 80 YARDS, with an arrow pointing down the lane. School Lane was an unmade narrow track. The school authorities had tried for years to find out who owned the land in order to make a properly surfaced road, but without success, so it remained as it was. To the right of the lane were the gardens of the Sandfields estate, and several tenants had put in gates giving access to the lane, so that their children had a short cut to school. On the left of the lane were the school playgrounds; they were in a sunken area with an open-fronted shelter at the end of the playground. A railing divided the boys' playground from the girls' continuing into the shelter. The girls' playground was nearest the lane and the infants shared this with the girls. In the girls' playground was a large climbing frame bought in 1954 to mark the Centenary of the school.

David had been on an official visit to the school the previous term to meet his new teacher, Mrs Baguley, and had chosen his coat peg in the cloakroom ready for his first day. Now was the time to remember that he had to " look for the picture of the swan" at the end of the row nearest to the classroom door. However, it was not yet time to go into school and the children and their mothers had to wait in the lane until Miss Perrin blew her whistle promptly at 9am.

All the children in the playgrounds stood perfectly still on hearing this shrill blast, which was followed by a second longer blast to bring the children into school. The way into the school for the infants, from the lane, was via a small gate adjacent to the back door of the schoolhouse, passing between the end wall of Class IV Juniors classroom on the left and the newly constructed toilet block on the right.

Entrance to the school from School Lane

David and Roland said goodbye to their mothers outside the infants' cloakroom door where Mrs Baguley was waiting to greet them. They and a few other new children were to join the large class of infants. The children found their right coat pegs and hung up their coats. Gathering her class together, Mrs Baguley escorted them into the school building for the first time, leading them straight to the room where Morning Assembly was held. This involved going across the courtyard, through the girls' cloakroom, now full of damp coats, and into the large classroom occupied by Class IV Juniors. There were five classes at the school, one infant and four junior, and they were all gathered together in this one classroom waiting for Miss Perrin to begin Morning Assembly.

Children were packed into this classroom. Some were sitting in the desks, others were sitting on them whilst more were standing beside the desks, between the desks, and anywhere they could find a space! The new infants were the last to come in and felt lost and bewildered standing in this crowded room not knowing what to do or what was going to happen. This scene was to be repeated every morning for there was no school hall in which to hold the daily assembly.

Mr Donaldson, the teacher of Class I Juniors, was standing by the window overlooking the courtyard. Beside him was an open fireplace protected by a wire-mesh guard. A fire was burning brightly giving warmth and cheer to the room. The door opened and Miss Perrin appeared carrying the Bible. Everyone stood up and Morning Assembly began. David recalls that on that first day he could not see Miss Perrin once the assembled school had stood up, but hearing Miss Perrin presented no problem at all!

After a hymn, a prayer and a reading from the Bible, several notices were read out to the children. At this point Mrs Baguley withdrew her class of infants and led them back across the courtyard, through the infants' cloakroom, and into their classroom beyond. David noticed the faded green door to the classroom; most of the other doors in the school were the same colour. Next to the classroom door was a small office area occupied by Mrs Gale, the School Secretary, who was also the first-aid 'nurse'. This office was really part of the infants' cloakroom. No School Secretary at this school ever had a proper office; there wasn't even a staff room for the teachers.

The infants' classroom was large, or so it seemed to a small boy on his first day at school. One wall of the classroom divided the infants' room from the junior girls' cloakroom, and against this wall was a sand tray. There were also two cupboards, and between them was a trolley on which stood a radio-a large valve set (pre-transistor days) with many push-buttons vertically down the front, used by the whole school to listen to the Schools Broadcasts. Mrs Baguley's desk was next to an open fireplace in red brick.

Two blackboards were in this room, an oblong one on the wall behind her desk, and a square one on an easel to the right of it. This was often necessary as not all the children could see the blackboard on the wall from where they were sitting. The easel stood in front of another door that led to the stockroom. This door also gave access to and from the Class II Juniors room as the classrooms were parallel yet staggered. On this door was hung a card of coloured spots, looking rather like a display of coloured dominoes; these were to help the class to count in maths lessons. On another wall were the letters of the alphabet with pictures, from A for apple through to Z for zebra. The room also had an old piano, and in a corner were several large items of unused furniture stored under covers.

David sat with his friend Roland on this first day and they learned to form the letters of the alphabet with chalk on a slate! Later, when they had mastered the letters, they graduated to pencil and paper.

If using slates in 1955 seems incredible, then it has to be remembered that there were long years of austerity following the end of the Second World War and a shortage of supplies, especially paper and pencils, due to a shortage of the raw materials that went into their making. Possibly the slates had been brought out of store to ease the difficulties during this time.

The daily routine soon became part of everyday life to the new children in Mrs Baguley's class of infants. Morning Assembly in the crowded room of Class IV Juniors, with Miss Perrin leading the daily service, was followed by a return to the classroom when the register was taken. There were up to 50 children on the register in those days, all the infants being in one class. Early attempts at the three Rs were usually carried out in the morning, with a break for milk and playtime. The new infants were given a small bottle containing a third of a pint of milk and a paper straw to drink it through, - a new experience for most of the children, particularly as straws were not generally available in the shops. Some children found this difficult to deal with at first, but gradually got used to it. Milk was now free to all children, and teachers had to encourage them to drink it as part of the campaign for improving the health of the nation's children. Some of the older children in the top class were chosen as milk monitors, and they brought the crates of milk into the classrooms after the milkman had delivered it to the school.

Milk time was followed by playtime. Mrs Baguley had shown her new infants how to get into the playground on their first day. Hand in hand they had followed her from the infants' cloakroom where they had collected their coats, into the small courtyard at the back of the school, through the school gate and out into School Lane where they walked along for a few yards, passing the back door of the schoolhouse, until they were at the head of the steps that led down into the girls' playground. The infants had to play in this playground, and the flight of steps was easier for small children to manage, the steps being wide and shallow.

The other steps giving access to both playgrounds started farther along by the classroom wall; they were very steep with a square platform halfway down. At the bottom of this flight was another square platform with two steps on each side one pair leading into each playground The girls went left and the boys went right.

These steep steps were the scene of several accidents over the years, and the infants were never allowed to use them but the girls could use either flight. The infants were always let out to play a few minutes before the juniors to allow them to reach the playground quietly and safely before the rush of the bigger children.

The steps can be seen in the photograph below.

After the first few weeks, the infants went out to play unescorted, and David sometimes found that he was the first one out, and by himself in the lane; but he soon saw that he was not quite alone An elderly lady, Mrs Perrin, who was Miss Perrin's mother, was often there at that time, sweeping the back doorstep of the schoolhouse and generally watching out for any small children who might wander off down the lane instead of down into the playground. She always had a smile for the children and she was very much part of the school as she was always about.

There were other hazards too, to look out for in those first winter days. The boys' toilets would often freeze-up and Mr Hall, the plumber, would be there with his blow-lamp trying to unfreeze the cistern or mend burst water pipes. The boys would be warned to look out for Mr Hall and take care! He never smiled; his was an unenviable task and he did not have much to smile about!

David would always meet up with his friend Roland in the playground. They would talk endlessly about steam trains, an interest they shared. However, Roland's passion for such trains continued into the classroom and sometimes intruded into lesson time. He also had a habit of drawing up an empty infant chair, putting his feet up and chattering on. At first Mrs Baguley quietly explained that chairs were for sitting on only, but Roland took no notice and continued with this habit. Each day the same situation was repeated, Roland with his feet up on a chair, chatting away, and now getting told off by Mrs Baguley but to no avail. This soon came to the attention of Miss Perrin and she too spoke to Roland and told him he was not to do this, but Roland persisted. He got a nasty shock one day when Miss Perrin appeared suddenly in the classroom via the communicating door with Class II Juniors classroom. Roland was caught with his feet up on the chair, disobeying her orders!

Shortly after this episode David was moved away from his friend Roland and found himself sitting at one of the desks at the back of the room and promoted to pencil and paper! No more of the slates and chalk. He had moved on.

A school photograph of David Porter, taken when he was 11 years old in 1961.

The school building was the same as it had been for years. Basically T shape, the area was divided up by timber and glass panelled walls making five classrooms with a corridor through the middle of the school giving access to the classrooms. Most of the rooms still had the old style desks with inkwells and hinged folding lids. The seats folded up and down as one piece and the children sat in pairs. There were four rows of five desks for a class of 40, more desks being added as the class grew.

The infants' room, however, had tables and small wooden chairs, as well as some old-style desks. On dark winter days the fire would be lit and the lights would be on all day. They had a clear glass shade above each bulb and they hung by chains from the high ceiling.

David had not been at school very long when he realised that Miss Perrin was a strict disciplinarian. There were school rules and all the new children were soon made aware that Miss Perrin expected them to be obeyed. After a few verbal warnings she punished offenders with strokes of the cane! The humiliation of being caned was often as painful as the actual punishment, and most children

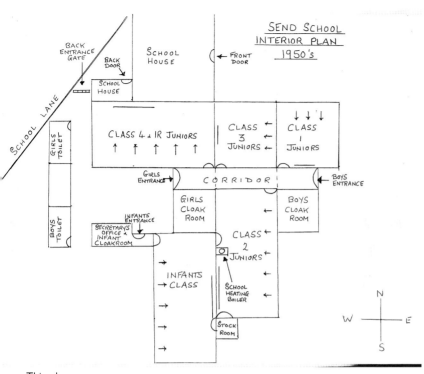

SEND SCHOOL
INTERIOR PLAN
1950's

This plan, showing the interior of Send School, was drawn from memory by David Porter.

punishment, usually on the spot. The infants had to share the junior girls' playground, which must have been annoying to the girls on occasions. The little boys in particular would spoil their games, out of mischief. One of the favourite occupations for the girls was to make houses out of the fallen leaves. Rooms with spaces for windows and doors would be formed into shape by lines of leaves. Each girl would make her own house and sometimes a whole line of houses side by side would appear on the playground floor. On a gusty day the wind would often blow these creations apart, but small boys could cause the same destruction even more quickly by running impulsively through the area and scattering the leaves!

When that happened tempers would boil over and the girls would shout in frustration at the offenders to go away, but occasionally an enraged girl would take a swipe at the nearest small boy. Hitting an infant was totally frowned upon and retribution was swift. Teachers on playground duty, had a clear view of both playgrounds from their position close to the top of the steps, and one of them would appear immediately to take charge of the situation. Some teachers would just remove the little boys and give them a 'talking to' but Mrs Donaldson, Class III Juniors teacher, would not tolerate unkindness by any girl towards an infant. She would go straight for the junior girl, dismissing any protestations, and administer several hard slaps to the girl's legs. This also had the effect of letting other girls know what Mrs Donaldson would do if this happened again.

took care not to attract her attention.

Miss Perrin could be kind and gentle with the infants, whom she never caned, but just knowing what could happen kept them in awe of her, and she ruled the school with the proverbial rod of iron. Parents, too, went in awe of her and did not come to the school without an appointment, except on parents' evenings.

However, she did raise the educational standards within the school, and the children were expected to work hard at their lessons. More children were getting to grammar schools from the state primary schools, and the Scholarship had been replaced by the Eleven Plus exam. Grammar school education was now free to all who won a place, so all the children in the top class sat the Eleven Plus exam and Miss Perrin made sure they were well prepared for the tests. Send School pupils gained more grammar school places than the national average, and had done so since 1941 when Miss Perrin took over the school.

Other teachers at the school administered

Most of the time though, the girls would mother the infants, helping them to tie shoelaces and fastening their coats on cold days, and kindly acts would be noted by the staff, as well as unkind ones. Boys were often called out from their playground by the supervising teachers if they had been fighting or misbehaving. They would then have to stand facing the school wall until playtime was over. Sometimes this was the end of the punishment but if the offence was serious enough the culprit would be sent to wait in the corridor for Miss Perrin to bring out the cane. As the partitions that divided the school into classrooms did not reach the ceilings, the children in the classrooms that were close to the scene of the canings could hear (and almost feel!) the punishments.

These minor offences or punishments were not reported in the school log-book. However, Miss Perrin had a Punishment Book in which she was required by the authorities to record details of punishments administered, but this book was lost when the school closed.

Among David's memories is that of reading to Mrs Baguley from the Janet and John books. These were post-war reading books with bright pictures, about two children named Janet and John who jumped, and played and rode their bikes just like other children. David did not know it then, but these books were part of the new 'look and say' method of teaching children to read. Single words appeared at first on the pages with the pictures, and the child learned the whole word by sight, with more words being added as they progressed through the book and built up their vocabulary by sight. Phonetics, letter recognition and word building were taught as well, but the reading depended very much on whole-word recognition. The children easily followed the stories of Janet and John and identified with their play activities. The reading scheme had large wall pictures, and flash cards to reinforce the learning, and the teacher had die-stamps to reproduce the pictures on paper for the children to colour and try to write the words themselves. There were many critics of this method of teaching children to read, because it was a different approach, but it was successful as it gave children an easy, enjoyable introduction to reading. The Janet and John readers remained in the infant classrooms for many years until the pictures became dated and they were replaced by new reading schemes.

Reading usually took place after morning play and the afternoons were spent on arts and crafts and sometimes music. The children were encouraged to sing, and play on the tambourines, triangles, cymbals and drums, accompanied by Mrs Baguley on the piano. This noisy session was possibly not appreciated by the other teachers in the school!

• • • • •

Since Send Primary was a church school, the vicar of St Mary's, the Reverend Cyril Sylvester was a frequent visitor. Prayers were said every day-at morning assembly, at the end of morning lessons, before afternoon school began, and before going home. If a class had PE or games as their last lesson, then the going-home prayers would be said in the playground.

On Ascension Day all the children had to go to St Mary's church for a special service. Carefully supervised by their teachers, a long crocodile of children, walking in pairs, would wend its way up Send Hill and down the other side to reach the parish church tucked away in the corner of the parish, close by the River Wey. It was a long walk but the children knew that after the service was over, the rest of the day was a holiday.

The Reverend Sylvester took the service, and his sermon to the children echoed the school's theme of discipline and good behaviour, and he warned of the penalties in a future life for those who transgressed. He had a loud voice and thumped the pulpit with his fist to get his message across. Children received the message with mixed feelings ... However, when his sermon was over, Mr Sylvester would lean forward, smile at the children and wish them a happy holiday!

*****

A Harvest Festival was held every autumn at the school, when the girls' side of the playground shelter was transformed into a farm shop to sell the produce donated by the parents. Vegetables, jams and marmalade were quickly sold alongside cakes and other produce, and the proceeds were given to charity.

Christmas time was the message of the Nativity, also a time of concerts and parties and Christmas decorations. The school was transformed with the decorations made by the children in their classes, and a post-box was set up within the school for children to send Christmas cards to each other. The cards would be made in class and Mrs Baguley encouraged the infants to write their own words. Envelopes had to be supplied from home and then, suitably addressed with the friend's name and class number, they would be posted in the school post-box. Miss Perrin chose 'postmen' from children in the top class and the cards would be sorted daily by them and delivered to the appropriate classroom. It was very exciting when the postmen came to the classroom. ... "Would there be one for me? " was the question on every child's face. "No? Tomorrow, perhaps ...".

His first Christmas at school was special for David Porter. There was to be a concert given by the school children, including the infants, for their parents, using the stage at St Bede's Secondary School.

For several weeks the children rehearsed a simple Christmas play about 'The Christmas Tree', some of the infants in the front row having to hold the decorations that were being placed upon the tree. A song was sung by all the children and told the story. As each decoration was named, the infant holding it had to step forward to highlight the article, working along the row as each verse was sung. The children were all rehearsed by Miss Perrin who was producing the show. David had a pink candle to hold and was anxious to play his part well.

However, it was one thing rehearsing at school in the classroom, but on the big night there were studio lights and an audience out front. The stage was crowded with children all wearing their best clothes. David's hands got wet with perspiration and the candle started to get slippery. Panic set in! Would he remember to step forward at the right moment? Would he drop the candle? But Miss Perrin was there to lead them through each step and the sheer force of her presence, and not wanting to let her down, ensured that the show went well.

The curtain came down to thunderous applause. Flushed with success, the infants basked in Miss Perrin's praise.

"Well done! Well done!" she said again and again and everyone went home happy .

Chapter 18

The Red Cross Years and After

In January 1956 the overcrowding in the school reached crisis point and Miss Perrin wrote in the log book;

"Owing to increasing numbers an additional Infant Class has been formed as from today. The local Red Cross hut is being used as the extra classroom space, temporarily, with Miss Palmer as class teacher".

Miss Palmer was promoted to Deputy Head and took the older infants to form the new class at the Red Cross hut. This was situated in Sandy Lane, close to the end of the Sandfields estate. The younger, Class II Infants, stayed at Send School with Mrs Baguley and were joined by the new ones just starting school. So in September 1956 when David, Roland and other infants started their second year of school, they too moved into the Red Cross hut with Miss Palmer, the earlier class returning to Send school to start their junior years. It was a very different classroom that greeted them: there were no desks since the class had to use the tables belonging to the Red Cross, but they had their own chairs.

Morning Assembly with Miss Palmer was also a different affair from that at the main school. In a quiet atmosphere with the children sitting around her on their chairs, there was time and space to enjoy the daily routine. Although there were more than 40 children in this class it was very much like a large family. Miss Palmer got to know all her class well and the children got to know each other. There were no distractions from other classes and less noise. Miss Palmer was a teacher of many years' experience, having been at the school since 1926, and she was a kind and gentle person. Discipline was still maintained, but by co-operation rather than punishment and Miss Perrin never appeared to visit or interfere with the arrangements. Most children loved being in the Red Cross hut with Miss Palmer and learned their lessons well.

Playtime outside in the garden of the old Red Cross hut 1956

David remembers spelling tests before play, with those getting the highest score going out to play first! He also remembers arithmetic lessons and small coloured wooden sticks being used to help the children with their maths. The sticks were made into bundles of ten held together with elastic bands, to use when adding and subtracting in double figures.

The infants who had school dinners had to return to the school at midday and they were escorted both ways by Mrs Gale, the School Secretary, who made the double journey each day via Farm Lane, which was the shortest and safest route to and from the canteen.

However, every week there were intrusions into the school day on Monday and Wednesday afternoons when the Red Cross reclaimed their premises for their own use. Then the infants had to use the pavilion in the recre-

Mrs Gale
escorting the
'canteen group'
at lunchtime,
1956

Infants setting
out with their
chairs to
the pavillion
in Send
recreation
ground, 1956

Infants sitting
outside the
pavilion on the
recreation
ground on a
sunny day,
1956

ation ground. They had to cross Sandy Lane to enter the recreation ground and then walk across the grass to the pavilion carrying their chairs. In wet weather the children were instructed to walk with the chairs over their heads to keep themselves and the chair seats dry!

The pavilion had a stove to heat it and this was supposed to be lit for the class but often it was stone cold. In the winter it could be a miserable time, but the situation had its compensations in the summer when the children would sit outside for their lessons, and Miss Palmer read stories to them.

The Red Cross class joined the rest of the school for all school functions, but for the medical inspections, Miss Cribb, the Health Visitor came to them. She took a keen interest in all the children, remembering names and family connections.

In the Spring Term the children were taught Maypole Dancing. At the Red Cross hut the Maypole was placed in the centre and fitted neatly up into the ridge roof, whereas at the school it had to be set up in the playground. There was no music, but the infants were taught the basic moves by Miss Palmer; three children had to sit at the bottom of the pole to keep it steady.

Miss Perrin always trained a team of Maypole dancers from the school for the annual May Day celebrations held on the recreation ground in the village, and she will be remembered for insisting that the dances were perfectly done. If the Maypole Dance went awry on the day, she would stop the music, chide the children and start again at the beginning. And all this in front of the audience! (See picture in next chapter.)

For the Autumn Term in 1957, David and his class returned to Send school, and another class of infants went to the Red Cross hut. But this was to be the last group. Two new classrooms were being built on a site in Send Barns Lane. In September 1958 the Red Cross hut was vacated and Miss Palmer moved into the New Instalment, as it was called, in charge of two classes of infants.

Back in the old school David and his class were now juniors, and so went into the crowded classroom for Morning Assembly. Now, though, they saw it from a different aspect. No longer were they at the back of the room as little infants, only hearing the service. They were part of the mêlée that took place prior to the arrival of Miss Perrin, to get possession of one of the desks or else be left standing. The boys usually managed to get the desks, so the girls sat on them, completely blocking the view. Being old the desks often rocked under this weight! Because of the crowding there was a temptation for the girls sitting on the desks to annoy the boys by kicking those in the desks in front of them. Such torment had to be tolerated because to make a fuss would bring further trouble from Miss Perrin!

During the junior years the children were taught to use pen and ink instead of pencils, and to learn to join up their letters, known as 'running writing'. Wooden pen-holders with steel nibs were given out by the teacher. The nibs got crossed if pressed too hard and became scratchy, which of course spoilt the writing. However they were not too freely replaced, as steel was still in short supply. The inkwells were made of china and had a small recessed hole just big enough to dip the nib into. A brass cover could be slid across the inkwell when it wasn't in use. The ink was made up from powder mixed with water, and the inkwells were topped up daily from a can with a long thin spout by the ink monitors who could be trusted with this task. Each child was given a small piece of blotting paper and expected to use it to saturation point.

Mischievousness sometimes led to ink-pellets made from ink-soaked pieces of blotting paper being catapulted across the classroom with the aid of a ruler. The targets were often the girls sitting at the front of the room, perhaps in revenge for the kickings at Morning

Assembly. If caught by the teacher, the culprits had the rulers turned on them for rapping their knuckles!

By 1959 David and Roland were in Class 1R in the room used for Morning Assembly. There the old desks had been replaced by tables, still called desks, that had pen-grooves and inkwells. The boys were determined to bypass the free-for-all rush and get their own desks each day for assembly, so they agreed a plan whereby they left their raincoats at home as often as the weather allowed, and taking a short cut via the girls' entrance, went straight into the classroom after the second whistle. This put them ahead of those who had to stop to hang up their coats in the cloakrooms!

Morning Assembly was also the occasion for Miss Perrin to draw attention to the school rules and give reminders about the standards expected of the children by her and the staff. As infants they had been spared this as they had been removed by their teacher. Now they were part of this routine and for some children it was a time to dread. Notices were read out, offences were commented on and the culprits named and shamed, but there was also a time for reflection; as for example, when a boy got knocked over on his way to school and prayers were said for his recovery and reminders given to be careful on the road.

There was sadness too, when Miss Perrin announced in May 1960 that her mother had passed away. Mrs Perrin was so well known to all the pupils and she was always in evidence at playtimes - a pleasant old lady who always had a smile for the children. The classes went quietly about the school for the rest of the day…

Miss Palmer retired at the end of the 1960 summer term, having been at the school since 1926 and having spent her last two years in charge of the infants at Send Barns Lane. She was presented with a leather handbag and a cheque for £15 5s.0d from pupils and staff, and a travelling case from the Managers. She stayed on in the village after her retirement and continued to take an interest in school affairs. Her written memories and her photographs given to the Send and Ripley History Society some years ago have added considerably to the story of Send school.

Miss Iris Cox was appointed in September 1960 and took her place as Deputy Head in the Infants' Department in Send Barns Lane.

The last year in the juniors was looming for David, Roland and their classmates. They moved into the top class with Mr Donaldson as their teacher. This class had the old desks again and they missed the new tables and chairs of their previous year with Miss Wallis. Mr Donaldson made lessons interesting. He taught geography by bringing old AA manuals into the classroom and letting the class plan journeys using the maps, even to booking pretend overnight stays. He brought history to life by his stories about the dinosaurs and other prehistoric animals, encouraging the children to look at pictures and make papier-mache models of them, and he captured their imagination with tales of pirates on the high seas, and of space and time travel.

In that last year, Mr Donaldson and his class made a 'time capsule', containing drawings, photographs and stories written by the children and they included other memorabilia of the day. The capsule was put into a large glass sweet jar which was then put into a metal canister and sealed. A message on the exterior asked the finders to keep it hidden until a given date, and then it was buried in the school grounds. It has never been found despite intensive searching during the time the playgrounds were being landscaped into the gardens of the private home that the school has become. Did Mr Donaldson really bury the capsule? He said he buried it in secret to preserve its hiding place. Or is it buried forever under the tons of topsoil brought in to make the new gardens?

Mr Donaldson had a good sense of humour as can be seen in the cartoon overleaf that he drew for one of his pupils at the end of the summer term.

Cartoon reproduced by courtesy of Audrey Smithers from her autograph book.

David recalled all the games the children played in the playground during his last junior year - the same games that previous generations had played. There were no set seasons for games except 'conkers' in the autumn, but hopscotch, marbles, and skipping, all came in their turn, and that old favourite of boys' called "pile-on" (where one boy leans against the wall and the others all pile on until the whole lot collapses), never seemed to go out of fashion!

And there was that large climbing frame bought in the Centenary year of the school, at the far end of the girls playground. It was used in PE lessons and always under supervision.

Joy of joys in that last year, an old Rover car appeared in the girls' playground for all the children to play on. It came from Bill Challen who owned the garage in the village, and it survived at the school for a long time, delighting the children with hours of imaginative play.

*****

Teachers came and went, and Supply Teachers filled the gaps until the next new teacher was appointed. One Supply Teacher in particular was always welcomed by the children. She was Mrs Sybil Somerfield, Miss Perrin's sister. She had two sons, Nick and James. James was in David's year and had mobility difficulties. His mother brought him to the school door by car and he sat in the front desk in each classroom. He was a popular boy, and at playtime he had a little group of friends known as Jim's Club who played with him by the schoolhouse as he couldn't get down the steps to the playground. His brother Nick, who was some years older than James, endeared himself to the boys by marrying Kyra Grace, a pretty young teacher at the school!

Nick Somerfield and Kyra Grace were married in July 1961 at Send Church by the Reverend Cyril Sylvester, and this wedding day photograph shows the whole family together.

This photograph shows the three Perrin sisters, Sybil, Cicely and Stella, together. Cicely was the sister who started at Ripley school with Stella in 1920.

Jack Grace had been a pupil at Ripley School at the turn of the century.

From left to right are Mrs Sybil Somerfield and her husband Denis, Nick's brother James, Stella Perrin, Peter Wicks (almost hidden), and his wife Cicely, Nick and Kyra, Mary Brock a family friend, and Mr and Mrs Jack Grace, Kyra's parents.

David and Roland said goodbye to the junior school in July 1961, both boys looking forward to going to their next school, St Bede's, in the autumn. As he left the school for the last time David saw his mother waiting at the end of School Lane to meet him; he was surprised to see her since he usually walked home on his own. But perhaps she was remembering his first apprehensive day as an infant all those years before, and wanted to share a moment of nostalgia with him on his last day at Send Primary School.

Chapter 19

Changes Ahead

In the picture are Michael Clack, Roger Leper, Colin Green, Paul Ritchens, Michael Turner, Ian Jones, Martin Fry, Darryl Freeman, Paul Freestone, and Peter Jones.

Mr and Mrs Donaldson left Send Primary at the end of the summer term 1961, to take up teaching posts in other schools. They were replaced by Mrs Joyce Jenkins who was appointed in September 1961, and her husband Norman Jenkins, who joined the school in the following January. Mr Jenkins's special talent was in music and soon the children were participating in recorder groups, choirs and musical presentations. They won praises and awards for their entries at the Woking Schools Music Festivals.

• • • • •

An additional classroom was opened on the Send Barns site in February 1962 and the reception infant class moved in. All the infants were now together, and the children in the top class moved up to the junior school each September when they were seven years old.

The two schools although on different sites were both part of Send Primary and under the headship of Miss Perrin, with a Deputy Head at Send Barns. The playing field at Send Barns Lane was used by the whole school on Sports Day. The picture above is of a group of six-year-old boys in 1962 starting the egg and spoon race, the "egg" being a potato!

A School Crossing Patrol was set up at Mays Corner in 1962 and Mrs Pat Clack, née Gibbons, a former pupil at the school as mentioned earlier, was appointed to take charge. There had been concern for some years about the increased traffic on Send Road and the Managers had finally agreed to this new appointment. Pat was the 'Lollipop Lady' for seven years, making sure that children crossed the roads in safety, until she took up other duties in the school.

Miss Perrin and the children of Send Primary School were regular participants in the May Day celebration that was held annually on the recreation ground in Send. This was a village event with stalls selling produce and bric-à-brâc, and a tea-tent to serve refreshments. A brass band would be engaged to play for the afternoon and all groups in the village co-operated to make it a happy occasion, the highlight of the afternoon being the 'Crowning of the May Queen.'

The May Queen and her two attendants, chosen from amongst the girls at the school, would enter the recreation ground in a decorated Land-Rover, be driven around the field for all to see and then ascend to a throne for the coronation. This was usually done by the girl who had been May Queen the previous year but sometimes a celebrity was asked, and one year Loelia, Duchess of Westminster, who lived locally, graciously accepted the task.

The May Queen in the picture is Jenny Harris in 1956, one of the first May Queens. Her attendants are Georgina Wells and Carol Woodhams.

A team of maypole dancers, trained by

Photograph of Jenny Harris as May Queen, 1956

Miss Perrin, would then perform the dances, and red, white and blue ribbons would be woven in and out as the dancers went round the Maypole to form intricate patterns to the delight of the audience. There were three dances and the final one was called the 'Spiders Web'. This would sometimes go sadly wrong, whereupon Miss Perrin would stop the music, sort out the children, and then resume the dance! But when it was all over, Miss Perrin would praise the children for their efforts. "Well done! Well done!" she would say with enthusiasm, and they all basked in her praise and went home happy.

There was a fancy dress competition on the day and even the pre-school children would dress up and join their older brothers and sisters in the parade hoping to win a prize. All entrants were given 6d just for entering the competition!

Here is another May Queen, Linda Peacock, in 1965, surrounded by the children who had entered the fancy dress parade that year.

In the picture below are:
Vivienne Meyer, Valerie Clack, Glynis Sale, Duncan Fry, Richard Wilkinson, Janet Meyer, David Pound, Ruth Pound, Darryl Freeman, Martin Fry, Susan Voller, Penny Anderson, and Richard Jenkins

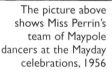

The picture above shows Miss Perrin's team of Maypole dancers at the Mayday celebrations, 1956

Chapter 20

The Final Years

The **Woking Review** sent reporters to the school in 1965 to gather copy for its 'Around the Villages' series. They took photographs of the children in their classes and interviewed Miss Perrin who told them that the number of children on the school roll at that time was 327 and that accommodation was very limited. Despite the new infant classrooms at Send Barns Lane, where Miss Dorothy Marshall was now the deputy head, there was still not enough room at the old school for so many children. To ease the problem an extra classroom had been erected the previous year on the garden alongside the boys' playground.

Miss Perrin also told the Woking Review reporters that one of the biggest problems faced by the school had always been the lack of a large assembly hall. Annual events such as Speech Day had to be held at St Bede's School and there was no parent-teacher association as there was nowhere to hold meetings. However, she was encouraged by the great interest shown by the parents.

Eleven children had been awarded grammar school places after the Common Entrance examinations earlier in the year, and other children had had successes in activities outside the school such as art exhibitions and essay and handwriting competitions which reflected well on the school and its teaching. The children had raised money for Oxfam, the Star and Garter Home at Richmond, and the Earl Haig Poppy Fund. That year, as in previous years, a collection had been made for the Church of England Children's Society, and a group of children had been taken to London to a special ceremony in the Royal Albert Hall, where they had presented the purses to a member of the Royal Family. Another party had visited Belgium in June, the first overseas visit made by the school which had also entertained needy children from Austria and West Germany when they were staying in Send under the International Help for Children Scheme.

Miss Perrin presented the school to the newspaper as being forward looking and involved in the world outside the village, whilst also being caring and helpful to less fortunate people. She concluded the interview by emphasising that there was a real shortage of trained teachers and that she had difficulties in filling staff vacancies.

The staff shortages already mentioned meant that Miss Perrin had to rely heavily on Supply Teachers. Amongst these at the time were Mrs Dorothy Lord, Mrs Barbara Meyer, Mrs Nessie Fretwell, and Mrs Sybil Somerfield, who all lived near the school and could be called on at short notice.

There was a change of School Secretaries in the 1960s too. Mrs Gale was followed by Mrs Peacock, and then from 1964 to 1968 Mrs Joan Harris was in the post; when she left, Mrs Pat Clack was appointed in her place. Mrs Clack, with all her previous connections with the school was now back as the last School Secretary.

The rapid development of housing estates in the village in the mid 1960s meant that more and more children were applying for admission and a bigger school was needed. Plans were in hand for new premises to be made available. A new Church of England secondary school was being built at Stoughton in Guildford and it was proposed that all the pupils at St Bede's school should be transferred there when it was completed, leaving the secondary school premises to be used as a junior school for the parishes of Ripley, Send, Wisley, Ockham and the Clandons, all of whom needed more school accommodation.

Many parents were reluctant to lose the

secondary school in Send and were concerned too, that they might be unable to afford the daily fares to and from the new school. However, St Bede's had a strong parents' association which fought a determined battle with the education authorities to ensure that free transport would be provided for all pupils transferring to secondary schools outside their village. The parents insisted that this commitment be in perpetuity, and extracted promises to that effect from the authorities.

A meeting chaired by the Rev. Cyril Sylvester was held in St Bede's school in 1971 for the parents of the junior school children. Mr Sylvester explained that the future for the juniors would be in St Bede's school once the transfer of the secondary pupils had taken place. Then they too would be transferred to the new Church of England secondary school in Stoughton, at the age of eleven. He was somewhat dismayed to have this assumption challenged by a large group of the parents who wanted a choice of secondary schools for their children. They wanted the George Abbott School at Burpham to be included in that choice. Not only was it nearer to Send than Stoughton but it was a school with an established reputation of excellence and although a secondary school it also had a grammar stream. This situation caused a fierce debate, as the church had always provided the education for the children of Send and Ripley, and had expected to continue to do so in the new C of E school at Stoughton. But parental pressure prevailed and the catchment areas for the George Abbott School were changed to include the children from St Bede's.

However a total re-organisation of secondary education in Surrey was due to take place in the 1970s and comprehensive education for all children was to replace the former secondary separation, and the last

Eleven-Plus exam took place in 1972. Comprehensive education aimed to give all children better opportunities and a wider range of subjects, and they would be taught in ability groups within each subject. All Secondary schools were to be renamed Comprehensive schools.

*****

Miss Perrin was due to retire at the end of the summer term in 1971. She had been headmistress of Send Primary School for 30 years, during which time the number of children on roll had doubled. She had given every encouragement to those who applied themselves to their schoolwork but punished those who broke the rules. She was known as a strict disciplinarian, but the children respected her and her judgment, and she had a loyal staff.

A village party was held on the evening of the 17th July 1971 in the hall at St Bede's School in honour of Miss Perrin's impending retirement. About 200 parents and past pupils attended and Miss Perrin was presented with a cheque for £130.

On the last day of the summer term the juniors were escorted to Send Barns Lane where Morning Assembly was held in the playground of the infants' school. This was a special assembly to mark Miss Perrin's last day as headmistress. Several of the Managers were there and Miss Perrin was presented with an electric sewing machine as a retirement present.

Below is the last entry she wrote in the logbook. There was no emotional farewell note after her long years of service. Her work

School closed at 3 p.m. today for the summer vacation when I concluded my services as Headmistress of the school.

Stella E. Perrin
30ᵗʰ July 1971.

was finished, and she just signed off!

She left the village when she retired and went to live in Kent to be near to her sister Cicely, the sister who had started at Ripley School with her in 1920. She lived there in active retirement for many years, and then moved to Wales to be near her nephews.

After Miss Perrin's departure the school faced its final year in the old building. No new head-teacher had been appointed so Mr Jenkins took temporary charge of the juniors and Mrs Lucy J Wickens, the Deputy Head based at the infants school, took overall charge of both sections.

The plans were firmly in place to close the junior school at the end of the summer term and to transfer the children to the St Bede's school premises in September 1972. Amongst the last children at Send School was Christopher Martin Brown, photographed there in 1972, aged ten. He and his classmates would be in the top year when they moved to the new junior school for the Autumn Term. It was Christopher who brought home the old book left behind by Riverdale School that had shared Send School's premises during the war;

Christopher Martin Brown, 1972

he could hardly have known that it would form part of the school history in later years!

A new Headmaster, Mr R Hall had been appointed to St Bede's Junior School and some of the teachers at the juniors were trans-ferring there with the children, including Mr and Mrs Jenkins, John Turley, and Mr Culver, along with some of the staff from Ripley School. The last term became a transition period when cupboards were cleared and stock packed up ready for the move. While the children were excited about the move to St Bede's, the teachers were no doubt looking forward to having their own staff-room at last. Perhaps surprisingly, there was no nostalgia about the last few days; there were no parties at the school for the children or the staff. The school just closed its doors after 118 years of educating the Send children in that building.

The school remained empty and forlorn for a few years, with leaves covering the play-grounds and the gardens overgrown. The schoolhouse, unoccupied since Miss Perrin's departure, looked shabby with peeling paint-work and broken windows. The Earl of Onslow had reclaimed his ownership of the site under the School Sites Act of 1841 which allowed him to do so, since the building was no longer being used for education, the pur-pose for which it had been given by his prede-cessor.

The Send Youth Club, (the Send Teens) had approached Lord Onslow requesting the use of the old school premises as a meeting place for their members. At first this had seemed a possibility and there was much fund-raising towards this happening. However, their hopes were dashed when Lord Onslow decided to sell the buildings to be converted into a private house.

The old school-house, attached to the school, was demolished in an accidental gas explosion a few months prior to the sale in 1976.

In the years that followed, the former play-grounds were landscaped with the addition of tons of topsoil to form delightful sunken gar-dens, and successive owners have made the old school into an attractive dwelling, which still retains a recognisable exterior. It is named The Old School.

The Old School, now a private dwelling.

Epitaph

St **Mary's Parish Magazine** for March 1996 reported the sad news that
Miss Stella Perrin had died at the age of 84 years.
Her ashes were returned to Send to be buried in the churchyard.
A Memorial Service was held in St Mary's Church in July 1996
and was attended by many past pupils from the Send Primary School
"who remembered her with gratitude and affection".

The church had recently been completely redecorated and, coincidentally,
the work was carried out by the firm owned by Miss Perrin's great-nephew,
David Somerfield, Nick and Kyra's son.

"It is sad," reported the Parish Magazine, "that she did not see the superb result."

Pupil Lists for the School at Send

1854-1972

A

1942	Anne	ABBOTT
1943	Janet	ABBOTT
1971	Carol	ALDEN
1971	Frederick	ALDEN
1971	Alun	ALDRIDGE
1962	Glenys	ALDRIDGE
1966	Heather	ANDERSON
1954	Dawn	AMOS
1965	Penny	ANDERSON
1960	Christopher	ANSCOMBE
1962	Graham	ANSCOMBE
1954	Richard	ANSCOMBE
1942	Richard	ANSELL
1962	David	ARMITAGE
1971	Heather	ARMITAGE
1968	Amanda	ARNOLD
1963	Mandy	ARNOLD
1962	Melanie	ARNOLD
1962	Tommy	ARTHUR
1942	Brian	ASPINALL
1943	Thelma	ATEA
1966	Carole	ATHERTON
1971	Lindsey	ATKINSON
1971	Philip	ATKINSON
1960	Barry	ATTER
1962	Christine	ATTER

B

1886	Alice	BAIGENT
1879	Annie	BAIGENT
1882	Charles	BAIGENT
1888	Edward	BAIGENT
1878	Eliza	BAIGENT
1884	Elizabeth	BAIGENT
1923	Elsie	BAIGENT
1892	George	BAIGENT
1890	Jessie	BAIGENT
1939	Joan	BAIGENT
1894	Joseph	BAIGENT
1941	Kathleen	BAIGENT
1918	Marjorie	BAIGENT
1971	Andrew	BAILEY
1897	Eunice	BAILEY
1942	Lilian	BAILEY
1971	Martin	BAILEY
1954	John	BAINES
1971	Angela	BAKER
1923	Edgar	BAKER
1917	Frank	BAKER
1954	Janet	BAKER
1952	Shirley	BAKER
1942	Tommy	BAKER
1971	Roderick	BALCHIN
1935	David	BALCOMBE
1962	Janet	BALES
1971	Ann	BALLARD
1971	Janet	BALLARD
1971	Christopher	BANCROFT
1971	Robert	BANCROFT
1956	Sheila	BARFIELD
1881	Ellen	BARKER
1885	John	BARKER
1885	Mary	BARKER

1884	William	BARKER
1971	Stephen	BARLOW
1942	Bernard	BARNES
1929	Dorothy	BARNES
1971	Alison	BARNETT
1971	John	BARNETT
1971	Michael	BARNETT
1957	Carol	BARRATT
1971	Glenn	BARRATT
1971	Wendy	BARRATT
1960	Heather	BARTLETT
1962	Jasmine	BARTLETT
1903	Alice	BARTON
1897	Anna	BARTON
1906	Charles	BARTON
1904	Ethel	BARTON
1901	Eveline	BARTON
1895	Letitia	BARTON
1897	Nellie	BARTON
1950	Anna	BATCHELIER
1950	Howard	BATCHELIER
1971	Christopher	BATEMAN
1971	Mark	BATEMAN
1954	Diana	BATES
1954	Howard	BATES
1949	Kenneth	BATTEN
1953	Diana	BEAKS
1953	Richard	BEAKS
1962	Roy	BELCHAMBER
1971	Peter	BELL
1971	Susan	BELL
1962	Anne	BELLETT
1881	Ada	BENNETT
1883	Walter	BENNETT
1971	Jacalyn	BERRY
1943	Mary	BERRY
1943	Christine	BEST
1943	Keith	BEST
1966	Sylvia	BICKNELL
1956	Jacqueline	BIDDLE
1961	Andrew	BIGGS
1962	Rosalind	BIGGS
1962	Shirley	BIGGS
1971	Andrew	BIGWOOD
1971	Caroline	BIGWOOD
1929	Les	BIGWOOD
1860	Alfred	BIRD
1858	Louisa	BIRD
1867	Emily Jane	BISHOP
1871	George	BISHOP
1875	Mary Ann	BISHOP
1869	Robert	BISHOP
1873	Sarah	BISHOP
1895	Lucy	BISLEY
1971	Julian	BLACKBURN
1971	Kevin	BLACKBURN
1962	Janet	BLACKWELL
1876	Albert	BLAKE
1887	Clara	BLAKE
1872	Eliza	BLAKE
1866	Emma	BLAKE
1889	Frank	BLAKE
1869	Henry	BLAKE
1859	Mary	BLAKE
1862	William	BLAKE

Year	Name	Surname
1971	Bronya	BLAKEY
1971	Jonathan	BLOOMFIELD
1971	Robert	BLUNDELL
1971	Sally	BLUNDELL
1960	Phillip	BOIT
1954	Rosemary	BOIT
1870	Ruth	BONNER
1968	Christopher	BOTTOMLEY
1971	Mark	BOTTOMLEY
1954	Christine	BOWDITCH
1954	Richard	BOWDITCH
1934	Albert	BOWERS
1952	Christine	BOWERS
1969	Daryl	BOWERS
1960	David	BOWERS
1962	Eileen	BOWERS
1923	Fred	BOWERS
1952	Fred	BOWERS
1923	Geraldine	BOWERS
1936	Harold	BOWERS
1952	Harold	BOWERS
1954	Jane	BOWERS
1950	Jeanne	BOWERS
1943	Jeffrey	BOWERS
1969	Keith	BOWERS
1971	Kevin	BOWERS
1952	Mary	BOWERS
1971	Maxine	BOWERS
1971	Verona	BOWERS
1952	Wendy	BOWERS
1971	Paul	BOYCE
1954	Brian	BOYCOTT
1954	Geraldine	BOYCOTT
1886	Annie	BRACKLEY
1886	Isaac	BRACKLEY
1878	Lottie	BRACKLEY
1876	Rose	BRACKLEY
1881	Thomas	BRACKLEY
1952	Amy	BRADSHAW
1952	Brian	BRADSHAW
1962	John	BRADSHAW
1956	Paul	BRADSHAW
1966	Roger	BRADSHAW
1943	Hilary	BRAY
1885	Joseph	BRAY
1883	William	BRAY
1896	Amy	BREWER
1904	Andrea	BREWER
1890	Annie	BREWER
1889	Arthur	BREWER
1957	David	BREWER
1896	Elizabeth	BREWER
1895	Ernest	BREWER
1902	Frank	BREWER
1904	James	BREWER
1954	Jimmy	BREWER
1929	Kathy	BREWER
1893	Lillie	BREWER
1962	Linda	BREWER
1956	Maureen	BREWER
1971	Michael	BREWER
1887	William	BREWER
1954	Andrea	BROMAGE
1954	George	BROMAGE
1956	John	BROMAGE
1971	Margaret	BROMLEY
1896	Arthur	BRONFIELD
1876	Edwin	BROOKS
1895	Edwin	BROOKS
1873	Elizabeth	BROOKS
1893	Elizabeth	BROOKS
1896	George	BROOKS
1890	Henrietta	BROOKS
1896	Walter	BROOKS
1866	William	BROOKS
1892	Archibald	BROOMFIELD
1923	Brian	BROOMFIELD
1890	Edith	BROOMFIELD
1887	James	BROOMFIELD
1971	James	BROOMFIELD
1896	Lilian	BROOMFIELD
1889	Walter	BROOMFIELD
1950	Brian	BROUGH
1950	Pat	BROUGH
1954	Christine	BROWN
1971	Christopher	BROWN
1971	Christopher M	BROWN
1954	Doris	BROWN
1956	Jill	BROWN
1954	Pat	BROWN
1960	Sonia	BRUIN
1971	Christopher	BRYANT
1971	Susan	BRYANT
1923	Cissie	BUGG
1923	Harvey	BUGG
1923	May	BUGG
1869	Edward	BULLEN
1867	Henry	BURCHETT
1864	Stephen	BURCHETT
1962	Helen	BURGESS
1867	Elizabeth	BURNETT
1875	Emily	BURNETT
1873	Thomas	BURNETT
1870	William	BURNETT
1923	Cissie	BURNS
1923	George	BURNS
1923	Ian	BURNS
1942	Ian	BURNS
1942	Norman	BURNS
1923	Raymond	BURNS
1923	William	BURNS
1886	Charles	BURROWS
1888	Montague	BURROWS
1890	Samuel	BURROWS
1878	Cecelia	BURT
1954	Keith	BURT
1954	Raymond	BURT
1870	Edward	BUTLER
1885	Edwin	BUTLER
1896	Eliza	BUTLER
1895	Elizabeth	BUTLER
1866	Ellen	BUTLER
1868	George	BUTLER
1857	Hannah	BUTLER
1864	James	BUTLER
1963	Stephanie	BUTLER

C

Year	Name	Surname
1923	Brian	CABLE
1923	Keith	CABLE
1923	Kenneth	CABLE
1889	Edith	CAKEBREAD
1894	Eliza	CAKEBREAD
1887	Ernest	CAKEBREAD
1891	Henry	CAKEBREAD
1971	Stephen	CAKEBREAD
1954	Brian	CARPENTER
1923	Cissie	CARPENTER
1950	Cissie	CARPENTER
1971	Deborah	CARPENTER
1923	Desmond	CARPENTER
1923	Frank	CARPENTER
1971	Heather	CARPENTER
1971	Jill	CARPENTER
1952	Audrey	CARTER
1886	Benjamin	CARTER
1966	Christopher	CARTER
1954	Desmond	CARTER
1971	Hannah	CARTER
1867	Henry	CARTER
1885	James	CARTER
1888	Jesselina	CARTER
1971	Joanna	CARTER
1891	Mary	CARTER
1894	Mildred	CARTER
1962	Patricia	CARTER
1962	Robert	CARTER
1870	Samuel	CARTER
1971	Stephen	CARTER
1874	William	CARTER
1962	Wendy	CARTLEDGE
1959	Christine	CARTNEY
1971	Caroline	CASWELL
1954	Valerie	CASWELL
1971	Deborah	CHALDECOTT
1968	John	CHALDECOTT
1971	Michael	CHALDECOTT
1968	Roger	CHALDECOTT
1943	Audrey	CHALLEN
1914	Marjorie	CHALLEN
1943	Marjorie	CHALLEN
1954	Mary	CHALLEN
1943	Peter	CHALLEN
1940	Raymond	CHALLEN
1952	William	CHALLEN
1942	Ben	CHANDLER
1873	Charley	CHANDLER
1971	Philip	CHANDLER
1942	William	CHANDLER
1886	Alfred	CHANNON
1882	Edith	CHANNON
1882	Emily	CHANNON
1879	Kate	CHANNON
1883	Norris	CHANNON
1886	Ada	CHARMAN
1896	Alan	CHARMAN
1857	Albert	CHARMAN
1862	Alfred	CHARMAN
1886	Alice	CHARMAN
1883	Annie	CHARMAN
1888	Arthur	CHARMAN
1923	Arthur	CHARMAN
1897	Ben	CHARMAN
1888	Charles	CHARMAN
1890	Daisy	CHARMAN
1865	Emma	CHARMAN
1860	George	CHARMAN
1887	George	CHARMAN
1866	Grace	CHARMAN
1860	Henry	CHARMAN
1924	Hilda	CHARMAN
1890	Hugh	CHARMAN
1897	Joan	CHARMAN
1954	Joan	CHARMAN
1864	John	CHARMAN
1903	Joseph	CHARMAN
1952	Joseph	CHARMAN
1891	Kate	CHARMAN
1903	Kathleen	CHARMAN
1862	Louisa	CHARMAN
1884	Louisa	CHARMAN
1922	Marjorie	CHARMAN
1862	Mary	CHARMAN
1885	Nellie	CHARMAN
1966	Paul	CHARMAN
1922	Reg	CHARMAN
1954	Rodney	CHARMAN
1881	Edward	CHARMAR
1885	Ellen	CHARMAR
1877	Fred	CHARMAR
1883	Robert	CHARMAR
1879	Walter	CHARMAR
1962	Paul	CHATFIELD
1896	Phyllis	CHEAL
1943	Angela	CHEESEMAN
1943	Arthur	CHEESEMAN
1962	Brian	CHEESEMAN
1943	Rosemary	CHEESEMAN
1971	Timothy	CHIVERTON
1963	Michael	CLACK
1965	Valerie	CLACK
1942	Angela	CLARK
1945	Anthony	CLARK
1942	Bobby	CLARK
1930	John	CLARK
1942	Monica	CLARK
1945	Raymond	CLARK
1971	Tania	CLARK
1971	Gordon	CLARKE
1964	Amanda	CLEVERLY
1962	Roger	CLEVERLY
1964	Amanda	CLEVERLY
1971	Andrew	CLEW
1966	Sandra	COBBETT
1956	Richard	COLBORNE
1960	Kevin	COLE
1962	Nicola	COLE
1953	Bobby	COLEMAN
1953	Royston	COLEMAN
1867	Ann	COLLIER
1871	Emily	COLLIER
1865	Hannah	COLLIER
1863	Harriett	COLLIER
1869	Sarah	COLLIER
1890	William	COLLINS
1954	Cathy	COLLYER
1954	Frances	COLLYER
1953	Harriett	COLLYER
1882	James	COLLYER

Year	Name	Surname
1855	Mary	COLLYER
1954	Roy	COLLYER
1950	Sally	COLLYER
1880	William	COLLYER
1971	Timothy	COLMER
1943	Derek	COOLING
1896	Arthur	COOMBER
1903	Eileen	COOMBER
1903	Harriett	COOMBER
1889	Lizzie	COOMBER
1894	Walter	COOMBER
1903	Caroline	COOPER
1954	Eileen	COOPER
1903	Ivy	COOPER
1950	Ivy	COOPER
1962	Susan	COOPER
1866	David	CORLNIDGE
1873	Frank	CORLNIDGE
1871	Hannah	CORLNIDGE
1971	James	CORNWALL
1971	Tina	CORNWALL
1954	Caroline	CORPS
1954	Edwina	CORPS
1971	Andrew	COURT
1864	George	COURT
1865	William	COURT
1971	Graham	COWDRY
1950	Edwina	COYLE
1950	Elsie	COYLE
1920	Gladys	CRADDOCK
1923	Marjorie	CRADDOCK
1924	Mary	CRADDOCK
1922	Olive	CRADDOCK
1930	Winifred	CRANE
1971	Stella	CRITCHER
1942	Mary	CROUCHER
1942	Michael	CROUCHER
1966	Susan	CROW
1971	Tina	CROW
1971	Allison	CUDE
1962	Ann	CUMBER
1971	Caroline	CURME
1971	Graham	CURME
1942	Arthur	CURTIS
1942	Michael	CURTIS

D

Year	Name	Surname
1971	Christopher	DABBS
1962	Colin	DABORNE
1954	Wendy	DABORNE
1892	Agnes	DANCE
1932	Alice	DANCE
1890	Ann	DANCE
1932	Arthur	DANCE
1894	Minnie	DANCE
1863	Arthur	DANIELS
1861	Florence	DANIELS
1860	James	DANIELS
1858	Mary	DANIELS
1865	Millicent	DANIELS
1856	Ruth	DANIELS
1855	William	DANIELS
1886	Alfred	DARLING
1863	Anthony	DARLING

Year	Name	Surname
1903	Bertha	DARLING
1893	Caroline	DARLING
1891	Elizabeth	DARLING
1882	Ellen	DARLING
1903	Elsie	DARLING
1924	Elsie	DARLING
1904	Frank	DARLING
1924	Frank	DARLING
1860	Frederick	DARLING
1858	John	DARLING
1883	John	DARLING
1886	Julia	DARLING
1865	Mary	DARLING
1879	Mary	DARLING
1889	Sarah	DARLING
1904	Sylvia	DARLING
1930	Tony	DARLING
1954	Wendy	DARLING
1855	William	DARLING
1874	William	DARLING
1887	William	DARLING
1930	William	DARLING
1954	William	DARLING
1876	Ellen	DAVEY
1874	Mary	DAVEY
1971	Alison	DAVIES
1955	Andrew	DAVIES
1971	Bronwen	DAVIES
1942	Albert	DAVIS
1942	Tony	DAVIS
1971	Amanda	DAWES
1962	Betty	DAWES
1971	Wendy	DAWES
1904	Albert	DAY
1903	Frederick	DAY
1971	Lorraine	DEDMAN
1960	Ann	DENT
1962	Geraldene	DENT
1954	Michael	DENYER
1960	Graham	DEW
1909	Frederick	DIXON
1971	Ian	DIXON
1971	Julia	DIXON
1909	Michael	DIXON
1971	Simon	DIXON
1955	Anne	DOCHERTY
1954	Steve	DOCHERTY
1971	Steven	DOCHERTY
1929	Dennis	DOE
1956	Elisabeth	DOE
1955	Mary	DOE
1950	Michael	DOE
1955	Roland	DOE
1971	Marionne	DOHERTY
1971	Anthony	DOLDIN
1971	Janet	DONNE
1971	Sarah	DONNE
1968	Karen	DONNELLY
1971	Martin	DONNELLY
1971	Cherry	DUGGAN
1956	Ann	DUNN
1929	Ernest	DUNN
1929	Frederick	DUNN
1962	Gillian	DUNN
1957	Jeffrey	DUNN

E

Year	Name	Surname
1865	Anne	EDAM
1856	George	EDAM
1860	Mary	EDAM
1862	Sarah	EDAM
1893	Ernest	EDE
1892	Ethel	EDE
1895	Flora	EDE
1888	Arthur	EDIS
1895	Elsie	EDIS
1887	Harry	EDIS
1890	Sydney	EDIS
1893	Wallis	EDIS
1865	Ann	EDOM
1869	Frederick	EDOM
1971	Alison	EDWARDS
1971	Andrew	EDWARDS
1971	Ceri	EDWARDS
1854	Mary	EDWARDS
1953	Annie	ELLIOT
1954	Elizabeth	ELLIOTT
1856	Thomas	ELMS
1962	David	EVANS
1955	Paula	EVANS
1955	Susan	EVANS
1960	Janet	EVE
1954	David	EXALL
1952	Susan	EXALL

F

Year	Name	Surname
1875	George	FAGENCE
1902	Annie	FAITHFULL
1942	Dennis	FAITHFULL
1911	Edith	FAITHFULL
1906	Elizabeth	FAITHFULL
1859	Frederick	FAITHFULL
1864	George	FAITHFULL
1906	George	FAITHFULL
1942	Gerald	FAITHFULL
1943	Gordon	FAITHFULL
1859	Harriett	FAITHFULL
1923	Harry	FAITHFULL
1932	Hazel	FAITHFULL
1915	May	FAITHFULL
1923	Terry	FAITHFULL
1943	Terry	FAITHFULL
1899	Tom	FAITHFULL
1866	William	FAITHFULL
1904	William	FAITHFULL
1943	William	FAITHFULL
1886	Charles	FARLEY
1890	Edgar	FARLEY
1894	Gertrude	FARLEY
1892	Charles	FARNFIELD
1885	John	FARNFIELD
1866	James	FARR
1895	Alois	FAUST
1892	Mary	FAUST
1894	Therese	FAUST
1890	Williamine	FAUST
1875	Mary-Ann	FERYER
1860	Eleanor	FIELD
1857	Jane	FIELD
1865	Lucy	FIELD

Year	Name	Surname
1960	Anthony	FINN
1955	Siobhan	FINN
1962	Terry	FINN
1957	Jeanette	FLAMONDE
1957	Suzanne	FLAMONDE
1923	Jack	FLIPPARD
1959	David	FLOOD
1961	Susan	FLOOD
1962	Michael	FLOWERS
1922	Jack	FORD
1923	Janet	FORD
1971	Peter	FORTUNE
1968	Elizabeth	FOSTER
1971	Helen	FOWLER
1971	Rebekah	FOWLER
1971	Ruth	FOWLER
1971	David	FRAMGER
1950	Janet	FRANKLIN
1950	Jean	FRANKLIN
1960	Malcolm	FRANKLIN
1971	Gary	FRANKLIN
1963	Darryl	FREEMAN
1971	Nigel	FREEMAN
1956	David	FREESTONE
1962	Donald	FREESTONE
1962	Paul	FREESTONE
1936	Cynthia	FRENCH
1953	Dorothy	FRENCH
1896	James	FRENCH
1936	Jean	FRENCH
1936	Ken	FRENCH
1895	Kenneth	FRENCH
1894	Mary	FRENCH
1894	Mildred	FRENCH
1891	Robert	FRENCH
1953	Vaureen	FRENCH
1952	Alan	FRIEND
1900	Dorothy	FRIEND
1936	Jim	FRIEND
1900	Percy	FRIEND
1952	Raymond	FRIEND
1953	Roland	FRIEND
1956	Roy	FRIEND
1934	Sam	FRIEND
1962	Martin	FRY
1965	Duncan	FRY
1923	Alan	FULLER
1920	Dorothy	FULLER
1882	Edith	FULLER
1887	Ernest	FULLER
1920	Gordon	FULLER
1923	Irene	FULLER
1923	Les	FULLER
1889	Lily	FULLER
1920	Lorna	FULLER
1879	Louisa	FULLER
1903	Robert	FULLER
1903	Sybil	FULLER
1870	Alfred	FULLICK
1863	Andrew	FULLICK
1923	Edie	FULLICK
1875	Ellen	FULLICK
1873	Frederick	FULLICK
1867	George	FULLICK
1864	Jane	FULLICK

1923	Sybil	FULLICK
1872	Abraham	FURLONG
1869	Henry	FURLONG
1871	Sarah	FURLONG
1865	William	FURLONG

G

1971	Sally	GADBURY
1923	Doris	GADD
1922	Edie	GADD
1922	Lily	GADD
1954	Linda	GADD
1908	Nellie	GADD
1920	Walter	GADD
1920	Audrey	GALE
1922	Frank	GALE
1920	Freddie	GALE
1920	Irene	GALE
1922	John	GALE
1923	May	GALE
1930	Audrey	GARDNER
1930	Bert	GARDNER
1930	Sheila	GARDNER
1880	Alice	GARMENT
1893	Arthur	GARMENT
1875	Elizabeth	GARMENT
1881	Fred	GARMENT
1882	John	GARMENT
1892	Mary	GARMENT
1923	Patricia	GARMENT
1924	Ruby	GARMENT
1854	Ruth	GARMENT
1883	Ruth	GARMENT
1879	Sarah	GARMENT
1886	Stephen	GARMENT
1884	William	GARMENT
1872	Ruth	GARTON
1923	Bert	GENT
1930	Patricia	GIBBONS
1943	Pamela	GIBBS
1962	Peter	GIFFIN
1962	Mark	GILDING
1968	Sarah	GILDING
1923	Alan	GILES
1890	Albert	GILES
1962	Catherine	GILES
1886	Esther	GILES
1901	Harold	GILES
1894	Helma	GILES
1889	James	GILES
1901	Marina	GILES
1942	Marina	GILES
1922	Phyllis	GILES
1942	Phyllis	GILES
1924	Reg	GILES
1887	Rosina	GILES
1962	Susan	GILES
1896	Walter	GILES
1890	William	GILES
1971	Dominic	GILL
1971	Tracey	GILL
1960	Peter	GILLET
1962	Roland	GILLET
1961	Rosemary	GILLET

1971	Elspeth	GLYNN
1971	Janet	GLYNN
1943	Sheila	GODDARD
1971	Amanda	GODFREY
1949	Bobby	GODFREY
1971	Teresa	GODFREY
1956	Clive	GODSMARK
1957	Eric	GODSMARK
1966	Linda	GODSMARK
1954	Alan	GOLD
1954	Evelyn	GOLD
1971	Diane	GOLDUP
1971	Tandy	GORDON
1943	Kyra	GRACE
1971	Dawn	GRAYHAM
1971	Nicholas	GREAVES
1954	Caroline	GREEN
1962	Colin	GREEN
1954	Evelyn	GREEN
1971	George	GREEN
1935	Henry	GREEN
1954	Henry	GREEN
1934	John	GREEN
1971	Michael	GREEN
1933	Millie	GREEN
1954	Millie	GREEN
1934	Rose	GREEN
1944	Theresa	GREEN
1952	Angela	GREGORY
1952	John	GREGORY
1966	Kathleen	GREGORY
1950	Alec	GRIBBLE
1950	Angela	GRIBBLE
1955	Roger	GRINSTEAD
1871	Alice	GRISH
1869	Elizabeth	GRISH
1868	Laura	GRISH
1909	Ewart	GROVE
1942	Ewart	GROVE
1892	Florence	GROVE
1923	Geoffrey	GROVE
1942	Geoffrey	GROVE
1895	Leonard	GROVE
1887	Mabel	GROVE
1942	Sheila	GROVE
1920	Stuart	GROVE
1857	Arthur	GROVES
1923	Edie	GROVES
1903	Elsie	GROVES
1865	Esther	GROVES
1903	Frank	GROVES
1923	Norman	GROVES
1860	Sarah	GROVES
1923	Vernon	GROVES
1923	Walter	GROVES
1966	Martin	GUEST
1968	Michael	GUTTERIDGE

H

1922	Edie	HACK
1922	Ernie	HACK
1922	Freddy	HACK
1923	Jennifer	HACK
1950	Jennifer	HACK

1923	Trevor	HACK
1923	Bill	HACK
1950	William	HACK
1954	Malcolm	HAINES
1885	James	HALE
1942	Georgina	HALE
1942	Trevor	HALE
1968	Sarah	HALL
1875	Edith	HALLAM
1873	Fanny	HALLAM
1868	Frederick	HALLAM
1863	Henry	HALLAM
1866	Joseph	HALLAM
1962	David	HAMPSHIRE
1950	Georgina	HAMPSHIRE
1954	Hilda	HAMPSHIRE
1922	Kathleen	HAMPSHIRE
1950	Kathleen	HAMPSHIRE
1954	Michael	HAMPSHIRE
1960	Sandra	HAMPSHIRE
1905	Hilda	HAMPTON
1905	Yvonne	HAMPTON
1971	Malcolm	HANKIN
1870	Edward	HARDING
1872	Kate	HARDING
1874	Rose	HARDING
1876	Samuel	HARDING
1873	William	HARDING
1879	Annie	HARMS
1896	Bertie	HARMS
1860	Charles	HARMS
1865	Frederick	HARMS
1861	Henry	HARMS
1891	Jesse	HARMS
1863	John	HARMS
1893	Leonard	HARMS
1888	Mabel	HARMS
1854	Thomas	HARMS
1886	William	HARMS
1965	Andrew	HARRIS
1871	Anne	HARRIS
1867	Eliza	HARRIS
1874	Frank	HARRIS
1865	Frederick	HARRIS
1876	Henry	HARRIS
1956	Jenny	HARRIS
1955	Lawrence	HARRIS
1869	Thomas	HARRIS
1962	Ann	HARVEY
1942	Charles	HARVEY
1962	Philip	HARVEY
1942	Yvonne	HARVEY
1943	Mary	HAY
1896	Arthur	HEAD
1893	Blanche	HEAD
1896	Charles	HEAD
1892	William	HEAD
1971	Denise	HEALEY
1971	Karen	HEALEY
1971	Carole	HEBBERD
1971	Mark	HEBBERD
1965	Rosemary	HEBBERD
1967	Stephen	HEBBERD
1855	George	HEDGCOCK
1952	Albert	HEDGES

1952	Arthur	HEDGES
1955	Ruth	HEGGOTT
1971	Adrian	HENSON
1889	Agnes	HEPBOURN
1885	Frederick	HEPBOURN
1891	James	HEPBOURN
1894	Rosina	HEPBOURN
1954	Arthur	HEPBURN
1882	Harriet	HEPBURN
1896	Henry	HEPBURN
1896	James	HEPBURN
1884	Jane	HEPBURN
1923	Peggy	HEPBURN
1929	Rene	HEPBURN
1954	Susan	HEPBURN
1971	Michael	HERBERT
1971	William	HERBERT
1881	Alice	HERSEY
1879	Arthur	HERSEY
1902	Arthur	HERSEY
1876	Frederick	HERSEY
1868	George	HERSEY
1873	Jane	HERSEY
1865	John	HERSEY
1902	Joyce	HERSEY
1871	William	HERSEY
1962	Andrew	HEWETT
1971	Jill	HEWETT
1971	Mark	HEWITT
1966	Paul	HEWITT
1873	Caroline	HEWS
1863	George	HEWS
1865	Thomas	HEWS
1971	Richard	HEYER
1971	Tina	HICKS
1883	Alfred	HILL
1878	Bertha	HILL
1885	Emma	HILL
1943	Gordon	HILL
1882	James	HILL
1880	John	HILL
1971	Madeline	HILL
1872	George	HILL
1960	Lesley	HILL
1876	Mary Ann	HILL
1960	Michael	HILL
1962	Carol	HILLMAN
1943	Joyce	HILLMAN
1943	Linda	HILLMAN
1971	Katherine	HINKMAN
1971	Wendy	HINXMAN
1952	Beryl	HOARE
1952	Linda	HOARE
1942	Beryl	HOBBS
1933	Connie	HOBBS
1933	Irene	HOBBS
1968	Jennifer	HOBBS
1908	Connie	HOBBY
1903	Sheila	HOBBY
1903	Sydney	HOBBY
1956	Pauline	HOLDFORTH
1962	John	HOLLAND
1966	Veronica	HOLLAND
1942	Albert	HOLMES
1942	Sheila	HOLMES

1897	Albert	HOLT
1884	Alice	HOLT
1890	Cecil	HOLT
1892	Charlotte	HOLT
1903	Christine	HOLT
1903	Elsie	HOLT
1883	George	HOLT
1885	James	HOLT
1893	Phillip	HOLT
1887	Sarah	HOLT
1895	Walter	HOLT
1889	William	HOLT
1954	Christine	HOOK
1954	Joyce	HOOK
1954	Susan	HOOK
1953	John	HOOKER
1953	Joyce	HOOKER
1968	Peter	HOOKINGS
1971	Rosemary	HOOKINGS
1962	Philip	HOOLEY
1966	Lorraine	HOTSON
1903	Ethel	HUGGINS
1903	John	HUGGINS
1934	Les	HUGGINS
1962	David	HUGHES
1963	Raymond	HUGHES
1923	Dianne	HUMPHRIES
1908	Ethel	HUMPHRIES
1962	Carol	HUNT
1942	Dianne	HUTCHINSON
1942	Eric	HUTCHINSON
1948	George	HUTCHINSON
1966	Helen	HUTCHINSON
1952	Margaret	HUTCHINSON
1942	Stephen	HUTCHINSON
1971	Michael	HUTHERT
1885	George	HUTTON
1884	Robert	HUTTON
1882	William	HUTTON

I

1963	Nicola	IDDON
1942	Margaret	INGRAM
1942	Terence	INGRAM
1950	Alfred	IRVINE
1962	Carol	IRVINE
1957	David	IRVINE
1954	Keith	IRVINE
1954	Terence	IRVINE
1954	Malcolm	ISTED

J

1873	Alfred	JACKMAN
1904	Alfred	JACKMAN
1966	Anita	JACKMAN
1857	Ann	JACKMAN
1943	Ann	JACKMAN
1904	Annie	JACKMAN
1905	Arthur	JACKMAN
1942	Barrie	JACKMAN
1863	Caroline	JACKMAN
1875	Charles	JACKMAN
1942	Edith	JACKMAN

1875	Edward	JACKMAN
1870	Eliza	JACKMAN
1860	Ellen	JACKMAN
1909	Elsie	JACKMAN
1868	Emily	JACKMAN
1861	Emma	JACKMAN
1897	Ernest	JACKMAN
1924	Ernest	JACKMAN
1867	Harriett	JACKMAN
1883	Henry	JACKMAN
1971	Kim	JACKMAN
1887	Louise	JACKMAN
1897	Margaret	JACKMAN
1901	Mary	JACKMAN
1942	Michael	JACKMAN
1901	Myrtle	JACKMAN
1943	Myrtle	JACKMAN
1900	Nan	JACKMAN
1943	Nan	JACKMAN
1942	Philip	JACKMAN
1864	Rose	JACKMAN
1862	Stephen	JACKMAN
1873	Thomas	JACKMAN
1872	Walter	JACKMAN
1867	William	JACKMAN
1953	Anna	JACKSON
1956	Annette	JACKSON
1969	Cheryll	JACKSON
1954	Linda	JACKSON
1955	Marion	JACKSON
1953	Michael	JACKSON
1955	Peter	JACKSON
1894	Amy	JAMES
1942	Anne	JAMES
1942	Carol	JAMES
1892	Emily	JAMES
1890	George	JAMES
1971	Gary	JELLY
1971	Mary-Anne	JELLY
1968	Catherine	JENKINS
1965	Michael	JENKINS
1965	Richard	JENKINS
1971	Vivien	JENKINS
1971	Thomas	JIMMISON
1971	Adrian	JOHNSON
1869	Bertha	JOHNSON
1971	Ian	JOHNSON
1971	Lester	JOHNSON
1962	Margaret	JOHNSON
1962	Mary	JOHNSON
1864	William	JOHNSON
1954	Carol	JONES
1971	Edward	JONES
1962	Ian	JONES
1954	Jack	JONES
1956	John	JONES
1971	Kevin	JONES
1954	Linda	JONES
1887	Mary	JONES
1962	Peter	JONES
1971	Stephen	JONES
1954	Trevor	JONES
1971	Trevor	JONES
1971	Clive	JORDON
1971	Beverley	JOY

K

1971	David	KARN
1923	Christina	KAVANAH
1863	Louise	KEBLE
1971	Sharon	KEENE
1971	Steven	KEENE
1971	Andrew	KEMP
1954	Christina	KENT
1954	Jennifer	KENT
1954	Raymond	KENT
1971	James	KIGHTLY
1971	Robert	KIGHTLY
1962	Shirley	KILL
1954	Alan	KIMBER
1971	Howard	KING
1952	Pat	KIRBY
1952	Raymond	KIRBY
1963	Joanna	KNIGHT
1971	Lorraine	KNIGHT

L

1971	Simon	LAKE
1971	Susan	LAKE
1971	Timothy	LAKE
1952	Jacqueline	LAKER
1956	Kenneth	LAKER
1952	Pat	LAKER
1950	Ernest	LAKING
1954	Jacqueline	LAKING
1950	Rodney	LAKING
1971	Jacqueline	LAMB
1962	Sonia	LAMB
1971	Sheena	LAMONT
1864	Alice	LANGFORD
1859	Emily	LANGFORD
1865	Frederick	LANGFORD
1855	Harriett	LANGFORD
1861	John	LANGFORD
1857	Maria	LANGFORD
1966	Carole	LARCHER
1968	Paula	LARCHER
1971	Katie	LAVENDER
1971	Michael	LAVENDER
1920	Basil	LAWRENCE
1971	Elizabeth	LAWRENCE
1903	Ernest	LAWRENCE
1903	Jack	LAWRENCE
1920	Violet	LAWRENCE
1962	Philip	LEANEY
1874	Alfred	LEE
1886	Alice	LEE
1867	Delbert	LEE
1883	Edward	LEE
1863	Edwin	LEE
1870	Ellen	LEE
1885	Florence	LEE
1865	Francis	LEE
1876	George	LEE
1869	James	LEE
1871	John	LEE
1872	June	LEE
1881	Louisa	LEE
1867	Lucy	LEE
1877	William	LEE

1955	Alan	LEESE
1955	Aprille	LEPPER
1922	Basil	LEPPER
1929	Betty	LEPPER
1954	David	LEPPER
1926	George	LEPPER
1953	George	LEPPER
1924	Jack	LEPPER
1962	Janet	LEPPER
1962	Roger	LEPPER
1926	Ronnie	LEPPER
1942	Alfred	LEWINGTON
1942	Ronnie	LEWINGTON
1971	Steven	LEWINGTON
1962	Bobby	LEWIS
1968	Janet	LEWIS
1962	Karen	LEWIS
1904	Alfred	LILLYWHITE
1906	Dick	LILLYWHITE
1903	Florence	LILLYWHITE
1906	Frank	LILLYWHITE
1908	Elsie	LILYWHITE
1923	Thomas	LILYWHITE
1971	Julie	LIPTON
1971	Amanda	LIVINGSTON
1971	Jacqueline	LLOYD
1971	Kevin	LLOYD
1971	Leslie	LLOYD
1903	Margaret	LLOYD
1971	Susan	LLOYD
1903	Thomas	LLOYD
1938	John	LOADER
1938	Margaret	LOADER
1971	Robert	LOCATELLI
1971	Victor	LOCATELLI
1903	Jimmy	LOCKYER
1903	John	LOCKYER
1953	Archibald	LODGE
1962	Guy	LODGE
1953	Jimmy	LODGE
1957	Michael	LOEHR
1962	Robin	LOEHR
1890	Agnes	LONG
1886	Arthur	LONG
1892	Ebenezer	LONG
1894	Ernest	LONG
1888	Henry	LONG
1886	James	LONG
1864	Edith	LONGHURST
1870	Fanny	LONGHURST
1934	Jack	LONGHURST
1867	Laura	LONGHURST
1934	Leonard	LONGHURST
1936	Molly	LONGHURST
1936	Peggy	LONGHURST
1937	Peter	LONGHURST
1935	Robert	LONGHURST
1962	Steven	LONGHURST
1872	William	LONGHURST
1903	Archibald	LONGYEAR
1901	Constance	LONGYEAR
1901	Edith	LONGYEAR
1963	Stephen	LORD
1971	Elizabeth	LYONS
1968	Kathleen	LYONS

M

1971	Paul	MACKILLIGAN
1971	Paul	MAHON
1955	Susan	MAISTON
1968	Carolyne	MALBY
1943	Ann	MALLENDER
1943	Jackie	MALLENDER
1971	David	MANDEVILLE
1971	Rosemary	MANDEVILLE
1971	Julia	MANSBRIDGE
1971	Nicholas	MARRIOTT
1905	Constance	MARSH
1897	Gertrude	MARSH
1968	Jane	MARSH
1953	Jean	MARSH
1953	Jill	MARSH
1897	Kenneth	MARSH
1873	Alfred	MARSHALL
1954	David	MARSHALL
1860	John	MARSHALL
1858	Mary	MARSHALL
1863	Matilda	MARSHALL
1954	Sarah	MARSHALL
1954	Shirley	MARSHALL
1971	Andrew	MARTIN
1923	Christine	MARTIN
1960	Peter	MARTIN
1923	Sarah	MARTIN
1950	Christine	MASON
1950	Jean	MASON
1865	Elizabeth	MASSINGHAM
1923	Angela	MASTERS
1911	Charles	MASTERS
1907	Daisy	MASTERS
1913	Elizabeth	MASTERS
1917	Frederick	MASTERS
1929	George	MASTERS
1950	Jean	MASTERS
1942	Kenneth	MASTERS
1936	Patsy	MASTERS
1949	Roy	MASTERS
1942	Shirley	MASTERS
1971	Vicky	MASTERS
1942	William	MASTERS
1952	Angela	MASTROMARCO
1952	Ernest	MASTROMARCO
1966	Nicky	MASTROMARCO
1954	Peno	MASTROMARCO
1923	Betty	MATHIS
1908	Reginald	MATHIS
1923	Stewart	MATHIS
1923	William	MATHIS
1971	Alison	MATTOCK
1971	Gaynor	MATTOCK
1936	Betty	MAY
1936	Constance	MAY
1887	Florence	MAY
1895	Nellie	MAY
1923	Sidney	MAY
1954	William	MAYER
1971	Alison	MAYERSBETH
1971	Karen	MAYERSBETH
1971	Susan	MAYERSBETH
1923	Bernard	MAYNE

1962	Jane	MCCANCE
1960	Fiona	MCCANCE
1964	Neil	MCCANCE
1964	Nigel	MCCANCE
1962	John	MCCARTNEY
1966	Bonnie	MCDIARMID
1962	Janet	MCGINLEY
1957	John	MCGINLEY
1962	Barbara	MCHUGH
1962	Catherine	MCHUGH
1942	Allen	MCPHERSON
1942	Bernard	MCPHERSON
1942	Freda	MCPHERSON
1954	Alan	MEAD
1950	Janet	MEAD
1950	Roland	MEAD
1932	Frederick	MELLIS
1932	Roland	MELLIS
1971	Gillian	METHAM
1954	Charles	MEYER
1971	Helen	MEYER
1963	Janet	MEYER
1967	Vivienne	MEYER
1960	Rosemary	MICA
1971	Deborah	MIDDLETON
1874	Albert	MILES
1878	Alice	MILES
1864	John	MILES
1854	Joseph	MILES
1867	Louisa	MILES
1857	Lucy	MILES
1872	William	MILES
1971	Robert	MILLAR
1868	Ada-Mary	MILLARD
1892	Albert	MILLARD
1895	Alice	MILLARD
1890	David	MILLARD
1864	Eunice	MILLARD
1889	Frank	MILLARD
1903	Frederick	MILLARD
1903	Leonard	MILLARD
1886	William	MILLARD
1971	Deborah	MILLER
1971	Vanessa	MILLER
1971	Deborah	MITCHELL
1918	Flossie	MOLESEY
1918	Frank	MOLESEY
1923	Bernard	MONK
1855	Elizabeth	MONK
1874	Ellen	MONK
1872	George	MONK
1867	Harriett	MONK
1867	John	MONK
1877	Kate	MONK
1874	Lydia	MONK
1869	Mary	MONK
1873	Sarah	MONK
1895	Dorothy	MONNERY
1888	Frederick	MONNERY
1886	James	MONNERY
1893	Margaret	MONNERY
1971	Mark	MOONAY
1942	Bernard	MOORE
1942	Denis	MOORE
1942	Ronald	MOORE

1943	Bill	MOREY
1943	Denis	MOREY
1953	Bill	MORGAN
1953	Doreen	MORGAN
1962	Janet	MORRIS
1950	Doreen	MORRISS
1952	Janet	MORRISS
1950	Mary	MORRISS
1942	Michael	MORRISS
1887	Hugh	MUIR
1896	James	MUIR
1889	John	MUIR
1893	Mary	MUIR
1891	Walter	MUIR
1950	Janet	MUNDAY
1950	Robert	MUNDAY
1956	Carol	MURRAY
1891	Ellen	MURRELL
1888	Frederick	MURRELL
1896	George	MURRELL
1896	James	MURRELL
1943	Jane	MURRELL
1943	Jeremy	MURRELL
1885	Julian	MURRELL
1962	David	MUSSELL
1948	Joan	MUSSELL
1957	Linda	MUSSELL
1971	Philip	MUSSELL
1962	Teresa	MUSSELL

N

1971	Kim	NAYLAND
1954	Christopher	NEEVE
1954	Robert	NEEVE
1962	Anthony	NEVILLE
1962	Robin	NEVILLE
1875	Caroline	NEWBLE
1873	Elizabeth	NEWBLE
1868	Mary-Jane	NEWBLE
1971	Anna	NEWMAN
1954	Christopher	NEWMAN
1971	David	NEWMAN
1954	Michael	NEWMAN
1971	Paul	NEWMAN
1954	Stephen	NEWMAN
1958	Peter	NEWSON
1859	Caroline	NIBBS
1857	William	NIBBS
1960	Georgina	NICHOLLS
1876	Mary	NICHOLLS
1962	Sally	NICHOLLS
1854	Harriett	NIGHTINGALE
1854	John	NIGHTINGALE
1954	Beatrice	NOAKES
1944	Jennifer	NOAKES
1954	Stephen	NOAKES
1971	Brian	NOBLE
1971	David	NOBLE
1968	Paul	NOBLE
1971	Ray	NOBLE
1971	Roger	NOBLE
1949	Dennis	NOLAN
1950	Alice	NORMAN
1971	Amanda	NORMAN

1922	Beatrice	NORMAN
1924	Maureen	NORMAN
1950	Maureen	NORMAN
1971	David	NORRIS
1923	Charles	NUNN
1917	Dorothy	NUNN
1915	Emily	NUNN
1914	Florence	NUNN
1929	James	NUNN
1916	Myrtle	NUNN
1909	Sarah	NUNN

O

1923	Craig	O'BRIEN
1923	Dorothy	O'BRIEN
1965	Sharon	O'CONNELL
1952	Annette	OGILVY
1952	Craig	OLGILVY
1950	Annette	OLIVER
1954	Dorothy	OLIVER
1954	Jill	OLIVER
1955	Tom	OLIVER
1971	Jeremy	OSBORNE
1966	Elizabeth	OSMASTON
1968	Mary	OSMASTON

P

1892	Alfred	PALMER
1894	Bertha	PALMER
1966	Elaine	PALMER
1894	James	PALMER
1968	Margaret	PALMER
1895	Mary-Ann	PALMER
1890	William	PALMER
1922	Dorothy	PANTLIN
1922	Jennifer	PANTLIN
1922	Olive	PANTLIN
1924	Phyllis	PANTLIN
1885	George	PARKER
1966	Christopher	PARR
1922	Bill	PARRATT
1952	Bill	PARRATT
1952	Jennifer	PARRATT
1971	Marian	PARRATT
1923	Charles	PARROTT
1923	Jack	PARROTT
1962	Belinda	PARSONS
1968	Mark	PARSONS
1943	Peter	PARVIN
1961	John	PATRICK
1969	Valerie	PATRICK
1856	Eliza	PAULLICK
1866	Hannah	PAULLICK
1960	Angela	PAULTER
1971	Ann	PAY
1961	Linda	PEACOCK
1896	Arthur	PEARCEY
1885	George	PEARCEY
1893	Olive	PEARCEY
1890	Sydney	PEARCEY
1887	William	PEARCEY
1971	Penny	PEARSON
1886	Walter	PERREN

1884	William	PERREN
1903	Charles	PERRIER
1924	Christopher	PERRIER
1901	George	PERRIER
1901	Nora	PERRIER
1924	Winnie	PERRIER
1950	Brenda	PERRY
1950	Christine	PERRY
1952	Brenda	PERRYER
1953	Glenda	PERRYER
1957	Peter	PERRYER
1962	Susan	PERRYER
1968	Brian	PERRYMAN
1856	Emily	PETERS
1953	Fred	PHILLIPS
1953	Glenda	PHILLIPS
1950	Joan	PHILLIPS
1968	Helen	PHILPOTT
1924	Alan	PIERCEY
1922	Fred	PIERCEY
1922	Alan	PINK
1923	David	PINK
1934	Jack	PINK
1953	Margaret	PINK
1942	Tony	PINK
1953	Tony	PINK
1923	Vera	PINK
1942	Vera	PINK
1864	Eliza	POLLOCK
1971	Denise	POOLE
1955	David	PORTER
1956	Margaret	PORTER
1855	Caroline	POTTER
1863	Edmund	POTTER
1864	John	POTTER
1858	Mary	POTTER
1861	Thomas	POTTER
1860	Elizabeth	POTTERTON
1864	Emma	POTTERTON
1971	David	POUND
1954	Helen	POUND
1962	Ruth	POUND
1950	Margaret	PRATT
1950	Roger	PRATT
1971	Ken	PRETTY
1943	Gordon	PREW
1943	Peter	PREW
1942	Roger	PREW
1942	Yvonne	PREW
1971	Deborah	PRINCE
1971	Linda	PRINCE
1943	Edna	PRIOR
1971	Cindy	PRITCHARD
1942	Bobby	PRIVETT
1942	Yvonne	PRIVETT
1887	Albert	PULLEN
1855	Ann	PULLEN
1883	Annie	PULLEN
1950	Brian	PULLEN
1865	Charles	PULLEN
1971	Dale	PULLEN
1954	David	PULLEN
1971	Dean	PULLEN
1889	Edith	PULLEN
1881	Edward	PULLEN

1866	Elizabeth	PULLEN
1879	Emma	PULLEN
1892	Ernest	PULLEN
1877	Frederick	PULLEN
1890	Frederick	PULLEN
1857	George	PULLEN
1960	Gillian	PULLEN
1896	Harry	PULLEN
1862	Henry	PULLEN
1894	Henry	PULLEN
1954	Jack	PULLEN
1887	John	PULLEN
1865	Moses	PULLEN
1923	Robert	PULLEN
1934	Ronald	PULLEN
1954	Sandra	PULLEN
1893	Sidney	PULLEN
1934	Sonnie	PULLEN
1971	Tina	PULLEN
1867	William	PULLEN
1886	William	PULLEN
1885	Willis	PULLEN
1860	Emma	PULLING
1863	James	PULLING
1922	Ernest	PULLINGER
1924	Jacqueline	PULLINGER
1971	Michael	PURSEY

Q

1863	Harriett	QUELCH
1865	Henry	QUELCH

R

1971	Stephen	RACKETT
1855	MaryAnn	RAGGETT
1952	Alan	RALPH
1952	Jacqueline	RALPH
1903	Alan	RAWES
1898	Lance	RAWES
1901	Marjorie	RAWES
1906	Roy	RAWES
1903	Victor	RAWES
1895	Winifred	RAWES
1942	Henry	RAY
1943	Nelson	RAY
1942	Peter	RAY
1971	Sally	READ
1881	Ann	REED
1880	Henry	REED
1882	Herbert	REED
1971	Nicholas	REED
1971	Simon	REED
1854	James	REIGATE
1855	MaryAnn	REIGATE
1971	Stephen	RENAUD
1971	Lisa	REPKO
1962	Christopher	RHODES
1962	Nicholas	RHODES
1964	Sarah	RHODES
1959	Stephen	RHODES
1971	Kevin	RICE
1962	Colin	RICHARDS
1962	Josephine	RICHARDS

1965	Adrian	RICHARDSON
1967	Stephen	RICKETS
1933	Alan	RIXON
1933	Peter	RIXON
1971	Paula	RIDGE
1971	Sarah	RIDGE
1971	Suzanne	RIDGE
1960	Diana	RITCHENS
1962	Paul	RITCHENS
1920	Alan	ROAKE
1892	David	ROAKE
1954	David	ROAKE
1894	Helen	ROAKE
1890	Myra	ROAKE
1923	Pat	ROAKE
1952	Pat	ROAKE
1925	Robin	ROAKE
1861	Walter	ROAKE
1971	Dawn	ROBERTS
1943	Mary	ROBERTS
1971	Sarah	ROBERTS
1884	Alfred	ROKER
1859	Ann	ROKER
1888	Ann	ROKER
1895	Caleb	ROKER
1863	Elizabeth	ROKER
1886	Grace	ROKER
1856	Harriet	ROKER
1893	Harriett	ROKER
1882	Henry	ROKER
1883	Jane	ROKER
1971	Joanne	ROKER
1861	John	ROKER
1890	John	ROKER
1860	Kate	ROKER
1858	Mary	ROKER
1923	Pearl	ROKER
1869	Robert	ROKER
1858	Thomas	ROKER
1962	Michael	ROSKELL
1943	Graham	ROWLEY
1943	Pearl	ROWLEY
1971	Ernest	ROYLANCE
1971	Pauline	ROYLANCE
1971	Peter	ROYLANCE
1971	Christopher	ROYLE
1950	Frank	RUDKIN
1950	Graham	RUDKIN
1962	Julie	RUDKIN

S

1942	Dorothy	SADLER
1923	Trevor	SADLER
1942	Trevor	SADLER
1865	Alfred	SAIL
1863	Alice	SAIL
1862	William	SAIL
1902	Alfred	SALE
1888	Alice	SALE
1878	Annie	SALE
1909	Dorothy	SALE
1886	Edith	SALE
1884	Elizabeth	SALE
1902	Frederick	SALE

1965	Glynis	SALE
1971	Jennifer	SALE
1882	John	SALE
1895	Margaret	SALE
1880	Mary	SALE
1887	Nellie	SALE
1922	Alan	SALES
1922	Alfred	SALES
1949	Alan	SALISBURY
1971	Colin	SALMON
1971	Gary	SALMON
1968	Jacqueline	SALMON
1955	Philip	SAM
1956	Colin	SANDFORD
1942	Alan	SAPSFORD
1942	Harriet	SAPSFORD
1942	Marion	SAPSFORD
1923	Judith	SAUL
1908	Percy	SAUL
1971	Deborah	SAVAGE
1971	Nigel	SAVAGE
1971	Penny	SAVAGE
1950	Audrey	SAXBY
1950	Judith	SAXBY
1956	Jacqueline	SCURR
1956	Phillip	SCURR
1956	Stephen	SCURR
1958	Ian	SEAGER
1958	Roger	SEAGER
1959	Tom	SEAGER
1943	Audrey	SEARLE
1943	Elsie	SEARLE
1954	Roland	SEARLE
1971	Andrew	SEWELL
1942	Arthur	SEWELL
1923	Elsie	SEWELL
1942	Shirley	SEWELL
1906	Arthur	SEX
1906	Ronald	SEX
1962	Philip	SHADDOCK
1952	Billy	SHARP
1892	Charles	SHARP
1952	Doreen	SHARP
1888	Emmeline	SHARP
1894	Frank	SHARP
1890	Kate	SHARP
1971	Denise	SHAW
1971	Peter	SHAW
1955	Ann	SHINN
1954	Billy	SHINN
1954	Malcolm	SHINN
1967	Paul	SHINN
1966	Richard	SHINN
1954	Malcolm	SHUTTLEWORTH
1952	Michael	SHUTTLEWORTH
1954	Alice	SILVER
1954	Michael	SILVER
1865	Sarah	SILVERWOOD
1889	Ada	SIMMONDS
1904	Alice	SIMMONDS
1891	Edith	SIMMONDS
1894	John	SIMMONDS
1917	Monica	SIMMONDS
1917	Ruby	SIMMONDS
1886	William	SIMMONDS

Year	Name	Surname
1923	Ian	SIMPSON
1923	Monica	SIMPSON
1954	Ian	SIMS
1942	Jimmy	SIMS
1942	Sylvia	SIMS
1954	Sylvia	SIMS
1954	Jimmy	SINES
1950	June	SINES
1950	Olive	SINES
1893	Ada	SINK
1877	Alfred	SINK
1895	Arthur	SINK
1881	Blanche	SINK
1883	Caroline	SINK
1892	Mary	SINK
1896	Richard	SINK
1923	Robert	SIRMAN
1954	Jean	SIVYER
1954	Robert	SIVYER
1971	Brian	SKEATES
1971	Christine	SKEATES
1971	Karen	SKELTON
1971	Martin	SKELTON
1968	Jane	SLATFORD
1971	Stewart	SLATFORD
1890	Ada	SLAUGHTER
1874	Ada-Mary	SLAUGHTER
1892	Albert	SLAUGHTER
1888	Dora	SLAUGHTER
1866	Edith	SLAUGHTER
1869	Emily	SLAUGHTER
1883	Emily	SLAUGHTER
1873	George	SLAUGHTER
1895	Hilda	SLAUGHTER
1881	Margaret	SLAUGHTER
1885	Mary	SLAUGHTER
1870	Rose	SLAUGHTER
1942	Anne	SMALLBONE
1943	Jean	SMALLBONE
1942	Michael	SMALLBONE
1952	Anne	SMALLPIECE
1950	Clive	SMALLPIECE
1950	Hazel	SMALLPIECE
1943	Alan	SMITH
1877	Albert	SMITH
1894	Annie	SMITH
1886	Arthur	SMITH
1971	Brian	SMITH
1960	Christine	SMITH
1922	Clive	SMITH
1934	Doris	SMITH
1962	Douglas	SMITH
1885	Emily	SMITH
1934	Ernest	SMITH
1883	Florence	SMITH
1896	Frances	SMITH
1936	Frances	SMITH
1895	George	SMITH
1956	Gordon	SMITH
1962	Jacqueline	SMITH
1896	Jennifer	SMITH
1953	Jennifer	SMITH
1962	Lesley	SMITH
1888	Lillian	SMITH
1971	Mark	SMITH
1971	Martin	SMITH
1893	Mary	SMITH
1953	Maureen	SMITH
1886	May	SMITH
1971	Nadine	SMITH
1943	Pamela	SMITH
1954	Pamela	SMITH
1950	Peter	SMITH
1971	Peter	SMITH
1933	Phyllis	SMITH
1950	Phyllis	SMITH
1937	Ronald	SMITH
1954	Ronnie	SMITH
1881	Rosina	SMITH
1935	Stanley	SMITH
1922	Steve	SMITH
1935	Steve	SMITH
1950	Suzanne	SMITH
1890	Sydney	SMITH
1949	Ted	SMITH
1922	Victor	SMITH
1950	Victor	SMITH
1971	Vivienne	SMITH
1952	Wendy	SMITH
1887	William	SMITH
1952	Yvonne	SMITH
1943	Ann	SMITHERS
1954	Audrey	SMITHERS
1891	Caroline	SMITHERS
1882	Catherine	SMITHERS
1888	Charles	SMITHERS
1884	Fanny	SMITHERS
1896	Frederick	SMITHERS
1886	George	SMITHERS
1896	James	SMITHERS
1954	Janice	SMITHERS
1888	Martha	SMITHERS
1943	Peter	SMITHERS
1880	Sarah	SMITHERS
1881	Alice	SNELLING
1885	Anne	SNELLING
1879	George	SNELLING
1877	MaryAnn	SNELLING
1968	Andrew	SNOW
1971	Gabrielle	SOLLIS
1956	James	SOMERFIELD
1943	Nicholas	SOMERFIELD
1950	Ada	SOULSBY
1950	Tony	SOULSBY
1930	Ada	SOUTAR
1923	Ernest	SOUTAR
1923	Douglas	SOUTAR
1932	Harold	SOUTAR
1934	Marjorie	SOUTAR
1942	Douglas	SPEAR
1942	Norah	SPEAR
1943	Eddie	SPITTLES
1943	Ernest	SPITTLES
1923	Harry	SPOONER
1923	Norah	SPOONER
1954	Wendy	SPOONER
1962	Vanessa	SPREADBURY
1929	George	SPRINGETT
1923	Harry	SPRINGETT
1923	John	SPRINGETT
1923	Maisie	SPRINGETT
1943	Anthony	STAFFORD
1949	Alan	STANFORD
1942	John	STANLEY
1966	Leslie	STANLEY
1971	Richard	STANLEY
1971	Sally	STANLEY
1933	Sidney	STANLEY
1933	Susan	STANLEY
1957	Colin	STEDMAN
1891	Edith	STEDMAN
1875	Emily	STEDMAN
1879	Fred	STEDMAN
1929	Joan	STEDMAN
1886	Joseph	STEDMAN
1881	Lucy	STEDMAN
1859	Alice	STEER
1870	Arthur	STEER
1861	Ellen	STEER
1862	Francis	STEER
1862	Henry	STEER
1855	James	STEER
1866	John	STEER
1864	Margaret	STEER
1868	MaryAnn	STEER
1872	Thomas	STEER
1864	William	STEER
1863	Ann	STENNING
1873	James	STENNING
1867	MaryAnn	STENNING
1873	William	STENNING
1966	Andria	STEPHANIA
1962	Susan	STEPHANIA
1960	Teresa	STEPHANIA
1952	Arthur	STEPHENS
1952	Susan	STEPHENS
1894	Alice	STEVENS
1894	Annie	STEVENS
1896	Arthur	STEVENS
1886	Charles	STEVENS
1888	Edward	STEVENS
1896	Ellen	STEVENS
1903	Ellen	STEVENS
1894	Ernest	STEVENS
1932	Ernest	STEVENS
1891	Esther	STEVENS
1891	Fanny	STEVENS
1892	James	STEVENS
1903	Jessie	STEVENS
1932	Jessie	STEVENS
1904	Robert	STEVENS
1904	Wilfred	STEVENS
1932	Wilfred	STEVENS
1962	Donald	STEWART
1971	Kerry	STEWART
1971	Peter	STICKINGS
1971	Ruth	STICKINGS
1923	Daphne	STILES
1943	Maureen	STILLWELL
1966	Lynne	STOKES
1950	Robert	STONARD
1950	Sydney	STONARD
1886	Bertram	STONE
1923	Brian	STONE
1966	Christine	STONE
1960	Elizabeth	STONE
1886	Ernest	STONE
1894	Francis	STONE
1893	Helen	STONE
1882	Kate	STONE
1889	Margaret	STONE
1883	Mary	STONE
1877	Sarah	STONE
1954	Sydney	STONE
1954	William	STONE
1971	David	STRANGE
1971	Michelle	STRANGE
1954	Alfred	STREET
1954	Brian	STREET
1962	David	STREET
1880	Alfred	STRUDWICK
1934	Alfred	STRUDWICK
1888	Alice	STRUDWICK
1885	Annie	STRUDWICK
1906	Bernard	STRUDWICK
1934	Bernard	STRUDWICK
1936	Beryl	STRUDWICK
1906	Denis	STRUDWICK
1935	Dorothy	STRUDWICK
1905	Elsie	STRUDWICK
1935	Elsie	STRUDWICK
1886	Emily	STRUDWICK
1883	Ernest	STRUDWICK
1875	George	STRUDWICK
1905	Harold	STRUDWICK
1933	Harold	STRUDWICK
1904	John	STRUDWICK
1933	John	STRUDWICK
1971	Leslie	STRUDWICK
1909	Marjorie	STRUDWICK
1901	Percy	STRUDWICK
1971	Sharon	STRUDWICK
1901	Stafford	STRUDWICK
1950	Stafford	STRUDWICK
1971	Steven	STRUDWICK
1950	Victor	STRUDWICK
1936	Violet	STRUDWICK
1877	William	STRUDWICK
1956	Marion	STUART
1896	William	STURGESS
1878	Albert	STYLES
1881	Alice	STYLES
1934	Alice	STYLES
1871	Amos	STYLES
1883	Annie	STYLES
1912	Beryl	STYLES
1872	Caroline	STYLES
1912	Daphne	STYLES
1912	Doreen	STYLES
1938	Doreen	STYLES
1933	Dorothy	STYLES
1869	Edith	STYLES
1892	Edward	STYLES
1933	Elsie	STYLES
1865	George	STYLES
1874	Harriett	STYLES
1935	James	STYLES
1943	Janet	STYLES
1943	John	STYLES
1863	Lydia	STYLES

1934	Ruby	STYLES
1897	Alice	SUMMERS
1897	Charles	SUMMERS
1888	Flossie	SUMMERS
1895	George	SUMMERS
1923	Kenneth	SUMNER
1967	Lydia	SUMNER
1971	Deborah	SUNDERLAND
1954	Bill	SUTTON
1954	Kenneth	SUTTON
1956	Linda	SUTTON
1894	Steven	SUTTON
1954	Bill	SWAFFIELD
1954	Michael	SWAFFIELD
1954	Barry	SWEENEY
1954	Michael	SWEENEY

T

1964	Peter	TALBOT
1962	Susan	TALBOT
1971	Alan	TAYLOR
1892	Albert	TAYLOR
1861	Annie	TAYLOR
1952	Barry	TAYLOR
1897	Cecil	TAYLOR
1952	Cecil	TAYLOR
1971	Derek	TAYLOR
1971	Dian	TAYLOR
1887	Eleanor	TAYLOR
1857	Eliza	TAYLOR
1866	Emma	TAYLOR
1897	Frank	TAYLOR
1889	Frederick	TAYLOR
1870	George	TAYLOR
1896	George	TAYLOR
1954	George	TAYLOR
1903	Harry	TAYLOR
1954	Harry	TAYLOR
1876	Henry	TAYLOR
1868	James	TAYLOR
1971	Mark	TAYLOR
1901	Maureen	TAYLOR
1971	Paula	TAYLOR
1929	Stanley	TAYLOR
1859	Thomas	TAYLOR
1863	William	TAYLOR
1901	William	TAYLOR
1954	Arthur	TEMPLE
1954	Maureen	TEMPLE
1971	Ralph	THATCHER
1971	Julian	THOMAS
1971	Malcolm	THOMAS
1882	Ernest	THORN
1885	William	THORN
1971	Andrew	THURBIN
1971	Sally	THURBIN
1923	Desmond	TICE
1886	Edith	TICE
1892	Ellen	TICE
1896	Elsie	TICE
1888	Ernest	TICE
1885	Frederick	TICE
1950	Frederick	TICE
1887	Kate	TICE

1923	Michael	TICE
1954	Michael	TICE
1886	Rose	TICE
1950	Trevor	TICE
1857	Ann	TICKNER
1905	Ann	TICKNER
1956	Brian	TICKNER
1863	Catherine	TICKNER
1883	Charles	TICKNER
1890	Ernest	TICKNER
1866	Fanny	TICKNER
1887	Fanny	TICKNER
1905	Frederick	TICKNER
1890	Jack	TICKNER
1890	James	TICKNER
1883	John	TICKNER
1901	John	TICKNER
1885	Louise	TICKNER
1901	Lucille	TICKNER
1953	Lucille	TICKNER
1861	Martha	TICKNER
1855	Mary	TICKNER
1881	Mary	TICKNER
1878	Matthew	TICKNER
1954	Maureen	TICKNER
1962	Michael	TICKNER
1892	Richard	TICKNER
1954	Richard	TICKNER
1896	Rosaline	TICKNER
1876	Thomas	TICKNER
1889	Thomas	TICKNER
1905	William	TICKNER
1954	William	TICKNER
1943	Ronnie	TIDY
1971	Paul	TINKLER
1943	Ann	TIZZARD
1923	Elizabeth	TIZZARD
1943	Frank	TIZZARD
1922	Winnie	TIZZARD
1884	Arthur	TOLLEY
1879	Minnie	TOLLEY
1877	Alice	TOWERS
1897	Alice	TOWERS
1865	Elizabeth	TOWERS
1897	Elizabeth	TOWERS
1873	John	TOWERS
1896	John	TOWERS
1870	Thomas	TOWERS
1968	Carol	TRUSCOTT
1969	Irene	TRUSCOTT
1971	Janet	TRUSCOTT
1969	Julia	TRUSCOTT
1971	Pamela	TRUSCOTT
1970	Stephen	TRUSCOTT
1971	Victor	TRUSCOTT
1903	Alice	TRUSSLER
1877	Edith	TRUSSLER
1888	Ena	TRUSSLER
1879	George	TRUSSLER
1893	Harry	TRUSSLER
1890	Mary	TRUSSLER
1882	Ada	TUBB
1873	Elizabeth	TUBB
1871	Henry	TUBB
1878	James	TUBB

1880	Kate	TUBB
1886	Laura	TUBB
1866	Louisa	TUBB
1876	William	TUBB
1885	Agnes	TUBBS
1902	Annie	TUBBS
1902	Brenda	TUBBS
1888	Fanny	TUBBS
1886	Florence	TUBBS
1854	Harriett	TUBBS
1886	Annie	TULETT
1971	William	TUNNELL
1942	Brenda	TURK
1942	Edie	TURK
1971	Richard	TURLE
1971	Sally	TURLE
1895	Daisy	TURNER
1971	David	TURNER
1923	Edie	TURNER
1893	Edward	TURNER
1923	John	TURNER
1923	Maurice	TURNER
1885	May	TURNER
1971	Michael	TURNER
1929	Molly	TURNER
1962	Paul	TURNER
1888	Rose	TURNER
1961	Therese	TURNER
1961	Sheila	TYSON

U

1962	Eleanor	UNEY
1954	Valerie	UPSTONE

V

1885	Gertrude	VINCENT
1955	Diana	VINER
1957	Pat	VINER
1968	Ian	VOLLER
1971	Kenneth	VOLLER
1965	Susan	VOLLER

W

1952	Denis	WADE
1856	Ellen	WADE
1863	John	WADE
1954	John	WADE
1867	Rose	WADE
1963	Philip	WAKEMAN
1968	Robert	WAKEMAN
1937	Denis	WALKER
1909	Mervyn	WALKER
1960	Margaret	WALKER
1909	Thomas	WALKER
1936	Thomas	WALKER
1880	Fred	WALKER
1954	Christine	WALLACE
1963	Gary	WALLACE
1971	Lindsay	WALLACE
1955	Maralyn	WALLACE
1954	Mervyn	WALLACE
1890	Herbert	WALLIS
1971	Susan	WALLIS

1971	Lynn	WALTERS
1962	Ian	WANBON
1971	Jill	WANBON
1885	Albert	WAPSHOTT
1881	Alfred	WAPSHOTT
1879	Annie	WAPSHOTT
1883	Arthur	WAPSHOTT
1875	Caroline	WAPSHOTT
1867	Emma	WAPSHOTT
1873	George	WAPSHOTT
1865	James	WAPSHOTT
1877	John	WAPSHOTT
1871	Mary	WAPSHOTT
1869	William	WAPSHOTT
1971	Janet	WARD
1893	Julia	WARD
1962	Stephen	WARD
1954	Arthur	WARREN
1954	Christine	WARREN
1954	Rosemary	WARREN
1971	Malcolm	WARWICK
1971	Vincent	WARWICK
1886	Francis	WATERMAN
1881	Alice	WATSON
1896	Daisy	WATSON
1874	Edward	WATSON
1868	Elizabeth	WATSON
1865	Emily	WATSON
1893	Ernest	WATSON
1876	George	WATSON
1889	George	WATSON
1880	Henry	WATSON
1887	Jessie	WATSON
1872	John	WATSON
1876	Lucy	WATSON
1859	Phebe	WATSON
1855	Rhoda	WATSON
1891	Walter	WATSON
1865	William	WATSON
1878	William	WATSON
1884	Willis	WATSON
1971	Maxine	WATTS
1971	Vanessa	WATTS
1904	Arthur	WEBB
1894	Constance	WEBB
1938	David	WEBB
1938	Derek	WEBB
1904	Graham	WEBB
1935	Graham	WEBB
1903	Harold	WEBB
1935	Harold	WEBB
1893	Hilda	WEBB
1903	Ian	WEBB
1942	Ian	WEBB
1870	James	WEBB
1936	John	WEBB
1957	Kelvin	WEBB
1933	Mary	WEBB
1948	Nigel	WEBB
1896	Reginald	WEBB
1937	Roy	WEBB
1871	Sarah	WEBB
1938	Tony	WEBB
1971	Christopher	WEDGEWOOD
1971	Susan	WEDGEWOOD

1962	Brian	WELLER
1934	Jack	WELLER
1954	David	WELLS
1954	Georgina	WELLS
1950	Rodney	WELLS
1950	Violet	WELLS
1886	Albert	WHAPSHOTT
1886	Arthur	WHAPSHOTT
1889	Edith	WHAPSHOTT
1890	Edward	WHAPSHOTT
1892	George	WHAPSHOTT
1895	Gertrude	WHAPSHOTT
1889	James	WHAPSHOTT
1887	Kate	WHAPSHOTT
1923	Patsy	WHAPSHOTT
1894	Emily	WHEAL
1890	George	WHEAL
1895	James	WHEAL
1966	Janet	WHEATLEY
1971	Peter	WHEATLEY
1971	Robert	WHEATLEY
1971	Ruth	WHEATLEY
1956	Billy	WHELAN
1952	Gladys	WHELAN

1952	Patsy	WHELAN
1971	Karen	WHIFFING
1968	Paul	WHIFFING
1923	Brian	WHITBURN
1954	Brian	WHITE
1954	Sally	WHITE
1971	Jennifer	WHITING
1971	Timothy	WHITING
1952	Carlo	WHITTERN
1949	David	WHITTERN
1952	Dorothy	WHITTERN
1952	Owen	WICKAMS
1923	Jacqueline	WICKSON
1942	Jacqueline	WIGGINS
1942	Violet	WIGGINS
1923	Beryl	WILCOX
1955	Beverly	WILDE
1955	Jonathan	WILDE
1961	Richard	WILKINSON
1952	Beryl	WILLIAMS
1949	Denis	WILLIAMS
1964	Linda	WILLIAMS
1971	Nigel	WILLIAMS
1952	Owen	WILLIAMS

1950	Raymond	WILLIAMS
1968	Robert	WILLIAMS
1966	Sheila	WILLIAMS
1950	Wendy	WILLIAMS
1950	John	WILLIAMSON
1950	Wendy	WILLIAMSON
1950	John	WILLIS
1950	Michael	WILLIS
1956	Ruth	WILMOT
1952	James	WILSON
1952	Michael	WILSON
1923	Carol	WISDOM
1896	George	WISDOM
1967	Andrew	WOOD
1957	Susan	WOOD
1952	Bob	WOODHAMS
1954	Carole	WOODHAMS
1954	Clive	WOODHAMS
1966	Andrew	WOODS
1971	Tania	WOODS
1881	Albert	WOODYER
1878	Ellen	WOODYER
1971	Caroline	WOOLEY
1884	Arthur	WOOLGAR

1886	James	WOOLGAR
1880	Maria	WOOLGAR
1971	Clare	WORSEY
1923	Bob	WRIGHT
1960	Evelyn	WRIGHT
1923	Lawrence	WRIGHT
1953	Lawrence	WRIGHT
1952	Alan	WYATT
1968	Andrew	WYATT
1956	Charles	WYATT
1971	Rowland	WYATT
1883	Albert	WYE
1971	Caroline	WYE
1879	John	WYE
1886	Kate	WYE
1886	Mary	WYE
1875	Alfred	WYTE
1870	Henry	WYTE
1873	Lucy	WYTE

Y

1954	Patrick	YOUNG

The *Masters* and *Mistresses* of the *School* at *Send*

1854-1972

1854   Master - Frederick NORTH
Mistress - Mrs Sarah NORTH

1861   Master - Arthur R MARSHALL
Mistress - Mrs Mary MARSHALL

1873   Master - Thomas HOWICK
Mistress - Mrs HOWICK
Infants' Mistress - Miss HOWICK

1880   Master - Thomas Lewis VINCENT
Mistress - Mrs Mary Ellen VINCENT
Infants' Mistress - Miss Emma DIDDAMS

1889   Master - Lancelot RAWES
Mistress - Mrs Jessica RAWES
Infants' Mistress - Miss Emma DIDDAMS

1924   Headmaster - A James ROGERS
Infants' Teacher - Miss Ethel Read (from 1921)

1940   Acting Headmaster - Sidney Kenneth Penn
Infants' Teacher - Miss Annie Kathleen Palmer (from 1932)

1941   Headmistress - Miss Stella Eugenie Perrin
Deputy Head - Miss Annie Kathleen Palmer (from 1956)

1971-1972   Headmistress Mrs Lucy Josephine Wickens.

Sources

Managers' Minutes, Ripley School 1893-1924

Managers' Minutes, Send School 1854-71

Ripley Parish Magazines 1884, 1891,1902-1912

Kelly's Post Office Directories 1861, 1867, 1874

Russell's Guildford and West Surrey Almanack 1851,1854,1856,1861,1869

Ripley Parish Council Minute Books 1894-1908

Board of Education Memoranda, The Schools in Wartime

PRO at KEW [various papers]

National Society Papers, 1846, 1854, 1871,

A Short History of the National Society 1811-1961 by Burgess and Welsby

Dame Haynes Charity Minutes, 1871

Send Parish Magazines, 1889, 1894, 1897,1899,1910,1914,1921

Lasham's Guildford Almanack and Directory, 1861

Ripley Baptism Registers, 1900-1918

Send Baptism Registers, 1889-1922

Surrey History Centre, Woking
  (various papers reproduced by permission of Surrey History Service)

Census Returns for Send and Ripley, 1841-1891

Annual Reports of the Send Women's Institute, 1939-1945

Photographs from the Send and Ripley History Society Archives

Extracts from articles in the Send and Ripley History Society Newsletters

Log-books of the Ripley National (later C of E) School, 1885-1968

Log-books of the Send National (later C of E) School, 1922-1972

The Straight Furrow by Fred Dixon

Surrey Advertiser and County Times, 19 Dec. 1953